SAFAR

SAFAR

Finding Home, History, and Culture through Punjabi Food in the American West

MADHUSHREE GHOSH

BLOOMSBURY ACADEMIC

NEW YORK • LONDON • OXFORD • NEW DELHI • SYDNEY

BLOOMSBURY ACADEMIC
Bloomsbury Publishing Inc, 1359 Broadway, New York, NY 10018, USA
Bloomsbury Publishing Plc, 50 Bedford Square, London, WC1B 3DP, UK
Bloomsbury Publishing Ireland, 29 Earlsfort Terrace, Dublin 2, D02 AY28, Ireland

BLOOMSBURY, BLOOMSBURY ACADEMIC and the Diana logo
are trademarks of Bloomsbury Publishing Plc

First published in the United States of America 2026

Cover images:
Photo on the left: Jassi Saini with her son, Ajit (credit: Photo taken by the author)
Photo on the right: Early Punjabi Immigrants to America, circa 1910s (credit: Courtesy of the
California History Room, California State Library, Sacramento, California)
Food image © iStock.com/Нарине Нахшкарян, gold border © iStock.com/©smuay

Bloomsbury Publishing Inc does not have any control over, or responsibility for, any
third-party websites referred to or in this book. All internet addresses given in this book were
correct at the time of going to press. The author and publisher regret
any inconvenience caused if addresses have changed or sites have ceased
to exist, but can accept no responsibility for any such changes.

Library of Congress Cataloging-in-Publication Data

Names: Ghosh, Madhushree, 1970– author
Title: Safar : finding home, history, and culture through
Punjabi food in the American West / Madhushree Ghosh.
Description: New York : Bloomsbury Academic, 2026. |
Includes bibliographical references and index.
Identifiers: LCCN 2025050689 (print) | LCCN 2025050690 (ebook) |
ISBN 9798881842673 hardback | ISBN 9798765155752 epub |
ISBN 9798765155769 adobe pdf
Subjects: LCSH: Panjabis (South Asian people)–Food | Panjabis (South Asian people)–Social
life and customs | Panjabis (South Asian people)–Cultural assimilation | Panjabis (South Asian
people)–Ethnic identity | Panjabis (South Asian people)–California | Punjab (India)–Social life and
customs | LCGFT: Creative nonfiction
Classification: LCC DS432.P232 G55 2026 (print) | LCC DS432.P232 (ebook) |
DDC 305.8914210794—dc23/eng/20251218
LC record available at https://lccn.loc.gov/2025050689
LC ebook record available at https://lccn.loc.gov/2025050690

ISBN: HB: 979-8-8818-4267-3
           ePDF: 979-8-7651-5576-9
           eBook: 979-8-7651-5575-2

Typeset by Integra Software Services Pvt. Ltd.
Printed and bound in the United States of America

For product safety related questions contact productsafety@bloomsbury.com

To find out more about our authors and books visit www.bloomsbury.com
and sign up for our newsletters.

For our ancestors, our purvaj, who took the risk,
who accepted the challenge
For the next generations, look where we came from,
look where we are
For Sila and Hashi, eijo, aaro ekta
For GSG, for all and everything

Revolutions happen not only in grand moments in public view but also in small pockets of people coming together to inhabit a new way of being. We birth the beloved community by becoming the beloved community.

—Valarie Kaur, author of *See No Stranger: A Memoir and Manifesto of Revolutionary Love*

CONTENTS

ACKNOWLEDGMENTS

Safar wouldn't have been possible without the kindness and support of the American-Sikh community members, and the relentless academic researchers, historians, and cultural commenters of the South Asian immigration journey.

This is a work of narrative nonfiction where details have not been imagined or invented. All conversations were with the community members or referenced in research documents, books, documentary films, and reference materials as noted throughout the book. In cases where the community members wished to maintain their privacy and anonymity, I have taken all precautions to remove any identifying features, names, cities, or other details that would be counter to their request. In such cases, I have noted where the names, locations, and identifying features have been altered to preserve anonymity. Most of the stories were from interviews with members of the community, historical reference materials, and multi-year conversations with them, their family members, and/or friends. If there are conversations that may have happened within this community that were listed as presumed dialogue, it was confirmed by them or the next generation members and/or noted as such.

Thank you for the stellar editorial guidance and support, Deni Remsberg and the Bloomsbury US team, and to my amazing agent, Dana Newman, you're the very best and you know why.

In writing *Safar* to represent the stories of these fearless women, I am grateful for the seminal and groundbreaking research work done by Dr. Karen Leonard, Dr. Nicole Ranganath, Dr. Tejpaul Singh Bainiwal, Dr. Jayasri Majumdar Hart, and Dr. Vivek Bald. Thanks to Meena Venkataramanan, Jaweed Kaleem, and Sonia Chopra, whose articles and essays in the *Washington Post*, *L.A. Times*, and *Eater* informed the start of *Safar*.

Much thanks to the Punjabi-Sikh community of Imperial County, especially Robert and Karmen Chell, John and Esther Deen, the members of the gurdwara Sikh Temple of El Centro, Victor Dad (now in Scottsdale, AZ), and A. Singh. Thank you to the amazing woman who inspired me to write about Sheila Singh—may I grow up to be you.

In Yuba County, Fresno, Sacramento, and Central Valley area, I am deeply indebted to the Stockton gurdwara members, especially the Hon. Raj Singh Badhesha, Daljit Saini, Prabhjot Singh Lasher, Manjit S. Uppal, Harnek Singh Atwal, Kuljit S. Nijjar, and Mandeep K. Pelia. Gratitude to Uma Devi and Daljit Saini for sharing their Punjab Dhaba food, restaurant, and their lives. Thank you, Guy Branum, for sharing his Yuba City childhood stories on a rainy Christmas break in 2022.

In San Diego and southern California, I am grateful to the Saini family of Punjabi Tandoor—Ajit, Jagdish, Bakhtawar, Jaspreet Kaur, Kamaljeet Kaur, Satwinder Kaur, Lucky, and Sukhpreet Singh—*Safar* would be incomplete without your trust, faith, and friendship. Thanks also to Valarie Kaur for her kind support and fearless leadership in community activism.

During *Safar*'s research, I have had the good fortune in eating at many Punjabi and South Asian restaurants globally—listing them with thanks. I hope you choose to visit them too: Punjabi Tandoor (San Diego, CA), Gulab (Clovis, CA), Little India (Yuba City, CA), Punjab Dhaba (Fresno, CA), Shan-e-Punjab Dhaba (Fresno, CA), BiBi (Mayfair, London), Tayyabs (Whitechapel, London), Darjeeling Express (SoHo, London), Charista (Shoreditch, London), and The Knight (Ladbroke Grove, London).

Special thanks to the librarians and curators at the San Diego public library, the Stanford Library (Special Collections), U.C. Berkeley (The Bancroft Library), U.C. Davis Pioneering Punjabis Digital Archive, South Asian American Digital Archive (Samip Mallick), and Imperial County Historical Society, who were instrumental in providing research data and in confirming digitized records of the families arriving in the American West over a century and a half ago. Earlier versions of Chapter 23 were published in *San Diego Magazine* and *Spruce Eats*.

A book is an academic endeavor without soul if not for the friends and family members who make this multi-decade project worth persevering. Thank you to my long-gone and always inspiring parents, my sister and her husband, and my beloved framily, Chiwoniso Kaitano, Marcie Frank, Stacey Seeloff, Michele Bigley, Talia Kolluri, Katie Freeman, Ramnit Bassi, Sarah Thyre, Mini Paul, Sam Sarwar, Lisa Sellers and Raj Tawney. As always, thanks Nancy Frank—look, another one.

Much of the work was completed on flights, airports, friends' homes, and cafes. Thank you to Casa Chandy (Brooklyn), the Conservatory (Talmadge), Kettle & Stone (Mission Hills), Tahona's (Old Town San Diego), The Knight of Notting Hill, JFK, SFO, CDG, LHR, and San Diego airports, where *Safar* became what it is.

Thank you, Sheila, Uma, and Jassi, for letting me tell your stories, and for your grace and trust. Thank you to the nameless mauna Sikh in the 1993 Thai Airways flight from Delhi to LAX, who told me a story I've followed for three decades.

And finally, thank you, Gary S. Greer, for inordinate patience, consistency, a different perspective, and joy.

AUTHOR'S NOTE

Safar, "the journey" in Hindi, Urdu, and Persian, phonetically translating to "suffer," arrived in my life three decades ago as a need to understand what our journey has been as immigrants to a country that continues to treat us with suspicion. It also started my lifelong exploration of belonging and understanding homesickness.

As a young graduate student in Long Island in 1993, when phone calls were expensive, and airline tickets even more so, I relied on recreating my Ma's recipes. Through food, I hoped to bring home in my tiny New York apartment. Food has always represented comfort, a connection, a string bridging the present to the past, and homesickness has been no different.

I am not a historian, a food anthropologist, a chef, or a travel expert. What I am is an immigrant to America, who arrived over three decades ago with two suitcases, a scholarship to a graduate degree in biochemistry, with a strong sense of home. As the daughter of refugees of the 1947 Partition of India by the British, stories of displacement, of longing for what was home are part of my DNA. It is with this intense need to understand how we came to be, and why we leave a place we love so much that allowed me to explore *Safar*.

While I am not a Punjabi (i.e., not from the northern state in India that was divided between India and Pakistan in 1947), my family is from Bengal—which too was divided, into West Bengal (where my parents moved to as children during the partition migration), and now the country of Bangladesh. I barely speak Punjabi, my Bengali food is very different from theirs, my Bengali customs, Hindu traditions, our history, and my personal agnostic attitude are very different from this community. And yet, both our people were transformed by the trauma of colonization, famine, displacement, and partition. That connection is what has led me to understand what made this community come to America, in particular, the American West, and what made them stay.

We have many histories and stories of Punjab, from a broader lens, or from the perspective of freedom fighters, mostly male. *Safar* arose from a need to understand it from the women's perspective, and how they live now.

As with *Khabaar*, I continue to *not* highlight scripts that aren't English, primarily to insist that our languages deserve the same respect as our colonizers'. If you read an unfamiliar word, let it marinate in your mouth, speak it once, twice, see how it makes you feel. Sometimes, it's a beautiful surprise when you realize you've always known it, you just didn't know you did.

*

During my trips up and down California, meeting women and their families who tell me their stories, I realized a gap in what was being said, and what was left whispered or unsaid. To follow the Sikh path, to follow a patriarchal family construct, these women have led lives in accordance, in service. Also, the women of *Safar* are strong, resilient, intelligent, considerate, and trailblazing. However, most are also extremely private. It is the culture, it is the norm—do not air out your grievances in public. No talk of generational trauma, no talk of the partition, no talk of the second-class status of women, the patriarchy, or even their own personal desires. What good will it do? Log kyaa kahengein? What will people say?

I have met these women over the years as their lives transformed, as did mine. We shared our secrets, we confided in our sorrows, we built surprising friendships over the years. However, for some, it has been hard to share their personal lives, some of it secret for decades. In certain sections, as noted, I have changed their names, cities, and other identifying notes, in respect of their families, and next generations. The storyline remains the same; I hope you feel their lives through these words.

What started as a short exchange with a Punjabi-Mexican farmer from Yuba City in 1993 on a Thai Airways flight from New Delhi, led me to travel from San Diego to Fresno to Sacramento and beyond, understanding this community, the one that holds the agricultural Central Valley together, the one that has transformed what California is now—in food, in travel, in community.

*

I joke that I've gone to more gurdwaras than I have Hindu temples as an agnostic. The women have been kind and have indulged my whimsy, while I respected their devotion to Sikhism. Alongside, I have eaten and made their food that reminds us of home and brings us back to what we seek—belonging, a sense of place, community.

Author and activist Valarie Kaur said in *See No Stranger: A Memoir and Manifesto of Revolutionary Love*, "True understanding is not possible unless we risk changing our worldview. Otherwise, we think we have built bridges to one another, but the bridges are rooted in sands that can shift with the tide."

With *Safar*, I hope that when you meet Sheila, Jes, Jassi, Uma, and their families, you see a world you understand a bit better, food that connects us, and love that encompasses all. To me, that is home.

PART ONE

WHY WE TRAVEL

1

Why We Travel and How This Happened

I realize I tell the same story in different ways, no matter what I write. Most of us do, but sometimes we call it fiction, and sometimes we say it's someone else's story.

It is August 1993. I am at the Indira Gandhi International Airport for the first time in my life taking an international flight out of my city, New Delhi. My two new suitcases from Palika Bazaar are packed with MDH masalas, a few pots and pans that Didi, my elder sister, has bought with her salary from her new nonprofit job. Didi has also bought me my first rust chanderi sari with a gold and maroon border—just in case there are Indian student gatherings in Stony Brook, the university in Long Island I am headed to, to get my PhD in biochemistry. I am living my family's dreams. My parents' hopes. My ambition. My ancestors' desires. To be the generation that was able to achieve what they could not. The pressure isn't so much that one cannot perform. One knows one's role in this. To be successful. To complete the education. To head back home.

Home is New Delhi. The Bengali refugee neighborhood of Chittaranjan Park. Back to my immigrant's success story. That was the plan. Simple. Easy. The start of it. And to end back home.

Home was to be Chittaranjan Park. New Delhi. I call the place I grew up, home. But I also adopted San Diego as my home. Two continents. Two ways of life. Both are home. Both are what I pine for when I am away. This makes me search for the meaning of home in what I do—work, food, writing, life.

August 1993. Baba walks me to the departure gate. He has enough connections with people who respect him that make it possible for him to get as close to the Thai Airways flight as he can. He holds my hand luggage like he used to carry my school bag to the bus stop near Market I. He will not let me carry it even though I am twenty-two, his youngest daughter whom he called his son. I remain, according to him I remain the son he never had, the daughter who does what a son should. I let him. This may be the last time he will carry my bag. But I don't know that yet, and at twenty-two I am brash enough to think we are amar, immortal, and that nothing will ever touch us.

"Achcha, cholee," I say, taking his leave.

He doesn't look at me, but hands my bag over. "Don't forget your traveler's checks. It's like cash—you lose it, you lose money. Make sure it's safely tucked in."

"Okay."

"Don't talk to riffraff. Watch how you behave. And who you talk to."

"Achcha."

We say many things to each other, but in silence.

The airport attendant says, "Madam ji, it's time," like it's a death sentence.

It actually is—I will never live with my parents or in the house I called my home again—but I don't know it yet.

Across the tarmac, through the glass doors, I spot my sister waving like it's a happy occasion. The one thing we Ghoshs are good at is pretending everything is okay. Except for Didibhai. Didibhai, our cousin, stands next to Didi, tears rolling down her face—the only one in the family who is unabashedly emotional. Ma stands a little apart—I know she is slowly dying of grief, her eyes say so, watching her youngest leave—but I cannot break down now. I cannot show anything so that later the family may think I am weak and wavering. Ma mimes, jal khash, don't forget to drink water, moving her hand as if holding a glass to her lips. I smile, because even when she's sad, she still has her idiosyncratic mannerisms—her pinky is raised like a white English lady. Throughout our lives, we have made fun of my Ma's idiosyncratic mannerisms—the bone china tea set, and Bengali desserts on white plates with gold trim. Ma, the most intelligent woman I have ever known. And yet, it is me who goes abroad to study. The one who doesn't understand literature or language as well as her or her elder daughter. The one who can work hard but doesn't understand oblique taunts. Who isn't the smartest. I shouldn't be the hope of the family. I shouldn't be getting the PhD. Being the youngest means I am indulged. I may be good, but am I *that* good? Regardless, here I am—me—in Baba's shirt, thick jeans, hair tied in a long braid that Ma plaited one last time. Me, waving goodbye to the only family I've known.

*

It's been more than three decades since that August night. That's the day my journey starts. The family, always mine, is now in memories.

Somehow, when I travel now, I am seeking home. That comfort. That familiarity. That love. Even though the family is no longer on this earth, I try to make each place resemble the home I used to know. Much like Spider-Man—the curse and the dream remain intertwined. I, the eternal immigrant, forever in search of home.

The Thai Airways plane is large, and the attendants are very considerate. I cry into my handkerchief, hoping no one can see my tears. After all, Baba had said to stay alert and not talk to anyone—who knows who they may be? My handkerchief is thick—almost a small, soft towel—great for Delhi summers to soak up sweat, a bit too much in this cold, air-conditioned, metal tube of a flight. The red flowers printed on the blue-bordered square piece of absorbent material, is just . . . too much, too much desi. I pretend not to cry. I start that practice in that flight—to pretend everything is fine—even when the world around me crumbles.

The people from Punjab in Northern India are Punjabis. They are Sikhs,[1] following Sikhism, but also Hindus and Muslims. Sikhs have long hair;[2] it's a part of their religion. But there are many men who cut their hair because it's easier, and they can "assimilate," especially in America. You're a mauna[3] Sikh if you have short hair.

The traveler next to me is Indian, likely from the north. I know he's Punjabi—you know that accent if you're Indian. He tells me he is Sikh, but with his short hair, I know he's a mauna Sikh.

He asks me where I am headed. "Amrikka?" he says, eager to talk.

New York, I tell him.

"Yuba City," he tells me.[4]

I don't know where that is.

"Arrey, that's where the farms are," he says, laughing, like everyone knows where farmers in America are from.

I thought they were in Iowa, I whisper.

Shaking his head confidently, he says, "California is where all the food is grown. Just like my Punjab."

"My father was Sikh, and my mother was Mexican," he offers, his eyes holding the anticipation of someone who expects questions. "Long time ago. When men couldn't go back home to marry. They married Mexican farm workers. Like my mother."

"Oh," I say, unbelieving. Which Indian will marry a Mexican, and that too so long ago? I think he's lying, but I don't say so. He looks like he's in his fifties, sixties even? Anyone above thirty is old to me. Sixties? Wow, that's decrepit, I think, like the mean twenty-two-year-old that I am.

The plane engines are so loud, they drown my thoughts. I try my mental math anyway. His parents are that much older—does that mean early twentieth century? A Mexican and a Sikh got married in . . . what was the place?—Yuba City. I know Punjabis marry Punjabis, just like Bengalis marry Bengalis. Why would a Sikh marry a Mexican? This doesn't even make sense. I don't believe him.

He smiles, eager to share, but Baba told me not to engage. I turn back to the window. I don't ask him his name. The flight attendant stops by with the drinks cart.

"Scotch," he says, loudly.

I move back into my seat. I don't come from a drinking family. Baba—the chain smoker—had always told us that Mahatma Gandhi had advised against alcohol and that's how we all won our freedom from the British. We—the

Ghoshs—wandered through society, disdainfully looking down our noses because being a teetotaler meant we were part of our freedom struggle.

When the mauna Sardar drinks his scotch from a little bottle, his kara, the steel bangle, the symbol of Sikhism glints in the light from the overhead lighting. A drinker. A Punjabi. A farming man.

I judge because that's how we have neatly put people in categories. A farmer. A man who drinks alcohol. A Punjabi. My assessment without much data.

Later, in my graduate school apartment in Long Island, I sign up for a book subscription because other Indian students tell me to. And the CD-box subscription because everyone else does. I'm trying to fit in. Assimilate. Become American. Then I buy a Rand McNally atlas. It shows up in a large cardboard box, tightly sealed. I look for Yuba City. It is way, way north near Sacramento. It's far away from New York where I am—which, I've been told, is the center of the universe. Yuba City looks like a small town. Not a city.

*

January 2023, three decades since the Thai Airways flight. I have already lived outside of India longer than I ever lived there. I still call India home. Home is always Chittaranjan Park, New Delhi 110019. This time, I return after almost four years because the Great Pause stalled our lives.

A friend drives me past the Shiv Mandir—the Shiv Temple—that used to be a dingy, one-room prayer hall on top of the hill across from our first house there. Now it has three huge buildings—no doubt where all the gods reside. It is a compound.

Baba and I, never religious, go to the Shiv Mandir every festival to get bhog, the rice and vegetable khichdi that devotees receive as blessings after prayers. Baba and I don't pray, nor do we fast. We go because bhog is delicious, and we are hungry.

In Hindi and Bengali, there's a phrase, payt pooja—worshipping your stomach by offering food. Like the stomach, too, is a god. That's what Baba and I—agnostics both—are good at. Honoring our stomachs.

Driving past the I block house, I see the single-story yellow house we lived in when I was six. I-1612. I call it the wraparound garden house.

In 1976, Baba grows his own Bengal in the vegetable garden—eggplant, okra, kumro/gourds, lau, beans, and tons of roses of all colors. That is Baba's heaven. That is my childhood.

Baba and I sit outside; in his hand, his khurpi, the little metal shovel with a broken wooden handle, me next to a bucket with water.

He digs, aerates the soil, adds khaad, fertilizer, saying, "Jal, aaro dao." Pour more water.

I do. He teaches me how to pick okra without destroying the plant, how to water the roots and not the leaves.

In 2023, that yellow house no longer stands. Instead, a huge, half-constructed four-story building stands covered in turquoise strips of tarp. Cement mixers in various stages of mixing slush, iron rods weld loudly on the cavernous ground floor. A condo-like building. Maybe a house for a multigenerational family. It is as concrete a place as Los Angeles.

"Where is the downstairs?" I ask illogically.

What I mean is the house stands on concrete stilts, and the ground floor, which in my childhood was the prized floor to live in, is missing.

"Ah, new city rules," my friend says, "all ground floors have to be on stilts, with dedicated space for folks to park."

It isn't my Delhi. I have officially reached the "in my days" age. I am that "old person" now.

Taking a selfie, I smile staring at the camera lens, my turquoise jacket matching the tarp covering the house that isn't my home anymore.

It feels like I have to travel even more to find the home that I left and even when I get there, I need to travel that much more.

The journey, the safar of searching for home, which began when I left it in 1993, continues in earnest in 2022. Where can I find my home when it doesn't exist anymore? How far do I travel to find that comfort?

*

Whenever I miss home, I visit Punjabi Tandoor. It's a standard North Indian Punjabi buffet-style, no-frills restaurant in San Diego. They have seen me young, and working in biotech, then going through a divorce—quite an anomaly in the South Asian immigrant community in America at the time. They have fed me Punjabi kadhi when I wanted home-cooked food, fried onion pakoras submerged in a yellow yogurt-based curry sauce sprinkled with dry fenugreek leaves, freshly ground cumin, and chilies. They have scolded me if I wasn't eating more daal, as their mothers would have insisted. They have welcomed me each time when I showed up with a "Bahut bhook lagi hai, what's on the menu today, I'm hungry."

When I enter, I am at home.

In India, we are all about khatirdaari, hospitality, and how to welcome someone so they feel they're part of your family. Punjabi Tandoor restaurant owners, the Sainis, are that.

Sometimes, people you wouldn't have ever interacted with in your home country become your own in your adopted one. The Sainis are Sikhs, a different religion from me, born a Hindu, a staunch agnostic. Unlike me, they are devout Sikhs, religious. They're restaurant people, Punjabis, and I come from a Bengali family from eastern India, the daughter of refugees. And yet, and yet, there's a connection, an apnapan, a closeness that's akin to family.

What do you look for when you sit across from a stranger at a table, a plate of food in between? Is it a conversation? Is it loneliness?

The Punjabi mauna Sikh from 1993 is how my safar, my journey starts. Over a hundred years ago, other immigrants from undivided India traveled to California for work. California—the land of America's produce. The land that reminds most of us of the land of five rivers, Punjab. The story is long, convoluted, and parts of it have already been forgotten. Most aren't alive anymore, and the children may misremember. I fill in the gaps by imagining and then guessing what may have happened.

I become friends with some of these travelers and grandchildren of these immigrants. But I also know I always become part of the story of the people I research, whether I intend to or not.

Why do I keep looking for the commonness? Is it necessary? As I get older, I am at peace with being alone mostly. I am at peace being lonely.

Us South Asians, we have traveled everywhere. We are everywhere. Our food has brought joy to many. Our food has morphed as we have moved, and with each safar, it changes that much more. But then, it stays the same.

This is our journey, our safar, *our story*. I want to take you to our California.

2

What Makes a Sikh?

The five Ks in the Sikh religion are the tenets Sikhs[1], live by.

1. The Kara: It's a steel bangle, and you spot it on a Sikh's right wrist, a pukka way of confirming their faith and adherence to it.

2. Kesh (hair, unshorn for men—hence their turbans and distinct beards, and for women, long hair in braids): Tied into a thick dark braid, the men wear it in a small bun on top of their heads, covered by a handkerchief for the boys, a larger, standard one for the adults. Not like the ones Muslims wear, but a distinct, oval shape.

    a   Long, colorful cotton cloths hang to dry every weekend. You know it's a Sikh house when you see the paghdi turban cloth fluttering in the wind.

    b. We meanly call our Sikh classmates names, that I am now ashamed of, but then we did because we were children—mean and unkind to others who we thought were different.

    c. You know a Sikh girl from her hair, kara, and eyes. And a Sikh boy from his hair, kara, and fearlessness. The Sikh army regiment is considered the fiercest in India.

3. The Kanga, or wooden comb, which they carry on their person. A sign of faith. I am told they carry plastic combs these days.

4. The Kachcha, or undershorts particular to those practicing the religion—I don't know much about that, but it represents a clean body and mind when in service of their religion.

5. The Kirpan, or the steel sword: A small knife—a sign of valor, of the need to defend the faith. Every practicing Sikh has one.

    a   In graduate school, a straggly bearded Sikh student would pull out a small tool to keep his turban in shape. I used to think it was a kirpan, but I am not Sikh, and I didn't know it was a tool to fix hair under the turban. After 9/11, when I had already moved from New York to Washington, DC, I heard he—now married—had cut his hair so he looked "normal." To assimilate. To not be mistaken for an Arab terrorist.

Punjabi Sikh at a Sikh festival, Fresno, California, 2025. Courtesy of the author.

3

The Safar, the Journey

The idea behind my safar journey to find home was to retrace the journey of Punjabis—in particular, Sikhs—to where I now live. The questions were simple—where they went, what they ate, and who they married. Very simple questions. Very complex answers.

Very shortly, I realize the exploration is tremendously internal. As a Bengali, who grew up in Chittaranjan Park, my focus on food, travel, and history has been very Bengali. But as a Delhi person, who grew up in South Delhi, and living next to Kalkaji, a predominantly Punjabi refugee neighborhood, I have been part of that life too. Both/and. Both true.

Look, I'm not saying we—Sikhs and Bengalis—are the same. What I started this journey for tells me more about me even as I absorb what happens to the Sikh community. But then, the journey transforms where they now call home. The person transforms the place. That's the story I seek.

*

Baba dismisses Punjabis in Delhi as "no-culture agriculture" people.

"All they do is eat makke ki roti, sarson da saag, and dance to balle balle," he says, mocking their food, their exuberant dancing, stereotyping the community.

That all of them own or have lost land during the 1947 partition.[1] That they don't believe education is the only way to success. That they drink whiskey, are loud and boisterous. What Bengalis hold dear, they don't. We are cultured, i.e., we sing classical and Rabindra sangeet. Our cuisine is refined. We aren't brash. Our educated women sing well. We believe in art. We aren't uncouth, like those no-culture agriculture Punjabis. I grew up believing that.

In South Delhi, the divide between our neighborhoods is stark. Chittaranjan Park for the bhadralok, well-behaved Bengalis; Kalkaji for the rough Punjabis. Both refugees of the partition. Oh, how cruel and how wrong can a child be?

No-culture agriculture. I repeat that, because that's what children do, mimic their elders' taunts. Later, when most of my friends are Punjabis, South Indians, Marwaris, and Biharis, I realize how similar we are. That the differences are what make us so attractive to one another. I start this journey of disproving Baba's theory of no-culture agriculture people.

*

It starts with food.

Punjabis—Sikhs following the Sikh religion, Hindus as well as Muslims come from hardworking generations of people of the land. Are they agriculture people?[2] Yes, most of them are. They are born in the land of five rivers, where the sun shines, and the monsoons strike perfectly at the right time to help grow the best wheat, rice, and produce. Bollywood movies are made of people having left their Punjab heading to London or New York, singing songs of the land calling them back. And music? Aren't they the people of the bhangra and gidda dancing? Are they not the dhol drum-playing musicians?

In my dramatic teens, I turn to poetry, as one does. It is Amrita Pritam's[3] cry to Punjab's poet Waris Shah in 1948, memorialized in "Ajj Aakhan Waris Shah Nu," that grabs me. Pritam's poem, a plea from a million daughters of Punjab, asks Waris Shah, a historic Punjabi poet, author of the tragic "Heer Ranjha" (a Romeo–Juliet story), to rise from the grave, and record Punjab's new tragedy, which was its partition—one part in Pakistan, and one in India, leading to a broken land filled with cries of the bereft, mourning the dead.

Poetry, much like music, connects us even when the words are of a language one isn't familiar with. Amrita looks at the partition through the lens of women. The grief of loss for the Sikhs in 1947 is what I, a Bengali, the daughter of refugees, have lived with.

Till they die, Ma and Baba talk about the partition like it just happened. They repeat those stories. How they cross over taking trains and buses. That Kolkata, the city they move to, is so noisy, and no one knows where their neighbors are now. Barisal for Ma and Dhaka for Baba is, was heaven.

Home is now Bangladesh for them, till they die. There, the food is better, the songs melodious, the weather sunny.

A place they never return to live. A place I still haven't visited because, for me, home is my Delhi neighborhood of Chittaranjan Park.

Bengali poet Jibanananda Das's poem "Tomra Jekhane Sadh Chole Jao," a call to a Bengal that used to be undivided, a love letter to an undivided land, roughly translates to "I will never lose her in the world's chaos, because she remains my Bengal's shore. . . . "[4]

A lament that they will never lose their land while in fact, they are landless, displaced, heading toward a divided country, while pining for a place that isn't theirs anymore.

Trauma travels through stories, through famine, through food. Only, we don't know it.

The partition of India in 1947 leads to a British Parliament-mandated division of British-controlled India into two independent dominions, India and Pakistan. Later, East Pakistan in 1971 becomes Bangladesh. The 1947 declaration leads to the largest human migration in history—Hindus move to India, Muslims to Pakistan. We are divided on the basis of religion.[5]

One million people are killed, and twelve million are displaced in the communal violence that erupts during the negotiations with the British.[6]

Shame guides our ancestors. Shame of losing homes. Shame of being victims. Shame of losing honor. Honor, the unsaid emotion, guides us. It's lost, and what good are we without honor?

Our ancestors talk about the partition, but not about the violence. In turn, we—the descendants—don't realize how deep that wound is. We don't appreciate what loss of country does to a people's psyche. We don't even realize that both Punjabis and Bengalis, the most affected groups, are so similar. We spend our time calling Punjabis no-culture agriculture people. We Bengalis, the fearful babus, clerks, the literary types who pontificate around dinner tables but cannot be like the fearless Sikhs.

The British divide and partition our minds. To date, we continue to highlight how we are different from each other.

Colonizers effectively bond us through famine, deprivation, and division.

*

In the middle of the Great Pause, as we also call the pandemic, I decide that to understand our safar, our journey, I need to explore where the ancestors landed in the early twentieth century in America. There's a special joy to know the people who dared to dream a better life.

I plan my route, assuming it will be a one-trip-and-done kind of safar. But I return many times. I develop a great fondness for the people whose stories I tell. Perhaps, this is what I am seeking? A connection with people, even if they seem so different than when I met the first mauna Sikh from Yuba City?

Our people's journey to the American West has been in waves. I have labeled them as the first, second, and third waves. I represent each wave with the stories of women who live these lives.

The Pioneers[7] start our migration to the United States even before India's independence. Sheila Singh, the sole surviving daughter of a Sikh father, Teja, and a Mexican mother, Marisol Singh, is a longtime California resident, a mother, the keeper of her parents' legacy. Sheila's name is a name I have given her—for privacy reasons, but also to tell her story while respecting her immediate family's concerns and wishes. Throughout this safar, I have made all efforts to change or remove any identifying characteristics or features of Sheila. But what I want to say is Sheila's story is the story of many Punjabi-Mexicans. Her personal life is her own, and I tell her story with respect. Sheila is also my mother's name, and I give this woman the respect I give my own Ma.

In Central Valley comes the Second Wave. Their place of worship, the gurdwara, is the Stockton gurdwara, a place of community, a place of religion, and a place of identity.

Jes Nijjer, the granddaughter of Punjabi farmers in Central Valley, daughter of a Selma farmer of grapes and California walnuts, is the Second Wave descendant who continues to align with her Sikh values while rejecting the intergenerational trauma bestowed upon her from her ancestors. She represents the generation(s)[8] brought up in American ways, with Indian values, familial guilt, generational trauma, and feminist ideologies. And how she chooses to live her truth.

In 1984, the killing of Bhindranwale, the Sikh leader, also called a terrorist by the Indian government and now martyred leader, in the Sikhs' holiest of temples radicalized many of the community.[9] Consequently, Indira Gandhi, the Indian prime minister, was assassinated by her Sikh bodyguards. In turn, there is an unofficial Sikh genocide.[10] When Sikh youth are targeted[11] in violent kidnappings, police-sanctioned torture, and through drugs, many families leave for the American West. This group is the Third Wave.

They aren't just farmers. They are truckers, dhaba owners, judges, trucking entrepreneurs, and scholars. Fresno-based Uma Devi, wife of Daljit Saini, helps run a social media favorite dhaba, or diner, off the freeway. Uma, a story of resilience post-trucking life in California.

*

When I return to Punjabi Tandoor, run by Jassi and her family—the very place where I belong in this country—I feel I return home.

The question of roots is a deeply complex one. It's not that one cannot uproot a tree. Yes, we can, and yes, the tree suffers before figuring out a way to survive.

With each wave I tell our stories. They are all different. They are all the same.

I share their food, their recipes that make them unique, and represent them. With each recipe, I give you a version that's mine, my own interpretation of what comfort is.

Their stories are ours, and I am honored to take you on this safar, this journey.

**

Makke Ki Roti (Maize/Cornmeal Flatbread, My Version)

Corn rotis are a Punjabi, a farmworker staple. I watched the women of Punjabi Dhaba, Fresno, make the rotis on a roaring gas fire one weekend. Here is my version of their recipe.

Ingredients

2 cups maize flour or cornmeal (makke ka atta)
1 teaspoon carom seeds
Salt as required
½ cup warm water
5 tablespoons ghee or vegetable oil
White butter

Recipe

1. Mix cornmeal flour, carrom seeds, and salt plus water to make the dough.
2. Cover the dough at room temperature for 30 minutes.
3. Make 6 medium-sized balls, then flatten them with a rolling pin.
4. Spread 1 teaspoon of ghee or oil on a flat pan or tawa.
5. Cook the rotis on medium-low flame, adding oil as needed.
6. Remove cooked rotis, and add white butter to each.
7. Serve with daal or sarson ka saag (mustard greens).

Corn roti/makke ki roti being made by Punjabi Dhaba cooks near Fresno's Golden State Boulevard, across Roady's truck stop and Arco gas station, 2025. Courtesy of the author.

PART TWO

THE FIRST WAVE

Sheila, the Punjabi-Mexican Daughter of Pioneers

Early Punjabi immigrants to America, circa 1910s. Courtesy of the California History Room, California State Library, Sacramento, California.

4

Brown Marriages and the Food They Created

Located in California's Central Valley, Yuba County, thirty minutes north of Sacramento, the state capital, is the leading US county producing peaches, prunes, and rice.[1] At the end of 2021, in the middle of the pandemic and right before the Omicron variant takes over the world, a short social media post[2] notes the passing of ninety-year-old Ali Rasul. Ali was the owner of Rasul's El Ranchero restaurant, located in Browns Valley, Yuba County.[3] He was the last survivor of thirteen Rasul siblings who grew up in Central Valley.

His daughter, Tamara L. Rasul English, on the private Yuba Sutter Facebook page,[4] notes that her father's restaurant was the first to offer "East Indian" food.[5]

"East Indian" food, a geographical misnomer, represented the Rasul family roots as much as the enchiladas and quesadillas were a nod to the family's Indian-Mexican heritage.

El Ranchero, on California's 440 Garden Highway, was frequented by Yuba–Sutter County farming locals until 1994, when Ali retired after four decades and closed the restaurant. Rasul's El Ranchero served cheese enchiladas in red sauce along with rotis, lamb curries, and Punjabi dishes. The post announcing Ali's death received 530 reactions as of March 2022, with over 100 comments from people who grew up going to El Ranchero.

Tamara writes, "Mexican food was served as well as curried dishes. . . . My father enjoyed cooking for and socializing with his customers and friends . . . for forty years. Thank you . . . for those memories."

Yuba City Facebook members reminisce about Ali. How Ali welcomed them, how a Mexican restaurant had Indian dishes, how the chef would entertain them when they were children, letting them make rotis on the side.

"Ali used to let us kids sit in his kitchen and make roties [sic] . . . he would always . . . take us back into the kitchen . . . we also used to call him Uncle Ali!!!!!" writes one, emphasizing with five exclamation points.

"Being about 10 years back then, I still vividly remember how delicious the flank steak enchiladas and roti were!" raves another.

El Ranchero closed nearly three decades ago. In 2025, people continue to reminisce about their childhood spent in a landmark restaurant of Yuba City.

His death is a reminder that this community and its collective memories are diminishing at an alarming rate.

*

I hear about the Punjabi-Mexican community[6] on my first flight out of India as a graduate student in 1993. I run that story in my head over and over for decades since that brief encounter.

You've heard this story many times. Here it is again, because memory fades, memory re-remembers. The story remains the same. The story is different each time I narrate it.

I sit next to a Punjabi from Yuba City, the son of a Sikh and a Mexican mother, on my flight to America in 1993.

"Yuba City, you know," he says, confident I know where it is. "In California."

"Near Los Angeles?" I ask.

"Sacramento, near the capital of the state," he nods vigorously, excited to share his story. "My father, he's a Sikh, he came to farm, married my mother. A Mexican."

I dismiss his story as falsehood. After all, Baba said to stay away from riffraff and maybe this fellow was just that. Riffraff. A farmer from Yuba City, and the rest of his story is all false. How could Indians and Mexicans marry, and that too in the beginning of the twentieth century? Impossible.

*

I head to the East Coast. Get my PhD in biochemistry, and then a postdoctoral fellowship in molecular biology. I am working at a startup in Rockville, Maryland, when 9/11 disintegrates the country in so many ways. Overnight, or so I think, people my color, we aren't liked. In upper-middle-class grocery stores near my apartment, I notice white women moving away from me in the fresh greens aisle.

In November 2001, I find my windshield smashed in the parking lot. On principle, I've resisted pasting an American flag on my car because I think a flag or the pasting of it has no bearing to whether I love America or not. But here we are, a smashed windshield.

I know what this means. It's too obvious for me to ignore it.

But, in the middle of my green card process, I can't fight back. Either I conform or else expect more windshield breaks. I give up, pasting a sad US paper flag I print off my work printer.

My immediate supervisor says, "Good you put that flag on."

Which is code-speak. Given the CFO of the company has already told me to be careful. "Don't wear salwar kameezes in public if you don't want to be killed, Madhu," he says, smiling. Well-meaning, is what I think.

People my color are suspect in the rest of America's eyes. The eyes that belong to a white America. Code-speak becomes the way to survive.

On September 15, 2001, Balbir Singh Sodhi, a turbaned Sikh gas station owner, an immigrant from Punjab, plants flowers near his Arizona gas station.[7] Frank Silva Roque shoots him five times. Roque mistakes the fifty-two-year-old Sodhi for an Arab Muslim, or as he had told his friends earlier, vows that he was going to "go out and shoot some towelheads" on the day of the attack. That day, Sodhi was planting flowers at the edge of his gas station to commemorate the 9/11 victims.

The year 2001 is also when the biotech and dot-com companies blossom in California. I move to the West Coast. I apply to ten biotech companies situated in beautiful glass and steel buildings facing the Pacific Ocean. I get call-backs immediately and choose a San Diego biotech near the beach. A new start. A fresh beginning.

Isn't this what America is all about?

*

Only when I arrive in California in 2002 is when I discover that Punjabi-Mexican families did exist. Still do. Yuba City, a town on a Rand McNally map, is a real agricultural town in California. So begins my two-decade exploration of what it means to be an immigrant and the question of belonging in an adopted country.

**

Desi Tacos (My Version)

A riff on Yuba City's El Ranchero restaurant run by the Rasul family—an American Punjabi-Mexican family, I made a version of tandoori chicken with desi, Indian spices in Mexican tortillas.

Ingredients

For the tandoori chicken
1 pound chicken thigh meat, chopped
1 cup avocado oil
1 teaspoon each garam masala, tandoori masala, cumin (ground), coriander powder, chili powder
2 tablespoons ground ginger
½ cup chopped jalapeños
1 cup each chopped onions, cilantro leaves, tomatoes
Salt and pepper
Lemon juice as needed

For the tomato chutney
½ pound cherry tomatoes
2–3 tablespoons avocado oil
3 tablespoons chaat masala mix
1 teaspoon chili powder
Salt and pepper to taste
Lemon juice as needed

For the tortillas
12 store-bought flour mini tortillas (serves 3–4 people)
Avocado oil
1 cup diced tomatoes
1 cup diced onions
3 cups chopped spinach
1 cup chopped cilantro
Lemon juice
Salt and pepper

Recipe

To make the tandoori chicken
1. Sauté the chicken on medium-low flame in avocado oil.
2. Add the garam masala, tandoori masala, ground cumin, coriander powder, and chili powder to the chicken.
3. Sauté for 2 to 3 minutes on medium flame.
4. Add chopped onions to the chicken and cover the pan to slow-cook the mixture.
5. Add diced tomatoes after 2 or 3 minutes, slow-cook.
6. Add salt and pepper to taste.
7. Add more spice mix, as per tolerance.
8. Dry the chicken mix on low flame and place in a bowl; set aside.

To make the tomato chutney
1. Heat the tomatoes on medium-low flame in the avocado oil.
2. Add the spices, and salt and pepper to taste.
3. Cook for 3 to 4 minutes, till the tomatoes soften.
4. Add more chaat masala as needed.
5. Pull chutney off flame, and add lemon juice to taste.
6. Blend the mix in a blender on high for 30 seconds.
7. Set aside.

Assembly of Desi Tacos

1. Heat the mini tortillas on medium-low flame, with 2 or 3 drops of avocado oil.
2. Coat one side with 1 teaspoon of tomato chutney per tortilla.
3. Add 2 tablespoons of chicken mixture in the middle of tortilla in a line.
4. Sprinkle 1 tablespoon diced onions, 2 tablespoons chopped spinach, ½ tablespoon tomatoes, ½ teaspoon cilantro.
5. Add ½ teaspoon of chutney on top to taste.
6. Sprinkle lemon juice to taste.
7. Serve hot and enjoy!

Making desi tacos in my San Diego kitchen. Courtesy of the author.

5

A Lot of Laws

Early 1900s, the First Wave of Punjabi farmers arrive on ships to the East Coast and the Pacific Northwest. By 1910, over five thousand Sikh men are already farming in California. The move is very simple—they are farmers or landowners in the land of five rivers, in British India's Punjab. As a group, these Punjabis of different religions—Sikhs, Hindus, Muslims—are termed "Hindus" by the United States.

But then, what about the other Indians? The Bengalis, the Biharis, the folks from Western India, or even the South? What was their story?

In the late nineteenth century, Muslim Bengali men, peddlers from what's now Bangladesh, arrive at Ellis Island, with bags of silks and embroidered cloths to sell.[1] Over time, they create a unique culture of blending Muslim Bengali lives by marrying Creole, Puerto Rican, and African American women on the East Coast. A story for another time.

Pre-partition Indians include men from what is now India, Pakistan, and Bangladesh. All identify "from 'Hindustan'" or as "Hindoostani."[2] Religion is not the marker of who they were.

This story is about those from pre-partition Punjab.

*

It would be easy for me to tell you that the Punjabi men travel for grand philosophical reasons. That they fight for India's independence and living in the "land of the free," but in general, that isn't the case.

What's documented is that the rich agricultural soils of Central Valley; of Imperial County, east of San Diego; of El Paso, Texas; and of Phoenix, Arizona, remind Punjabis of their state—the land produces food. They know how to grow food.

It is as simple as that. It is as complex as that.

*

To understand the journey of South Asians, we must understand the laws of the land to which they move.

The US Immigration Act of 1917[3] prevents Asians (and other nonwhite people) from becoming citizens, obliquely excluding people seeking refugee or immigrant status from the Middle East to Southeast Asia. A literacy test is imposed, effectively eliminating non-English speakers.

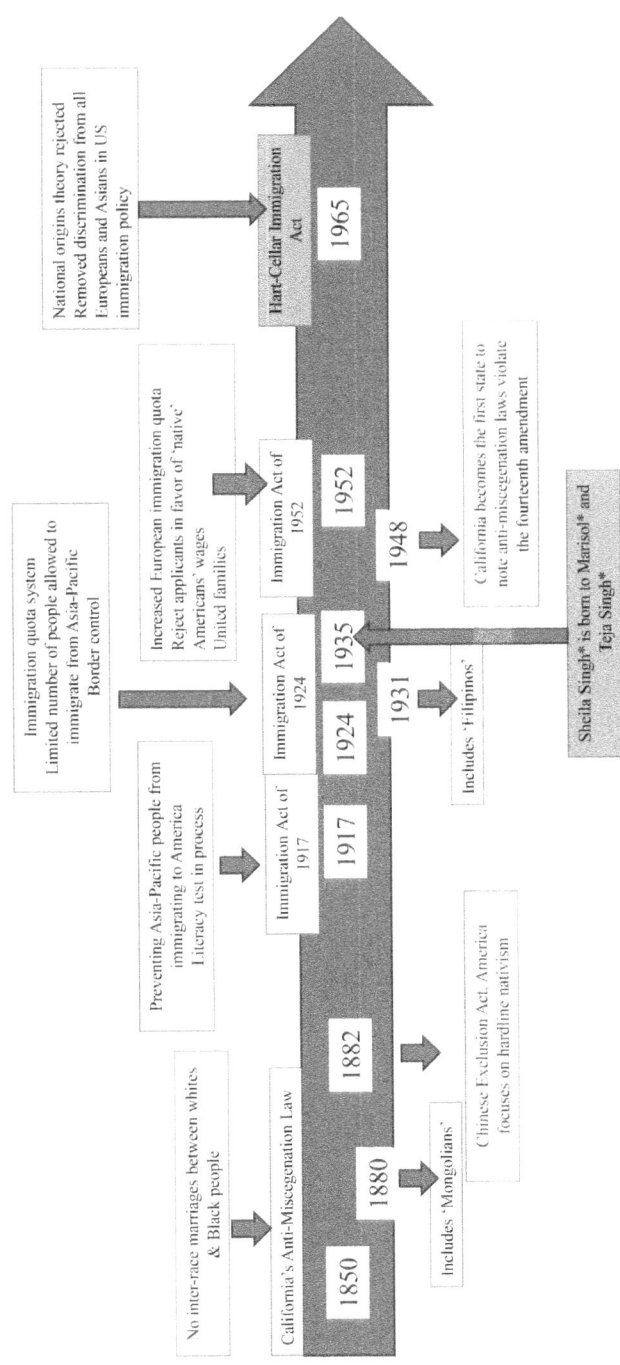

*. Names of the Singh family members have been changed to protect their privacy

Timeline of immigration and antimiscegenation acts and laws in the United States, 1850–1965. Created by the author.

I have henna designs on my hands on the day of my visa interview at the US Consulate in 1993. Henna is a plant found all over Asia, Africa, and parts of southern Europe—a plant called *Lawsonia inermis*.

Henna is used to dye body parts or to color hair globally, especially during weddings. Dry leaves, then grind, make a paste with almond oil and water. Fill it into a plastic cone, cut the tip, and draw intricate designs on your palms and feet. Temporary tattoos of paisleys, flowers, and intricate designs resemble bridal jewelry. For those days, the bride is pampered. In a patriarchal household, this might be the only time she'll be coddled. Once married, her role is in the kitchen and in producing children.

The dark green/brown paste dries on your palms. The longer you leave the paste on, the darker the temporary dye sticks to your skin. If the design is dark, it's said your husband will love you a lot. Allegedly.

In 1993, at my friend's wedding, her mother insists her best friends also get henna tattoos. Minor ones, but henna nonetheless. As a Bengali, henna is alien to me. These are North Indian rituals. Alien. I will be an alien in America soon.

My plan is to get my PhD. Then head back to India. After all, the parents are waiting for me to return.

*

The US Consulate in Chanakyapuri, a leafy, rich neighborhood in New Delhi, is large, overbearing, and we—my sister and I—wait in line for hours. It is an honor to be sent a letter from the State University of New York, telling the consulate that I am legitimate. I have my father's bank account details. I don't intend to fleece America. I am a good Indian.

"Your university invite?" asks the young man behind a glass counter when my number gets called.

"Your degree from Indian Institute of Technology?" he asks, thumbing through the pages.

My heart races. What if he denies my visa? I don't have a Plan B. The plan has only been to go to America. Get the PhD. What do I do if I don't get it?

He asks slowly, as if he knows I don't understand his American accent. "Why do you have henna on your hands?"

I am taken aback. What, what? "Oh," I say, staring at the paisley designs on my palms. "My best friend got married. She's from Uttar Pradesh. We had the ceremony the day before—"

"If you were the bride, you'd have the designs till the elbows, right? With the husband's initials hidden in the henna?"

How does he know? Uh-huh, I nod.

He vigorously stamps my Indian passport.

"Congratulations, Miss Ghosh. You've been approved."

Thanking him, I run out before he changes his mind. After all, I have no Plan B.

*

Who were these men who traveled from pre-partition India? Most—who served in the British Army overseas, like East Africa, China, Southeast Asia— migrated to Canada and the United States from central Punjab, mostly the warrior "races."[4]

More than 85–90 percent were Sikhs, and 10 percent Muslims, but were collectively termed Hindus or "Hindoos." Hindus were higher-caste Brahmins and Khatris.[5] Sikhs were Jats and Chuhras or Dalit/lower caste converted to Sikhism. Muslims were Rajputs, Arains (gardeners), or Pathans. The caste system they belonged to as Hindus, before converting, remains resolute, regardless of time.

But why America? The Punjabi men move from Canada when that northern country starts tightening admission requirements. Before 1907, less than 10 percent of applicants are rejected. In 1907, it is 28 percent and by 1913, that number explodes to over 50 percent.[6]

*

Didi, my elder sister, waits outside with Baba. Did you get it, did you get the opportunity to get to the land of the free?

I wave the papers at them. "Look, look!"

I tell them about the consulate officer's question. Didi says, "He must have been probing."

"What, about what?"

"That you were going to America to marry an American. And be a burden on the American economy. He could have rejected you, you know?"

Many of my college friends also apply, just like me. Student visas are limited. I am lucky to be selected. The wedding henna designs could have invalidated my application. I don't realize that till I see the "approved" stamp on my papers.

It's easy for America to reject an Indian student, especially a girl, from the possibility of a better life and education. Very easy. I come close on that summer day in 1993.

Three decades later, I wonder what my life would have been like if I couldn't go to America.

There is no plan B.

*

The Punjabis arrive in America via the Philippines, before moving to the mainland, and applying for citizenship. But, by 1917, the Immigration Act bars immigrants of the "Asiatic zone" and subjecting applicants to "literacy provisions."

In 2025, the United States now has a hardline nativism culture like in 1917. The Immigration Act or the Literacy or the Asiatic Barred Zone Act restricts immigration by creating new categories of inadmissible persons.[7] The act bars immigration from the Asia–Pacific region.[8] Following the Chinese Exclusion Act of 1882[9]—no Chinese, no Asians—this act now includes Indians (who are part of British-ruled India).

The act is amended by the Immigration Act of 1924,[10] creating the country quota system. Through border control and an application process, the US policy limits the number of applicants from the Asia-Pacific region. Both acts are then revised by the Immigration and Nationality Act of 1952.[11] The 1952 law increases European quotas but can also reject applicants who may affect "native" American wages. By native, they mean white. This act, however, also promotes family unification.

It will be decades before the 1965 Hart-Celler Act, which abolishes the national origins theory that used to restrict immigration from the Eastern Hemisphere.

In the 1920s, when our story starts, Punjabis are provided no such relief. There is a quota, there are rigid rules, and frankly, the United States does not want you, nor your family, to be here if you're Punjabi.

*

In 1993, I travel to America on an F-1 student visa. I do so because of the 1965 Immigration Act. This act lets South Asians like me to attend American universities, to work in laboratories for minimum wage, while getting a degree no girl in their family could ever have dreamt of.

An opportunity of a lifetime. America, the beautiful. America, the land of the free.

*

The 1917 law prevails. Punjabis, if they leave for India to marry women from their community, may not be allowed to reenter the United States.

Oh, but wait, there are more laws since 1850 in California. California's antimiscegenation laws prevent whites from marrying other races, i.e., whites and Blacks or "mulattoes."[12] It is expanded to include "Mongolians" in 1880, then Filipinos in 1931.[13]

Damned if you do. Damned if you don't.

*

In 1948, California becomes the first state to rule that antimiscegenation laws violate the Fourteenth Amendment.[14] This amendment guarantees citizenship, equal protection, and due process to all people born or naturalized in the United States.

Punjabis, restricted by these immigration and antimiscegenation rules till 1948, survive through enterprising ideas, hard work, and an unshakeable will to succeed in America.

6

Sheila, Daughter of the First Wave

The First Wave Punjabis, or the Pioneer Punjabis—comprising Hindus, Sikhs, and Muslims—are forced to determine how to survive in America, whom to marry, how to own land, and how to gain citizenship.

The American laws ensure that the only way the Punjabi citizens could survive as a community would be if they married outside of it.

It is then that Punjabi men consider Mexican farmworker women as potential spouses. Why? Because they are both classified under the confusing term *brown*. In a land of identity politics, brown encompasses multiple regions, countries, ethnicities. But brown they are.

*

Sheila is ninety in 2025. She lives alone in her house she moved into more than five decades ago, a few hours north of San Diego, near universities, global cuisines, and museums. But Sheila reminds me each time that she is a ranch girl from Arizona's Punjabi-Mexican community. She finds it surprising that people think Punjabi men married Mexican farmworker women for land.

"Ah, many were in the country undocumented, as much as many of the Punjabis were," she laughs. "This community existed because people of color couldn't marry white folks. The men figured out how to get land."

According to Dr. Leonard, it wasn't that Sikhs wanted to marry Mexican women to acquire land. Instead, it was an act to assimilate in an adopted country that had just made it difficult for them to exist there.[1]

In 1907, Sheila's father, Teja Singh, arrives in San Francisco along with his brother, Shakti. First, they farm near El Paso, Texas, working the fields owned by Anglo immigrants. Shakti, a religious man, decides to move to Stockton where he spends his years in service, at the gurdwara, the first Sikh temple in the American West.[2]

"My life is Ghadar and waheguru," he says, referring to the Indian independence movement and his Sikh gurus.[3]

The Ghadar party, a revolutionary pre-partition Indian expatriate group, is formed in 1913 in the American West.[4] It is started by mostly ex-British military Punjabi men, and in farming towns in the United States, Ghadar's mission is to overthrow the British. Ghadar in Punjabi and Urdu means rebellion. Religion doesn't mark them in their freedom quest. They are willing to do so through violence, words, and action.

Wedding of Punjabi Sikh and Mexican couple, Valentina Alvarez and Rullia Singh, 1917, southwest United States. Courtesy of the Department of Special Collections, Stanford University Libraries.

The Stockton gurdwara publishes *Ghadar*, the anticolonial newspaper. The revolutionaries create community, pray, and congregate at the temple. Some leave for India to wage strategic attacks on the British in India. They are among the first of twentieth-century India's freedom fighters.

Based on my many conversations with Sheila, we know Shakti is religious and lives near the Stockton gurdwara. Was he also a freedom fighter? We don't know. But religion, revolution, and the zeal for an independent India are all one and the same. To be Indian, to be a Ghadari, is just natural. The country's freedom is paramount.

*

Teja decides to assimilate, or whatever that means in those days. He removes his Sikh turban and cuts his hair. A mauna Sikh, he fits in. As Sheila says, he's a Sikh in name only.

In El Paso, he meets Marisol. Twelve years his junior, she's visiting from Chihuahua.

Sheila never gets a straight answer from Marisol about how her parents marry.[5]

Each time, Marisol says, "It was too long ago. Why do you need to know?"

Sheila has a romantic view of how Teja and Marisol connected. That they fell in love, got married—a Mexican girl, a Sikh man, more than a decade older than her. In love.

Likely, it was a union of necessity—he, needing a spouse, she, needing security. Teja, a lease-holding farmer, is financially secure. Marisol is looking for stability and building a family. Small ambitions. Simple life.

What's surprising is they fall in love. They build a life in a country foreign to both.

Teja teaches Marisol how to make cauliflower curry, rotis, chicken, the Indian way. The contemporary Punjabi-Mexicans liberally use curry powder.[6] Marisol and Sheila do the same.

Curry powder, a distinctly British invention, is first introduced in 1784 by Crosse & Blackwell. Inspired by Indian spices, it's a uniquely British instant masala creation. In fact, in the South Asian subcontinent, each region has variations of the garam masala, and each regional kitchen has variations of those variations.

In Imperial Valley, eighty-two-year-old John Deen proudly shows me his jar of McCormick curry powder spice. To him, it's the connection to Omer Deen, his Punjabi-Muslim First Wave father.

"We make all our vegetables using this, minus turmeric because of my wife's heart condition. This mix is so authentic," he adds with conviction.

I don't have the heart to tell him that turmeric is good for heart health. But it's authentic to him.

Sheila's Mexican mother makes it by slow-roasting and grinding the spices together. I decide to make garam masala inspired by Marisol's mix, as Sheila remembers.

*

John Deen at his wedding with Esther Queseda, May 1971, Calexico, California.
Courtesy of the author.

In the early twentieth century, around 378 marriages were performed between these agrarian communities, thus spawning a hybrid community[7] that has been in steady decline since the 1960s–1970s.

Dr. Karen Leonard notes, "Because they were similar, Punjabi men marrying Mexican women, marriages between 'brown' immigrants worked as their cultural similarities were significant."

Their children grow up with maternal Mexican influence. Their fathers are still considered of "foreign" cultural identity. Most children assimilate, either embracing the Mexican Catholic faith or marrying into Mexican or white American families, diluting the community.

Teja and Marisol settle down in White Settlement, Texas. Their family grows over the years to include four children. Sheila is the youngest and the most beloved.

When Sheila is six, Teja buys twenty-five acres near Phoenix. The Jewish family that sells Teja the land sells it even though Punjabi-Mexicans aren't allowed to own American land. Many such deals happen in those days. The government didn't need to know. The Anglos help the Punjabi-Mexicans because doing business with people whose word is honor is good business for all.

This land comes with a house, plus a kitchen garden. Marisol now takes care of farm animals—goats, chickens—and grows produce. The Singh children grow up with horses, cows, alfalfa, melons, chickens, and soybeans.

The implementation of the Alien Land Laws enables a resurgence of prejudice against "Asians." By 1933, Punjabis and the Japanese are indicted for conspiracy to evade the Alien Land Law.[8] All prejudices of old against Hindus are presented by five white defendants in 1933, with the caveat that "Hindus are not Caucasians or whites but are members of the Aryan race of India and ineligible for citizenship."[9]

Even though he prospers as a Sikh farmer and neighbor, Teja (and his family) must prove their assimilation in the American West.

**

Punjabi-Mexican Curry Powder (My Version)

A 2022 conversation with Sheila Singh resulted in a version of Marisol's curry powder recipe I've shared here.

Ingredients

3 tablespoons turmeric powder
4 tablespoons coriander seeds
2 tablespoons cumin seeds
2 teaspoons garlic powder
½ teaspoon ground cinnamon
2 teaspoons chili powder
1 teaspoon ginger powder
½ teaspoon nutmeg (whole)
½ teaspoon mace (whole)
2 teaspoons ground black pepper
1 teaspoon cloves

Recipe

1. Slow-roast coriander seeds, cumin seeds, chili powder, nutmeg, and mace for 2 or 3 minutes and take off flame; grind them into a fine powder and set aside.

2. Mix the garlic powder, ginger powder, black pepper, and cloves with the turmeric and rough grind them.
3. Mix the roasted spices with the mix from above.
4. Store in an air-tight container.

Red Beans Lentils/Rajma (My Version)

Ingredients

½ medium white onion, chopped
2 tablespoons ground ginger
3–6 medium garlic cloves, grated
2 tablespoons ghee
1–2 teaspoons avocado oil
1 tablespoon each cumin seeds and ground coriander seeds
1 dry red chili
1 teaspoon each ground garam masala and chili powder (Kashmiri chili)
3–4 medium tomatoes, chopped
Salt
1 cup black daal (soaked overnight)
½ cup cream, or kefir
Cilantro leaves (optional)

Recipe

1. Sauté the onions with ginger/garlic in ghee/oil on medium flame.
2. Add the cumin, coriander, and garam masala with the dry chili and sauté till onions turn golden brown.
3. Cook the chopped tomatoes with chili powder, salt to taste.
4. Add the softened black daal, plus 1–2 cups water.
5. Slow-cook on medium-low flame, covered, stirring occasionally.
6. Add half the cream/kefir and continue slow-cooking.
7. Garnish with cilantro leaves (optional) and a dash of cream before serving.
8. Eat hot with rice.

7

But What about the Japanese?

Of all the undesirables who come to our shores, (he says) this parasite, the Hindu, is the most degrading.

— *"The Hindu Question,"* The Holtville Tribune, *September 1910*[1]

While the Singh family has a Catholic mother and a Sikh father, Sheila doesn't recall being forced to either religion. Their friends, other Punjabi-Mexican families in Arizona, are of different religions. But they are all tight—not because of religion, but because of their similarities and closeness from the unique marriage bonds. Every month, the family heads to Imperial Valley—a long car drive from Phoenix. It is to visit the Sikh gurdwara on West Commercial Avenue in El Centro.[2]

Imperial Valley, less than two hours from San Diego where I live, accidentally becomes a racially diverse agricultural region by the early twentieth century.

In 1910, Imperial Valley has 1,322 farms, covering 223,602 acres worth $20.5 million, with more than 75 percent of the land farmed by Japanese and Punjabi farmers.[3] The land, leased from absentee Anglo landowners, is cultivated by immigrants.

By 1915, 8,156 acres of cantaloupes are cultivated in the Valley, and by 1920, Imperial Valley is the cantaloupe capital of the nation, thanks to the Japanese farmers. They harvest peas in November, a crop that doesn't ship before January. Imperial Valley benefits from Japanese immigrants.[4]

The Japanese farmers, similar to Punjabis, circumvent Alien Land Laws and lease land from Anglo farmers by forming corporations and partnerships with them, given their being barred from land ownership. Their relationships with banks, and ability to pay off loans with interest, make them "model" immigrants.

*

February 2025.

I drive to Imperial Valley to meet Bob and Karmen Singh Chell. Two hours from America's Finest City, the freeway transforms into windy roads. In El Centro, I turn to the Imperial Valley Pioneers Museum.[5] Eighty-year-old Bob in a checked shirt and serious expression shakes my hand politely. Karmen is the chatty one, they tell me.

"I can talk and talk and talk," she says, and doesn't stop. "We started this museum because people need to know about us."

Bob nods, his light eyes distant. They light up only when we discuss Nand, his father. "He was a hardworking farmer, a man of his word. All Sikhs were."

Karmen chimes in, "Bob's like Nand. Silviera, his mom told me!"

They have the easy camaraderie of a long-married couple. "Us Imperial Valley farmers never left. Why should we?" says Karmen. "Politics now makes this place different."

"How so?" I ask, curious. After all, in 2025, new indignities are handed to us in the form of creative executive orders to erase our identities.

"People fight over owning things all the time," she adds. "They're diverting water from here. Water makes California the best land. That's why these fires happen," says Karmen, her voice raised. "Now we fight every council representative for water for our ranches."

I still don't know if she's raging over Democrats or Republicans.

Quietly, Bob adds, "Politics isn't my problem. In the Valley, we lived with Filipinos, Japanese, Lebanese, Koreans. Everyone. It didn't matter we were different. For us, that was normal."

I believe his earnestness. While I'm grateful a reticent country farmer confides in me, I'm still not sure of their politics. I don't want to misrepresent them.

Do they care that the current regime may eliminate birthright citizenship? If that, then do they know that they—sons of Sikh and Mexican farmworkers— may not be citizens, after all? Bob, who doesn't speak Punjabi, visits the El Centro Sikh temple, but is far removed from the more traditional Second Wave Punjabis. They aren't similar, except perhaps the last names.

Even when they visit India, the Chells find commonalities in food and Punjab/Imperial Valley weather. Bob knows he's American. A Punjabi-Mexican, but American. A man who took over the farm from his ailing father when he was twenty, this farmer is a First Wave farmer. At age eighty, is he now not American? But he isn't Indian or Mexican, either. Does he realize what the administration is erasing?

Does he know?

*

December 7, 1941. Oahu, Hawaii. The Japanese launch a surprise air attack on the US Naval Base in Pearl Harbor using 353 fighters and dive and torpedo bombers. In over seven hours, Japan coordinates attacks on US-held Philippines, Guam, and Wake Island,[6] and on the British Empire in Malaya, Singapore, and Hong Kong.[7] Two thousand four hundred and three American casualties, two-thirds of them are part of the US military. America is now at war.

El Centro gurdwara, Imperial Valley, 2025. Courtesy of the author.

Two months after the attack on Pearl Harbor, people of Japanese ancestry are ordered away from Western America as part of EO9066, Franklin Delano Roosevelt's executive order.[8] The reasoning used is that of "military need." Over 117,000 Japanese people in America lose their homes and businesses.[9]

What does this have to do with the Punjabis?

In the 1900s, Japanese and Punjabi farmers in Imperial County experience the same racial prejudices—anti-alien laws, physical hardships, and no access to land ownership and difficult citizenship processes.[10] White farmland owners, however, continue to lease land to them.

After Pearl Harbor, the US government interns Japanese immigrant farmers in Arizona, leaving behind agricultural fields, businesses, schools, and places of worship.[11] Around 1942, Sikh farmers pool their resources to buy the Japanese monastery for $6,000.[12]

*

I drive down Commercial Avenue—a small street, surrounded by buzzing power lines, abandoned old recycling plants across railway tracks. When Nand Chell was alive, the Chell family went to the gurdwara for weekend prayers and roti at the langar. Every gurdwara has free food at their langar kitchen for all, regardless of religion.[13]

Commercial Avenue is an old road in an old town. It has seen life, and how. The rough sun isn't kind to the town, nor is the heat. The brush around the neighborhood is covered in desert sand. It feels like a street that represents this agricultural town—hot, dry, and now, forgotten. I miss the turn to the gurdwara building, even though my navigation system insists I have arrived.

In the distance, I notice the shape of the beige building, a curve that's familiar from all the photos of this gurdwara in archives I've pored over for more than two decades. I can barely see the fading Sikh symbol on the façade, the khanda—a symbol of Sikh weapons representing strength.[14] The front steps are torn out, wires hanging dangerously off the wall, the brown door shut, the gates with more khanda symbols in gold closed. Did the El Centro gurdwara close? When?

I head to the building. A couple of big trucks haul debris from the compound. I walk to the building "Sikh Temple" in all the photos I've seen it in. Somehow it looks forgotten, much like the rest of El Centro. The house of worship I've dreamt of for years now seems anticlimactic.

"Excuse me, is the gurdwara open?" I ask, tentatively.

The workers shrug.

"Don't know, but the lady took the food and closed the gate, so I think it is . . . ?"

Ah, the langar food. No Sikh begs, because the langar welcomes all in need. The smell of cumin and fried onions gives me pause.

She fed someone, this lady who locked the doors. The gurdwara is functional, still a place of Sikhs. Through the main door, I see the takht has the Guru Granth Sahib, the holy book on a plank above the carpeted floor, for devotees to pay respects.

The door is unlocked. I take my shoes off before entering this empty place of worship. The holy book is covered by an ornate chaddar. The Sikh symbol of the sword, the trident in orange flags—signifying the Sikh religion—is at every corner, on every saffron flag.

A small note next to the holy granth, the religious texts, highlights that Shahid Udham Singh[15]—a Ghadar party revolutionary who assassinated Michael O'Dwyer, lieutenant governor of Punjab in 1940—used to pray at the El Centro gurdwara before he left for England to carry out the assassination.[16]

*

Here's a story within a story. The 1919 Jallianwala Bagh incident occurs at a community garden in Amritsar.[17] On that day, people—activists and civilians—arrive at the garden. The activists are there to protest the Rowlatt Act, an act the British use to detain and arrest Indians without trial.[18] Coinciding with the Baisakhi spring festival, this gathering is huge, in defiance of the British orders. Brigadier-General Dyer orders British troops to fire on unarmed civilians. The sole exit is closed. Sixteen hundred rounds of ammunition are fired into the protestors and festival goers, killing 379 and wounding 1200.[19] Two decades later, in 1940, Udham Singh launches his revenge by killing O'Dwyer in London.[20]

O'Dwyer was Punjab's lieutenant governor during the Jallianwala Bagh massacre under Dyer's orders. An Irish nationalist, O'Dwyer didn't believe Indians were "fit" to self-govern but considered the Irish sophisticated enough to be free. O'Dwyer's killing may have been a case of mistaken identity, given that the names—Dyer and O'Dwyer—sound similar. An unrepentant Udham Singh is executed in months.[21]

Incidentally, Udham Singh, the revolutionary marries Lupe Hernandez in Imperial Valley and has two children before he leaves for England, abandoning his Sikh-Mexican family to be a freedom fighter.[22]

You can be passionate about freedom. You can also be a bad husband. Both can be true.

*

The El Centro gurdwara is silent. Prayers, ardas, have completed this Saturday afternoon. In the early twentieth century, Punjabis use this space to fight for India's freedom. Today, the silence speaks volumes. The next day, when I ask the granthis how many people come to worship, a volunteer Sikh woman says, "Twenty-five."

I've seen photos of many Sikhs in front of this Japanese monastery, now Sikh gurdwara. More than twenty-five. I prod again, "Ever more than that?"

"No, twenty-five max."

It is 2025, after all. For her, it must only be a place of worship. Not a historical place. A religious one. Does she realize how significant this small, decrepit building is to immigrants like us?

Adjusting her dupatta over her head, she offers chai in a paper cup with a few sweet laddoos—small garbanzo bean flour balls, soaked in sugared rose water—for me. I receive with thanks.

The Santa Ana winds in the Valley are picking up, heading westward through mountain passes from the hot pressure desert to the lower pressure California coast. My old car cannot handle the sudden gusts, nor am I an expert driver to manage in the night. The drive will be long, with me white-knuckled at the wheel, no doubt.

The historic El Centro gurdwara is getting a facelift—and for now, is a functioning gurdwara, but only barely.[23]

Perhaps during their spring festival of Baisakhi, it will buzz with people, music, prayer, and newly constructed concrete steps leading to the entrance door.[24] Perhaps. For now, it's a quiet place in need of attention.

*

Sheila and her family regularly drive from Phoenix to the El Centro gurdwara. It is, as are all gurdwaras, a meeting place for the community—the Muslims, Hindus, and Sikhs—a place to find prayer, jobs, celebrations of weddings, and births.

"It was a picnic! We ate at the langar. It was fun." Sheila's joy of her childhood remains palpable.

Our childhood memories of food and place are always filled with nostalgia. Especially if that childhood was a happy one. Sheila can only recollect the long drives through the desert to get to the gurdwara and the food. The curries, rotis, sweets.

She doesn't remember the prayers much, because likely the prayers were for adults. But she fondly recollects her friends—Elle, Lily, Elsie, some still alive. The Punjabi-Mexican children continue to be fast friends. Likely because there were only a few of them who shared the same unique history.

*

The Imperial Valley Punjabi-Mexicans, the Chells and the Deens—a Punjabi-Sikh-Anglo couple and a Punjabi-Muslim-Mexican couple—don't recollect how the El Centro gurdwara changed hands from the Japanese to their Punjabi community.[25]

Bob remembers his father collecting funds to build the gurdwara. John says there were Japanese families but doesn't remember what happened to them after the war. Punjabi-Mexicans hardly remember the Japanese families of Imperial County. After the war, most Japanese never returned for fear of violence against them.[26]

Instead, the Chells remind me of their disappearing cuisine. Karmen hands over a printed family recipe. "We always had avocados chutney at our family gatherings," she says proudly. "If recipes survive, we survive."

With time, the story morphs and characters disappear. The Imperial Valley Japanese are collateral damage in this story, disappeared.

Even the First Wave immigrants hardly remember them.

In Imperial Valley, the Sikhs are the dominant immigrant group, alongside Mexicans who farm the land. But twenty minutes from El Centro, the Riverview Brawley cemetery still has unkept graves of the Imperial Valley Japanese.

A shiny obelisk at the end of the cemetery tells the stories of unknown Japanese farmers, their children, who were buried there.[27] Most of the illegible scripts are worn.

If you talk about Imperial Valley now, especially if you talk to the children of Punjabi Sikh-Mexican farmers, you talk about Sikh farmers, not their Japanese neighbors.

**

Desi Cantaloupe Salad (My Version)

An homage to the Japanese Imperial Valley farmers,[28] this salad uses cantaloupe, a fruit they grew prolifically in the Valley, before the US government effectively imprisoned them during the war. Serves 3–4 people.

Ingredients

For the salad
5 cups mixed greens or spinach mix
1 medium onion, sliced
1 cup boiled beets, cubed
1 medium cantaloupe
½ cup each walnuts (toasted, optional)/cashews/raisins (fried in ghee)
Salt and pepper
2 tablespoons chaat masala
1 tablespoon roasted cumin powder
1 teaspoon Kashmiri chili
½ cup pomegranate seeds
½ cup chopped cilantro leaves

For the vinaigrette
1 cup single-source olive oil
½ cup lemon juice
Salt and pepper to taste

Recipe

1. Add the greens, onions, beets, and thinly sliced cantaloupes to a large salad bowl.
2. Add the nuts and raisins.
3. Add salt and pepper to taste, along with the masalas (chaat, cumin, chili).
4. Sprinkle pomegranate seeds.
5. To make the vinaigrette, combine all ingredients—adjust tartness to taste with more lemon plus salt and pepper.
6. Toss salad dressing on salad, mix, serve cold.

Masala Chai

A standard beverage in most Indian households, this chai is an offer I've received in every gurdwara I've visited during my safar.

Ingredients

4 cups water
1 teaspoon ground chai masala: equal portions of green cardamom, cloves, black pepper ground into a blended mix
1 tablespoon ginger, ground
½ cup milk, whole
Sugar to taste
3–4 teaspoons of CTC assam tea, or gunpowder chai

Recipe

1. Boil the water in a saucepan, medium-low.
2. Add the spices, with ginger, and set to boil.
3. Add the tea leaves, boil for 2–3 minutes.
4. Add the milk and sugar (optional), boil, and take off flame.
5. Pour the chai through a sieve to remove the tea leaves and spice debris.
6. Serve in teacups with store-bought Parle-G or Nice biscuits.

8

Sheila in Arizona

Every few months, Teja takes his family to Stockton, where his brother Shakti lives near the gurdwara. Shakti has ties to the Ghadar party,[1] the freedom fighters. But is he the ideal Punjabi?

Sheila remembers when Shakti was mean to her mother. "Ordering her around. Marisol, do this, clean the clothes, make food, make tea."

"Did your father intervene?" I wonder.

"Well," she pauses, "she told Teja, get him out of here, I am not his slave. . . . "

"And . . . ?"

"My father was very good to my mother. He made sure Jagat left soon."

Sheila's family may have been an exception to the norm, where the husband–wife relationship appears balanced.

Punjabi men from India generally lead patriarchal lives. Teja had to be an exception.

In Phoenix, Sheila's family lives near other Punjabi-Mexican families.[2] Some Sikh, some Hindu, and some Muslim. Religion for the First Wave Pioneer immigrants isn't paramount as is their national identity. Close friends, their children treat each other as siblings, no matter the religion.

The food is curries and vegetables, and roti. Indian food. The Dad family, Muslim, and the Singh family, Sikh—the food is Hindustani. The Mexican mothers make gobhi sabzi, cauliflower curry without potatoes, lentils.[3]

I often wonder how those desi recipes transfer orally from the Indian subcontinent men to their Mexican wives. Likely the dishes alter, the spice mixes change, and the curry becomes uniquely Punjabi-Mexican. Now, only childhood memories remain among their children, who may be misremembering.

"My father taught my Mexican mother how to make Indian food with no measurements," Sheila laughs, "a pinch of this and a pinch of that. But she made the best garam masala. From scratch."

*

Marisol grinds cinnamon, cloves, turmeric root with mustard, coriander, and cumin seeds into a paste with a ginger-garlic-onion paste. Using this paste with homegrown tomatoes, she makes chicken curry, even beef salan.

Beef, a no-no in India, isn't so in Arizona. Marisol uses produce from her vegetable garden to make curries—okra curry with tomatoes, onions, and a dash of ground cumin seeds, fried karela, or homegrown bitter melon curry, and cabbage or eggplant with scallions, garlic, and spinach.

Much like the Arizona First Wave immigrants, the Imperial Valley First Wave immigrants insist that they too grew up only on Indian food.[4] John Deen, a practicing Catholic who has lived in his Imperial Valley ranch home for more than four decades, is emphatic that his mother, Guadalupe, cooked only Indian food.

"How did she know to make Indian food?" I wonder.

"Oh, my father taught her," he says confidently.

Karmen Chell, however, confides, "The Punjabi-Mexican food was just adding veggies to tomato sauce. It was awful. No spices, really. It's only when I ate at an Indian restaurant that I realized how amazing the food is, this Indian curry."

Perhaps the recipes the Indians taught their Mexican wives were a version of what they themselves remember? After all, they left India decades ago, traveling through military service for British India. How could they remember recipes? Perhaps they deduced, and sometimes their memories faded? After all, spices and sauces were scant in the American West that could resemble Indian food.

It's also possible that soggy spinach with potatoes, and a can of tomatoes poured over it, is the best recipe the Indian men remember. Their Mexican wives replicate the same assuming this is from India, a country they'll never visit because home is America.

My version of these stories is that the curries of Punjabi-Mexicans in the 1930s–1940s likely weren't traditional. When people travel, so does their food. Sometimes, the new land and new food do not resemble what they thought was home after all.

*

As a graduate student in 1993 Stony Brook, I cook for myself. I often mistake coriander powder for jeera, cumin powder. The store-bought garam masala doesn't pack the punch Ma's spices did. Every mistake leads me to try harder, because each dish, if created like Ma's, connects me to home.

The one simple dish that everyone makes as a graduate student, and at which I fail miserably, is daal. It takes me a decade here before I finally create a daal worth eating, not burnt or bitter: a daal fragrant with asafetida, cumin, mustard seed seasoning, or a deeper-flavored one with homemade garam masala slow-cooked with onions and tomatoes in a heavy cream base.

I've often wondered if it takes me a decade to perfect a daal recipe, perhaps First Wave Punjabi family recipes also eventually end as a uniquely different type of cuisine.

Mexican-Punjabi food is neither Mexican nor Indian. It isn't fusion, but mostly Indian and Mexican dishes. Very rarely are Mexican spices mixed with Indian recipes, but it's more a combination of two styles.

Marisol regularly cooks lamb curries, rotis, saag, gobhi (or cauliflower), along with Spanish rice. Mexican staples of tamales and menudo are appropriate during Christmas and other Catholic holidays.

Much like Teja, Sheila doesn't like those much. "At heart, in a family of two girls and three boys, I had the desi gene," she giggles.

"I learnt to make the masala for chicken and beef curry from my Mexican mother," Sheila reminisces. Prepackaged garam masala was unheard of in those times.

*

The Rahmatullah and Dad families, Muslims, are fast friends with the Singhs and other Punjabi families in Arizona. Given the families were few and the culture in these biracial groups was so distinct, it is natural for the children to become fast friends.[5]

While the gurdwara in El Centro is a meeting place for all, many Muslim festivals are celebrated separately, as are Hindu or Sikh. The First Wave children acknowledge the religious differences, but they focus on their similarities and uniqueness as a community in America.

Most Mexican wives are at least a decade or two younger than their Punjabi husbands. Why? Likely because for the Punjabi men, after migrating through Singapore, China, or the Philippines before landing in the Pacific West, many years have passed, and they are much older as grooms.[6] As a result, there is an enormous generational, cultural, and value difference between couples—the men coming from strict patriarchal worlds, the women much younger, looking for more freedom, equality, and help in raising their family. The younger wives sometimes rebel—life on the ranches is harsh, lonely, and isolating—there is a divorce uptick in the Imperial Valley community.[7,8] Fifty-nine divorce petitions were filed between 1919 and 1969 in Imperial Valley.

Sheila doesn't think divorce is an issue in Arizona. She's confident that everyone lives in harmony. My opinion in 2025 is slightly different. I surmise the Arizona First Wave families live in harmony. But life usually means there is marital discord in some. In such a small Punjabi-Mexican community, it's possible the Mexican wives may not feel supported enough to leave or divorce their husbands.

*

When I move to San Diego, I volunteer as a dog walker in a seaside town. I fall in love with every mutt I walk.

A section of the shelter near the 5 freeway is cordoned off with no access to volunteers. Sometimes I see a chair in front of each kennel. I hear dogs leaning against the door, nails scratching the concrete floor. Sometimes I hear low voices, all women. Whispers of "Good boy, I'll take you out of here soon." Or, "A few more days, we're getting our new home."

Later, I find out that those dogs belong to women leaving abusive situations. The shelter keeps the dogs for as long as it takes the women to find a safe place.

According to Red Rover, nearly 50 percent of women don't leave their abusers because of their pets and nearly 25 percent return to their abuser when their pets are used as pawns in the relationship.[9] The same applies to women with children leaving abusive situations.

When we apply the same rules to early twentieth-century Punjabi-Mexican households, a Mexican wife leaving a marriage would mean leaving her children or providing for them as a single mother in an unfamiliar place with no support.

It's not all roses. Sheila may have experienced a stress-free childhood, but a Mexican mother in a Punjabi marriage trapped in Arizona would have limited means. We don't have data that prove either assumption, but given 35 percent of women experience abusive relationships in 2025, I wonder how many women's stories have disappeared over time.[10]

Dr. Leonard says that when these Mexican women do leave marriages, it's because of the support system of sisters that emboldens them.

"Most Mexican women came with their sisters, marrying into Punjabi families . . . " explains Dr. Leonard. "This meant the sisters could support each other."

Life for the First Wave Punjabi children is tough. They are brought up among Mexican, Anglo children in playgrounds of bullying and name-calling. Bob, quiet in his ways, grows up earlier than most. His father, Nand, is two decades older than Silviera, his Mexican mother. By age six, Bob helps Nand water the plants, manage the irrigation, and manage operations.

Karmen's dark eyes are sad when she adds, "Bob didn't have a childhood. When his father got sick, he was twenty. He stopped school and took over the farm. Twenty!"

Bob doesn't react as loudly as his wife. "It was hard, but it was life." Bob didn't pay any heed to name-calling.

Sheila remembers the Singh name, and her "half-and-half" status was cause for much name-calling by the Mexican children.

"They were mean, mean children," Sheila says, shaking her head.

Son of a Punjabi Muslim father and a Mexican mother, Victor Dad dismisses the bullying. "Yes, they called me gringo, half-and-half, Hindoo, but I got over it."

In 2025, I don't think current racial erasures, name-calling, and asking for proof of belonging to America are any different from what happened nine decades ago. But the First Wave children handle these differences quietly. Perhaps it's because they are taught to be model immigrants who assimilate. If you keep your head down and stay quiet, there will be no trouble.

The First Wave immigrants assimilate. It's a way of life.

*

A longtime Californian, Sheila, now nonreligious, is a passionate Democrat. Bob, a regular gurdwara student, heads to El Centro gurdwara only on special occasions. He doesn't comment on politics because it "doesn't involve him." John Deen, the son of a Muslim farmer and a Catholic mother, is a Catholic, a registered Republican who voted for Obama because he wanted to see a "Black man in the office of the president" during his lifetime.

The political and religious affiliations are all over the entire spectrum. What we know is that the First Wave children "assimilate" so well that most don't speak Punjabi or Spanish. The erasure of their origins means they remember Indian food as what the British called curry, rather than their fathers' regional cuisine. When asked about Rasul's El Ranchero, Sheila says, "I had no need to go to Imperial Valley or Yuba City for food. The Phoenix Punjabi-Mexicans were here, and food was great."

The First Wave children of immigrants remain brown, English-speaking Americans.

I want to take you through Sheila's journey, her safar.

**

Marisol's Chicken Curry (My Version)

Sheila's mother made chicken curry based on Teja's instructions. Her Oaxaca roots may have also influenced the recipe. Here is my version of Marisol's curry.

Ingredients

2 pounds chicken thighs (bone-in)
Avocado oil
Salt, chili powder, ground turmeric, black pepper to taste
Roasted ground garam masala (½ stick cinnamon, 4–6 cloves, ½ inch turmeric root, 1 tablespoon each mustard/coriander/cumin seeds, roasted, and ground by hand in a mortar-pestle)
½ cup ginger-garlic-onion paste (1 inch ginger, 3–4 cloves garlic, 2 medium onions)
½ cup water
4–6 medium tomatoes
Cilantro leaves, chopped

Recipe

1. Sauté the chicken thighs in a medium pan on low flame, in avocado oil.
2. Add salt, chili powder (to taste), ground turmeric (to taste).
3. Sauté the mixture on medium-low for 3–5 minutes.
4. Cook the ginger-garlic-onion paste for 5–7 minutes.
5. Add the ground garam masala and cook for 3–4 minutes.
6. Add water, and simmer for 3–5 minutes.
7. Stir the chicken in the sauce.
8. Add more salt, black pepper, or chili, as per taste.
9. Cover and steam-cook till the chicken is cooked.
10. Garnish with cilantro leaves, chopped.
11. Serve with rotis or rice.

Chell Family Pioneer Avocado Chutney (My Version)

Karmen Chell saved this recipe as a Chell family heirloom. Here is my version.

Ingredients

10 avocados, mashed
2 cups chopped cilantro
3 tablespoons chopped ginger
10 serrano chilies, finely chopped
12 jalapeño chilies, finely chopped
10 yellow chilies, finely chopped
3 cups mint, finely chopped
Crush red chili flakes to taste
3 cups green onions, finely chopped
1 medium onion, finely chopped
2 tablespoons avocado oil
Lemon to taste
Salt to taste

Recipe

1. Mix all ingredients in a large bowl with a spatula.
2. Add more salt, chili flakes, and lemon juice as per taste.
3. Cover and refrigerate for at least two hours.
4. Serve with poppadoms or tortilla chips.

9

Sheila, the Indian

Sheila Singh runs faster than her best friend, Lily. Dashing through the yard, she takes long steps up the staircase, her short hair bouncing with each step, her laughter catching in her breath.

She looks back, waving to her friend. "Come on, Lily!"

Sheila's dark hair is a beautiful brown, curled in the latest teenage fashion. Her laugh and flashing eyes hold a glorious world in them. Lily catches up, giggling. If you didn't know them, you'd think they were American—not quite white, but white enough.

It would surprise people when both speak Spanish and English well. Of course, their English is as American as the goras, the white folk. Because their fathers want them to assimilate and be pukka true Americans, speaking Punjabi will not do.

Also, it wasn't about religion, really, since Sheila is Punjabi Sikh-Mexican, and the other is a Punjabi Muslim-Mexican. Every month Lily and Sheila meet at the park. The Punjabi-Mexicans are tight-knit in Arizona.

They're that age when boys are of utmost importance. Now, let's not get too carried away—they are decent desi girls. Their skirts are long, with baggy blouses. Lily even has studious glasses. Usually, boys don't bother her. But Sheila carries her books in front of her so not to attract attention to her body, especially her bosom. Education is important. But they are teenagers, after all. One can't fault them for giggling, can we?

"You're my best friend, Lily," Sheila declares dramatically, spoiling it with a laugh.

"And you're *my* best friend," Lily says, meaning it.

In Phoenix, life is good, but Sheila is ready to head to California. She and Elle have enrolled in the secretarial business school near the college; she hopes to work in an office and live on her own.

The start of a wonderful life, the very start. Turning her gaze toward the boys who were following them at a respectable distance, Sheila laughs. It's a good life.

*

Indian immigrants are described as "the least desirable, or, better, the most undesirable, of all the eastern Asiatic races which have come to share our soil."[1] Dr. Leonard notes, "The [Mexican] women, often sets of sisters . . . married Punjabi partners. The women were really in charge of these relationships. They learned to cook a little bit of Punjabi food. The men liked Mexican food too. . . . It was a comfortable relationship."

In that "comfortable relationship" is a power dynamic. Indian/Punjabi men speak Punjabi, Hindi, some English, and a smattering of Spanish. The women, mostly collateral damage from the Mexican revolutionary war, are farmworkers. When their Punjabi supervisors propose marriage, it's a step up from their lives in Mexico. Even if the language isn't the same, the comforts of life help ease a uniquely arranged marriage.

Didi and I are daughters of the Ghoshs, daughters of a bank officer and a teacher. The daughters of children of refugees, we enroll at St. Anthony's Girls' Senior Secondary School in Hauz Khas, an upscale South Delhi neighborhood Catholic school. Daily, Baba ties our blue ties, and Ma braids our hair into pigtails held secure with blue ribbons. We polish our black shoes with leather polish under Baba's supervision. Heading to the bus stop, Didi holds my hand; she is three years older, and hence the wiser sister. We are well-behaved, obedient, well-dressed, and good students.

Every day, Ma instructs, "Make sure you speak English in school, not Bengali. And don't speak to those Hindi-speaking girls!"

"Why, why?"

Ma crunches up her face in disdain and, perhaps, worry. "You should be around other girls who speak English. The Hindi girls don't study, their parents don't value education."

In the seventies, middle-class families like ours acknowledge an English-medium education is the ticket to success. We don't question it. Being adjacent to English speakers makes us close to white.

We speak in English.

It's a different form of colonization when you speak, read, write, and think in your colonizer's language. I speak Bengali, but my Bengali is hesitant and obviously scrappy. I read Bengali at a five-year-old's comprehension, because no one taught us the language of our ancestors.

Kenyan writer Ngũgĩ wa Thiong'o said, "Writing in English, or making sure that literature is only available in English, you are starving the imagination of a majority of people."[2]

I read, write, and think in English in America. I continue to do so. I don't realize how colonized my mind is. In that, I don't even miss Bengali, or Hindi, or the poetry, the lyrics, even the scripts of these languages that actually make me, me.

In 1977, a seven-year-old me doesn't know that. I am happy I am going to a Catholic school. The nuns think I am smart. I articulate my thoughts in English with ease.

*

Teja grows corn, alfalfa, and soy on his farm. Marisol tends the chickens, ducks, and the vegetable garden. The children accompany Marisol to church and then head to the gurdwara as a family. The children are mostly Catholic because their mother is. Teja waits in his car for church service to be over to pick them up after mass.

Every few months, they head to Stockton gurdwara, the oldest one on the West Coast, to meet Teja's brother, Shakti. The Singhs meet other Punjabi-Mexicans, eat langar vegetarian food, pray. A place of community, it's when the family is almost fully Punjabi.

Growing up in two cultures, Sheila switches languages, foods, and how to be among goras easily. It is the only life she's known—a hybrid culture, a hybrid language, and in turn, a hybrid her.

Life for the Singhs is in Arizona even though India gains independence in 1947. Sheila, Arizonan as she is, however, is also as desi as Teja. The community is small—these Indian families—men from Punjab, Hindus, Sikhs, Muslims. Hardworking farmers who came two decades ago to farm, because that's what they are good at. Farm, earn, send money back to their villages, live.[3]

*

Ma and Baba marry in 1962—an arranged Bengali marriage of Bengali displaced families. They never called themselves refugees. *Refugee* is a term that Bengali babus, the educated class, reserve for the uneducated farmworkers and peasant class. No, they aren't refugees, even though I claim that word to describe me—the daughter of refugees. They call themselves "displaced."

In Kolkata, they marry in December. It rains that day, a lucky sign. Ma wears a pink brocade Benarasi sari that I still have in my closet, tissue thin, silver threads of embroidery. Baba slings an off-white Kashmiri shawl on his shoulder, over a kurta and a white silk dhoti around his torso.

A traditional Bengali wedding of a bank officer and a teacher. Educated people. Moving up in life. Two families joined forever. An introvert. An extrovert. A bookworm. A singer.

*

When Teja and Marisol marry, Marisol doesn't understand Punjabi. But that doesn't stop the marriage. Teja speaks English, farms, has money. They may perhaps be the only Punjabi-Mexican couple that Sheila knows of who marry for love.

I don't know if this happened, but I think this may have. So here we are. Here we are.

In their kitchen, Marisol tells Sheila stories. Marisol expertly throws rotis on the tawa, Sheila adds ghee to it.

"Primero me enseñó a hacer roti." This is how to roll a roti. Marisol tells a story of her and Teja.

Marisol adds, "Roti, roti." It isn't a tortilla, but a roti. Teja teaches her.

"¿Era que?" Sheila asks to confirm, like this is roti, pointing at the fluffy round dough heating on the flame.

Marisol smiles, patting the whole-wheat balls into round shapes. Rotis. Chicken curry. Daal. Teja remains Indian in what he likes to eat. She remains Mexican even when she cooks Indian food for the family.

Sheila hugs her mother. "Look at you, my Mexican mama!"

Her mother, not the demonstrative kind, pushes her away softly. Teja is the affectionate one, not Marisol.

Sheila sneaks a roti out of the bowl and runs out before her mother can catch her.

Marisol flips the roti, adding a dash of ghee on the low flame. She remembers the early days of her marriage, to a man who still cannot speak fluent Spanish. An older man, he shows her his love by bringing her the first harvest of fruits from the farm. Even now. Even after so many children. The first corn. The first peach. Always for her, Teja's wife, Marisol.

Every day, she becomes a good wife. Mexican, but good. Teja shows her how to be desi. Cook daal. Roti. Chicken curry. How to grind coriander, cumin, nutmeg, cinnamon, and cloves to make garam masala in the metate she brings from Oaxaca. Marisol knows to be desi even when she speaks Spanish.

"Is the food ready?" Teja asks from the dining room. He isn't impatient, nor is he the regular Indian man, demanding his wife be in the kitchen. He's a patient man, willing to assimilate, to be American, to show his love for his Mexican wife. Teja is a good husband.

"Sí," she replies, applying ghee to the last roti. As desi as this Mexican can be.

*

Ma teaches me how to use all the burners on the stove. Cook in thirty minutes or less, a whole meal. Don't slave over the stove; that's not what a woman should do.

"A woman should be at the dining table, talking politics with all," Ma announces with a smile.

Being a Bengali, politics, social causes, and conversations around them is how I grow up. Sometimes, uncomfortable conversations are how you parse apart issues. Ma makes me who I am.

Pass the salt or the butter—kind of conversation at the dining table is an alien concept to me. When I move to America, that's all I hear—the sign of a happy family is everyone at the table. The husband asking for things to be passed to him, the wife fussing over the food for the family. No conversation on politics. Or conversations on how to be better neighbors. Americans, for me, are oddly avoidant. How do you live avoiding life? Does anything matter to you other than your immediate family's needs? If not, then why not? If yes, then do you just pass the salt?

Sheila and Marisol connect deeply, two women in a time when conversations like these happen only around the kitchen stove.

I meet Sheila when she is eighty-seven, her parents long gone, her marriage over, her roots no longer in India, or even in Arizona. Sheila has the confidence of a woman who has lived her life alone. But she also has the poise of a woman who has been called beautiful all her life.

She still has that smile of her teenage years, her hair is sparse, her wrinkles are numerous, and her sense of humor remains wicked.

"I am as desi as my father was," she announces proudly.

When her brothers clamor for burgers, Sheila craves roti-sabzi and chicken curry. Much like Teja. She is her father's desi daughter.

For her age, Sheila is the perfect example of spry. The spark of joy when she greets me at her neat California home is that of a young person greeting a long-lost friend.

"Ah, ah, Madrooshi," she says, her arms outstretched in an uncomplicated and inviting hug, like she's known me forever. "Come on in."

Almost instantly, I feel like I am visiting family. I want to catch up like I would have if Ma were still alive.

I hand her the red flowers I drove two hundred miles from San Diego with, and a plate of naroos—coconut, with molasses, mixed with saffron and cardamom, topped with a surprising blueberry, my contribution to bringing a Bengali dessert with an American tinge to this dinner Sheila has organized for me.

We sit down with Dr. Leonard, then a serious eighty-four-year-old professor with very unserious pink dyed hair, and Sheila's younger daughter.

Dr. Leonard explains, "Well, I became friends with Sheila only after I started researching my book. We realized how much we like each other. It's been almost thirty years now!"

She hears about the Yuba City and Imperial County Punjabi Mexicans in the eighties from a student. Three decades ago, Dr. Leonard writes the stories of 378 such marriages between Mexican farmworkers and Punjabi farmers.

From the kitchen, Sheila brings a large pot of chicken to the dining table. Her handshakes slightly as she ladles the chicken with broth onto ceramic plates with intricate designs. She banters with Dr. Leonard, evidence of a long and strong friendship filled with jokes and stories. I am but a witness.

Across the dining table, I see a picture of Sheila's dog, Lulu, who passed away recently. The house feels like it misses the dog.

Her daughter confides, "I'm going to the shelter every day in case I can find a puppy to foster."

The living room is filled with photos of Sheila's parents. Her father when he landed in San Francisco. Her mother when she was young. A young Sheila with her mother. Photos of her daughters. The evening light slowly fades, but the room remains warm. Sheila has created a family and a life in California.

I am but only a witness.

**

Sheet Pan Chicken Thighs,
Inspired by Sheila Singh's Recipe

Ingredients

6–8 skinless boneless chicken thighs
1 cup chopped olives, kalamata and Castelvetrano
1–2 jalapeños, chopped
3–4 cups vegetables: onions (quartered), sliced zucchini, quartered bell pepper, medium tomatoes, halved
½ cup chopped parsley
Salt, chili powder, and pepper to taste
Optional: One cup cubed feta or paneer
Sauce: Mix quarter cup lemon juice, two teaspoons dried oregano, 4–6 cloves garlic, roughly chopped, half teaspoon chili powder, salt and pepper; whisk with ¾ cup of olive oil till the oil is emulsified

Recipe

1. Heat the oven at 400 degrees F.
2. On a large sheet tray, arrange the vegetables to cover the entire tray.
3. Add quarter cup of the Greek-inspired sauce and mix the sauce with the vegetables.
4. Place the salt, chili, and pepper-seasoned chicken thighs uniformly over the vegetables.
5. Add more olive oil as needed.
6. Toss the chopped olives evenly over the sheet.
7. Add more sauce over the pan, making sure to cover all the chicken and vegetables.
8. Bake at 350 degrees F for about 25–30 minutes.
9. Broil to char the vegetables and crisp the chicken for about 5 minutes, making sure not to burn the chicken.
10. Transfer into a flat-bottomed bowl; add leftover juice to cover the chicken.
11. Garnish with parsley leaves and optional paneer or feta cheese cubes.
12. Serve with toasted sourdough bread.

10

Sheila, the Student

It is the fifties, and the Punjabi-Mexican community is tight and small. They aren't very Indian, nor are they Mexican really, because seriously, who takes after their Mexican mothers when identities are forged through last names, and their last name is Singh or Abdullah or Dad or Rahmatullah?

Besides being desi, Sheila is ambitious, an anomaly. She learns to hide that and smiles to make herself nonthreatening, especially to the boys. She does well in school and when the final report cards show up, she knows she's headed to California.

Teja Singh agrees to business preparatory school for his daughter. She will learn to type and manage office business affairs, as young and competent women aspire to do in the fifties.

"Study hard, Sheila."

"Yes, Daddy," she agrees.

Her father has always told her she is destined for great things. But there's this question of boys.

*

There are a few things in the Ghosh household that are primarily Ma's or Baba's responsibility. During jackfruit season, Baba sits in front of the bothee—the sharp iron knife on a metal stand, places newspapers all around it to avoid staining the floor, and applies mustard oil on his fingers so the unripe jackfruit resin doesn't stick to them. He cuts the huge fruit expertly into pieces, removes the seeds, and cleans out the fibers, giving Ma the cleaned jackfruit. She expertly converts it into a curry with turmeric, cumin, and roughly ground cardamom, cloves, and cinnamon.

Later in America, I find out that vegans consider jackfruit a meat substitute.[1] But in the seventies, I am my Baba's helper, applying oil to his fingers so he can cut it for Ma to cook.

Every Sunday, he and I head to Market 1 in Chittaranjan Park to buy a fatty part of the goat from our local butcher. Ma converts the minced goat meat into keema curry.[2] It isn't that we thought this was a gendered role, though now I'm certain it was. But this is what Ma does, and this is what Baba does.

My Baba isn't the typical Bengali man. He cleans and cuts the meat, chicken, and vegetables whenever Ma wants him to. He washes his own clothes. He grows vegetables in our wraparound garden house. Ma is just smarter than him in so many ways, so she is the teacher who makes her daughters curious. And both of them make us hardworking.

*

As more Punjabi immigrants arrive in the United States in the early 1900s, the government imposes policies to decrease the immigration trend. Before 1907, fewer than 10 percent of applicants were rejected. After 1907, 50 percent or more were rejected.[3]

Punjabi farmers who arrive in America now cannot return to marry women from their communities. If they leave, they cannot reenter. If they stay, they can't own property. Under the Immigration Act of 1917 and the 1924 National Origins Quota Act, Punjabi men have a choice to make—keep their immigration status in the United States, marry women here, or return to British-occupied India.[4] Teja stays. And marries Marisol. This is Sheila's story.

Teja Singh likes music. Sheila watches her father sing in his language when he thinks he is alone. Teja admires all the college students who are musicians. They remind him of the 1907 India he left.

With his short hair, Western clothes, and Mexican wife, Teja has moved from San Francisco to El Paso to Phoenix. He has assimilated.

Now his littlest, Sheila, will be what she wants to be. With limitations, of course.

Let's not get too carried away. She's a girl, after all.

The first time Sheila meets Vidur is in her house. Her father invites a California college music group performing in Phoenix over to dinner. Vidur plays the tabla and the sitar almost like a professional musician. There are dancers, singers, and musicians in this group.

Marisol cooks up a storm. Chicken, sabzi, rice, daal, roti. The kitchen bustles with prep work, Marisol moving from the stove to the cutting board and back. Curries boil in the background. Sheila and her elder sister help with the tea.

The table is set, and everyone eats with gusto—the young college students are hungry for a home-cooked meal, and Marisol cooks very well. After drinking countless cups of chai, the musicians sit down for a gaana music session.

The Singh siblings sit in the living room. Vidur's tabla beats, the dancers from Holland's intricate steps captivate the family. Then, the harmonium player riffs a tune as warm-up, it's a joyous evening.

"Bravo, bravo," says Teja, adding, "waah, waah!" the Indian equivalent words.

Sheila's brothers coax the singers to sing more. After the usual amount of pretend resistance, they start again. Vidur riffs on the sitar, his fingers expertly flying over the strings. They sing a Mohammad Rafi song. Her brothers clap along; it must be popular.

Vidur's voice is strong, trained in classical music. His eyes follow Sheila like there's no one else in the room. Blushing, she heads to the kitchen.

Marisol looks up from the stove, suspicious. Sheila dashes back to the dining room. Vidur continues to play the beat. Sheila's heart races too fast to bear.

"Waah, that was great," Teja nods his head in appreciation.

Marisol hands more chai, with cookies, and onion fritters. The musicians marvel at how she has mastered Punjabi food.

Puffing out his chest, Teja proudly says, "She's good, Marisol. You cannot figure out if this was made by a desi or a Mexican!"

Someone pulls out their camera to record the moment. It's the older Singh siblings, then a Norwegian dancer, another desi dancer, Vidur, and then Sheila, and a dancer from Holland. In between the Dutch dancer and her, Vidur inserts himself, his arms wrapped boldly around both women. His dark hair matches his dark suit, his mustache is very admirable, and his smile lights up the photograph. In front of them, Marisol and Teja Singh sit, serious, like older couples do—with the gravitas of a long-married, prosperous couple.

Vidur hands his empty cup to Sheila. She makes sure her fingers don't touch his when she takes the cup. She's sixteen, from a respectable Indian family after all.

*

In 1993, I travel to Long Island for graduate school. I am the first Ghosh daughter in America. I spend my days in lab, working, studying, teaching. Every night, I return from the library around 11 p.m., sit before the television with my Honey Nut Cheerios and 2 percent milk, watching Jay Leno crack jokes I don't understand.

The silence around me is deafening. I am used to noises—vegetable sellers hawking fresh produce, street sweepers swishing their brooms, gurdwara's loudspeakers announcing morning prayers, Hindu temple priests clanging the cymbals, and Delhi city buses' belching exhaust air on the main road. New Delhi, my city, is noisy, loud, and shameless. Stony Brook is quiet, soft, mute. I don't fit in.

I miss my parents. I miss my bed. I miss home. Every weekend, when my roommate leaves for her parents', she encourages me to use her portable TV. In Long Island, every Saturday, a sad channel plays Indian film songs. A middle-aged man with a handlebar mustache interviews local singers who likely came to America on an H1-B work visa, harboring dreams of singing. The channel is speckled with snowy transmission, wavy videos. Every weekend, I watch the singers with cereal as dinner. I miss home.

I miss home even now, three decades later.

*

Two years later, Sheila meets Vidur the second time completely by chance. She has moved to the college town with Elle, her Punjabi-Mexican childhood friend from Arizona. She waits for her outside the grocery store.

A young man walks by, stops, and turns back. Dark eyes, short, the man carries himself with the confidence of a tall man.

"We met in Phoenix, yes?" he asks.

Sheila looks up, unsure.

She and Elle have been living in the boarding house studying at the city business school for a few months.

"Phoenix, when?" she plays along.

Elle steps out of the store when the man says, "Don't you remember? I'm Vidur, I played the sitar, from the university here. Engineering."

Of course she knows him, of course she does. Why is she even pretending that she didn't? Oh, oh, oh. Sheila cannot take her eyes off him. He is so handsome, she sighs like a Hollywood heroine.

Elle looks on in disapproval, but it doesn't deter him.

He says, "Come, let's have coffee?"

Both the girls say yes, because, why not? He opens the restaurant door, smiling when Sheila looks at him.

At eighteen, Sheila will soon get a job after school. A former farm girl, but now, she expects to be employed soon. The freedom she craved is here. She loves this life. I will do well. I will marry well. I will live well.

Vidur has an aura of power, like he commands attention, she decides, liking it.

"How's college?" he asks the usual questions. "How's your father? And brothers?"

Good, good, she nods. She's dizzy knowing that her crush is in front of her.

"It's been two years, yes?"

"Uh-huh."

They talk and they talk, and they talk.

The next weekend, Vidur invites them both to the city garden. Sheila doesn't say no.

It is the start of a wonderful relationship that she didn't know she needed.

Sheila is one of the first women in her Punjabi-Mexican community to go for higher studies. The university students are many, the campus is vibrant, filled with young people brimming with hope and idealism, and an uneven ratio of men to women. This is what she wants to do. Live better than her farmer father had and settle down as good Indian girls do.

Vidur is more than a musician. An engineer. This is the first coffee. And more. And more.

There are cinema dates, music sessions, sitting in cars, on park benches, on campus, more cafés and diners. Every morning Sheila wakes up to a joy she has never experienced. She is so in love that she could die.

*

The first time I meet my now-ex, I am a graduate student in Maryland. He lives with a bunch of Indian students in the apartment upstairs. He has a master's degree, a job, and a Toyota Corolla. He is tall, very handsome, with a thick head of hair. He sings like Mohammad Rafi. He consults for an IT firm. Nusrat Fateh Ali's qawwali music blares loudly from the stereo. The ground shakes, despite the ragged beige carpet. It's a Friday, and he's back for the weekend.

"Meet Madhu," says a roommate, excited to introduce me. I am the cool desi girl—Bengali, artsy, a science girl who can cook—different.

He—my now-ex—sticks his hand out. "Hello," he says formally. His eyes don't meet mine, but I don't notice. I love his voice.

The roommate says, "She cooks so well. Look at her jeans, aren't they rad?"

I am wearing hand-me-down jeans, paint splattered strategically all along the sides. Later on, he says I am trying too hard to be American. I stop wearing those jeans.

Nusrat brings us together. Music. Food. The fact that he's South Indian and yet he can speak in Hindi is a plus. He loves his parents. He will love me too.

I am in love.

*

Most of the students in the university come from the Punjab state in India, the divided one—America now allows brown people, Indians, to enter as immigrants for higher education.

Vidur is different. He's here to make it. Vidur comes to America to better his life. Like Teja.

Sheila is in love. He is bold. He is handsome.

"I love you, Sheila, you're mine," he announces dramatically.

She shakes her head. "Hush! What are you saying?"

Her heart races; she's doing things with him she never imagined she would. When he pulls her toward him, she doesn't hesitate. But then she is still her father's daughter when he wants more.

"No," she pulls herself away.

They're in his house—a rented apartment he shares with other engineering students. She straightens her skirt and smooths her hair, getting up.

"No," she repeats.

"Why? This is America. I am a man, and this is natural. Our needs. My needs. Why can't we—?" he says, lying in bed, his eyes confused.

"No," she whispers. How is this love? What will my parents say? What if I get pregnant? she thinks, alarm bells taking over her lovestruck beating heart. No. No. No.

"Sheila?" he asks, now concerned. He sits up.

She inhales before looking at him, "I can't. We have to get married."

He laughs, a sound that takes over the room in its echoes. "Stop it, I'm just a student, I can't afford to—"

Sheila picks up her books on the floor, her small leather purse next to them. "I have to go."

In her boarding room, across from Elle, Sheila cries into her handkerchief.

"What, oh, what have I done?" Sheila sobs. "I can't sleep with him. He doesn't even know if he wants to marry me."

"Ah, that settles it then," Elle, the judgmental one, says, her hand flicking the thought away dismissively.

Sheila's eyes well up again. Vidur was the man she loved. No woman can afford to get pregnant, least of all a desi girl from an Arizona farming town in the fifties. What would people say?

She calls him. "I will be with you only after we get married."

"Okay, but you can't work after we get married," he says decisively.

"Wait, I want to work. I want to earn money. How can—"

But she knows and he knows. There's no middle ground. It is the love of young people. Brash. Passionate. Headstrong. No meeting in the middle. No compromise.

"Don't call me again," she tells him, her sobs stuck in her throat.

She doesn't see Vidur after that. This feeling she has for him scares her no end. But then, he doesn't reach out either.

Now the deal is this. Sheila is beautiful and smart. She's an educated woman with brains. Why wouldn't men want to be with her?

Sheila works at the college's procurement and supply department. She meets other interesting single women. Together they visit museums, parks, cafés, and then head to parties together. She's doing well for herself, this Punjabi farmer's daughter.

*

My now-ex and I have been together for a few months when I start planning my married life. We will find jobs that will get us our green cards, me with my PhD, he with his IT degrees.

Two weeks after I tell my sister that I am in love, my now-ex calls me. "I'm moving to California."

"Huh, but what about me?" I ask, confused. It'll be a couple of years before I complete my PhD in Maryland. What about us?

"Madhu, it's only been a few months. It's not serious. Is it?"

I beg him, "Don't leave me."

I panic. My heart races—is this how one gets dumped? Is this what happens when you let a man into your heart? I believe in Bollywood. That once you love someone, it's your forever.

I run to him. I hate myself for groveling, but I cannot stop. Nor do I know this is narcissistic and abusive. I am in love. I wish my tears will melt him. He holds me, finally, letting me snivel.

I exhale, because I feel I won him back.

This becomes our pattern for the two decades we are together. He, trying to leave, he, telling me he's done. Me, running after him. Me, begging, don't go. Don't leave me.

*

At one such college party, Sheila meets her now-ex-husband. He is tall, handsome, a few years older, not a Punjabi, but Indian from another religion.[5] Different religion, different culture, foods. Indian nonetheless. His well-off family are businesspeople.

"Marry me," he tells Sheila on their second date.

He checks all the boxes, especially the one where the boy doesn't want to have sex before marriage. He will wait for her and the wedding night. It is time; she compromises. She nods, yes, I have to tell my father.

A few days later, she reaches out to Vidur. He picks up on the first ring when she calls him.

"I'm getting married."

"Don't," he says. "I must get my business running. Wait."

"No," she says, clutching onto the receiver.

"We were meant to be together, Sheila. Don't do this."

But the other boy has already proposed. She has already accepted. She hangs up, wiping the tears streaming down her face. This is the end.

**

Ma's Aloo Curry (Potato Curry)

Ma insisted that cooking not take over women's lives. One easy recipe she taught me was this versatile potato curry, a Bengali recipe I make often when I miss home, or what used to be home for me.

Ingredients

1 dry red chili
2–3 medium bay leaves, dry
1 teaspoon onion seeds (or kalonji)
5–6 tablespoons mustard oil
10 medium Dutch potatoes, cut into small cubes
2 tablespoons turmeric
2 tablespoons freshly ground cumin powder
1 tablespoon red chili powder
Salt to taste

Recipe

1. In a round-bottomed karahi/pan, combine the chili, bay leaves, and onion seeds and wait for the spices to sputter in oil on medium flame.
2. Sauté the potatoes in the spices.
3. Mix the turmeric, cumin powder, and chili powder in 2–3 tablespoons of water.
4. Add the mixture and sauté the potatoes for 2–3 minutes, adjusting oil, salt, and chili.
5. Pour 2–3 cups of lukewarm water, reduce flame to simmer, and cook for 4–6 minutes.
6. Once the water in the potato curry transforms into a rolling boil, switch off the flame.
7. Serve hot with rice, or pooris.

11

Sheila, the Homemaker

In 1957, Sheila marries in the little California town that is home for her now. Marisol and Teja are overwhelmed with joy. A farmer's daughter is marrying outside the community, into a business family. The wedding is how it should be—with celebrations of Indian songs, wedding customs, pomp, and prayer.

Sheila will make this marriage work. She cannot, will not think of Vidur. Her life is full—her husband, his work, his needs, cooking, making the house a home, everything a married woman needs.

After a few months, Sheila catches up with Elle. Sheila's hair is coiffed in the latest updo, her embroidered dress smart; she's beautiful.

"How are you really?" asks Elle.

"I'm good, why?" she says, adjusting her dress. Her dark eyes interrogate Elle.

"Vidur got married. A few months after you."

Sheila's heart pounds. She pretends to straighten her shirt. "To whom?"

"That girl, you know the one who used to make eyes at him at the dance hall?"

"Uh-huh."

Sheila laughs as if she doesn't care. "Good," she says with certainty.

On her way back to her husband, Sheila wonders if Vidur wanted to marry but maybe not her? Did it matter anymore? she thinks. At dinner, she fiddles with her wedding ring and smiles at her husband when their eyes meet.

*

Life unfolds whether we like it or not. Sheila becomes a mother. And again. Two rambunctious daughters, naughty beyond belief. The family in India asks her husband to return to help with the business.

"Sheila, pack up the house."

Even though her parents are getting old, and she misses the farm, she is now married. Family ties loosen. As the educated one who marries outside the community, Sheila feels less close to her siblings. Their lives are still around the farm, and they marry Mexicans. Hers? Sheila is a Californian married to an Indian. She's different. Her family is what she's created.

She prepares to go to India with her daughters and husband.

India, her father's land, has always fascinated Sheila. She follows all the news reels at the movies on India, the songs, the news. She heads to India, seeking her desi roots.

In 1958, a photographer takes a picture of her with her husband. She in her silk sari, her hair tied in a demure bun, her eyes still flash like they used to when they lived in California. Her then-husband in white, dapper, his arm on her shoulder, possessive. She looks happy. She isn't.

*

Our wedding is different. Usually, a traditional Hindu wedding means the groom and his family arrive at the bride's home, with music, and drums announcing their arrival. The groom folds his hands respectfully in front of the bride's parents. They welcome him with flowers, blessing him with Bengali jaggery-based sweets.

That's not my wedding. I plan it from San Diego, because Ma and Baba are old and I don't want them inconvenienced. Even then, they do all they can. They call family members, cousins, sisters, brothers, nieces. The wedding is in Hyderabad—at the groom's house. Because I don't want my parents to have to run around trying to be traditional and religious when I'm not. I want them to enjoy themselves.

But they are my parents, after all. Baba isn't happy that the South Indian family doesn't understand our rituals. Ma is worried the Bengali prayers won't be performed properly by the priest. No one addresses the issue: that we—my now-ex and I—haven't communicated in years. We are busy getting married.

He wears a silk kurta and dhoti I buy for him. I wear a red Benarasi sari Ma brought from Kolkata. We smile, we make all the right gestures. My parents look worried when they bless us.

When my now-ex holds my hand and pulls me around the fire, the sacred fire, promising to keep this union forever, I know in my heart he cannot promise that, that neither of us will keep that promise. I quell that thought and I declare, yes, I promise to be your wife, now and for the next seven reincarnations. I promise we will remain husband and wife.

*

Sheila learns to eat rice alongside chicken and vegetables. Her mother-in-law, a patient woman, makes desi dishes, basmati rice, and nuts sprinkled with raisins. The rajma is spiced with cumin and hot peppers and thin ginger slivers. There are a hundred ways to make chicken. Sheila now likes rice as much as roti.

Sheila now makes her signature apple pie, similar to what she used to make in Phoenix, but the dough is thinner, the cinnamon is stronger, and the butter from buffalo milk smells different. The pie is best like a thin-crust pizza. Her daughters love it, so she makes it when apples are in season. She assimilates, an Indian who is American trying to be desi, Indian.

The Indian city they move to is noisy. The cars speed. There are too many people on the roads. What seemed like a good adventure isn't fun. Her husband works long hours and complains he doesn't want to be here.

For Sheila, the children's lives take over. First, the younger daughter falls ill with a fever, and then the spicy food doesn't suit the elder one. Days are spent measuring children's hot foreheads, holding them as they throw up, or measuring cups of medicine to lower their temperatures. A young mother, Sheila is distraught watching her babies suffer.

"Please, let's go home," she pleads.

But her husband's brother needs him. What can he do?

Sheila wonders if she made a mistake marrying him.

*

The phone call, across oceans, comes to them from Sheila's sister.

"Our father," her sister says, her voice cracking through the line.

Teja, the Indian who married a Mexican, the Punjabi who taught his wife how to make roti and chicken curry, is gone. Marisol is alone in Arizona. Sheila looks at her two children, sleeping in bed. Sheila decides for herself.

"We're returning to California," she says.

For once, her now-ex-husband complies. Sheila can get her job back at the university, she knows that.

Less than two years after her exit to India, they pack up for their American city. Miraculously, the girls start to heal. Perhaps the food is the reason? Or is it the bright sunshine isn't that harsh in America?

What would her father have said that Sheila, the desi daughter of Teja Singh, couldn't live in India, her land? Or maybe her roots transplanted to California through Arizona. Perhaps this was to be home? Sheila wonders if Teja would be disappointed. No matter, she shakes her head, adjusting his photo in her living room.

Marisol visits Sheila twice every year, staying with her for a month at a time. Sheila works at the college, close to her home in a neighborhood lined with shaded trees. When Marisol visits, the food is made, the beds are clean, it is home, and home is this city in southern California, for her and her children, even when the marriage she envisioned isn't what it is.

"Marriage is hard," Sheila confesses to Elle on one of her weekly phone calls. "I guess this is life."

Elle's silence tells Sheila all she needs to know.

*

Occasionally, on her way to work, Sheila wonders if she will see Vidur driving down to his engineering offices. She hears he's a successful businessman in a city about an hour from her. Is he happy? she wonders. He must be. How many children does he have now? How could he marry so quickly after I got married? I am a married woman; how dare I begrudge him his life?

Shrugging, she heads to work, as she will for decades after that. She's nearing forty when she tells her now-ex-husband that she is done. It's time she lived her life.

"I want a divorce," she says, surprising herself.

But she feels at peace, even though in her circles, she might be the only divorced one.

Her daughters are outraged. "Mama, c'mon, we need you. Daddy needs you. There's nothing wrong in our lives, why are you doing this?"

Sheila tries to reason with them, "You won't understand—"

"I don't want to, Mama!"

Her husband agrees to a divorce with a caveat. He wants to be in his daughters' lives. They find him an apartment close to Sheila's. It's a new era. A new family. A new way of life.

*

By the time Baba dies, and three years later, Ma, I am broken. My back, weak, now hurts constantly, a disc in my spine protrudes painfully searing against my sciatic nerve. My now-ex argues about simple things. He punishes me for all disagreements by refusing to speak to me for weeks. My body, my heart, my mind, everything freezes into fright. Fear that my marriage would break down. I don't realize it's already broken.

In 2008, when the country goes into a roaring recession, biotech collapses in San Diego. I lose my job. I struggle to find employment. My now-ex says, "Well, go to Starbucks; at least be a barista."

My parents are gone, I have no family. Or else my father would have told him what I want to: "How dare you treat my educated daughter like this?" he would have said. "She has trained to be a scientist. Be a husband, not competition."

I don't say anything. It takes me fourteen months before I get a job leading teams of scientists in San Diego and in the UK.

Mocking me, my now-ex tells everyone, "Well, she took advantage of my health insurance when she was unemployed. She couldn't have her back surgery without me!"

I don't realize how unusually cruel he is. I am used to his disdain, taunts, silence, the fear.

The fear. The fear. The fear.

*

Every get-together has a hundred stories. Sheila doesn't remember what the celebration for the party was anymore, but there she is, newly divorced, working a steady job, her daughters still young, and her now-ex lives close by. An acceptable arrangement.

Being a divorcée in this community is isolating and yet liberating. She's finally living life on her own. This is what I think may have happened that day.

Her younger one asks for another helping of kheer. "Mama, please, it's so good," she says, pulling Sheila's hand. "Can we get some more?"

Sheila lets herself be dragged to the buffet table. The girl is still a picky eater.

At the chai station, she feels his presence before he speaks. His back turned, his hair still dark. He has put on some weight, but then which man wouldn't after college? His suit is tailored, and he looks good. Oh, so good.

Flustered, Sheila turns away, rushing her child to the table. "Get a bowl, more? No?"

He waits till he is alone with Sheila. Sheila hesitates, still.

"Sheila."

"Hello."

What else was there to say? Each with children of their own. One who couldn't, wouldn't leave his wife. One who chose to leave her spouse.

"You look good," he says. He sounds nervous, she thinks.

She looks at him. Love, fear, joy, hope. There are no words.

*

I move back to Maryland after a decade of this marriage. I work in a German biotech company. My now-ex tells me to go, and that he will find a job there soon. He doesn't.

Every month, I travel to Germany for work. I'm doing good work in women's health, in cancer diagnostics. If you see me at work, you'll say, "how confident she is," and usually I am.

But home—the townhouse I buy because my now-ex has promised to join me at it—is silent. My now-ex hasn't spoken to me for more than 214 days.

I tell this story over and over and even now, over a decade since this happened, I still marvel at how cruel this silence is. I want to save my marriage, but the days become weeks become months and still, silence from my now-ex.

The next year, I return to San Diego, pack my now-ex's things in one shipment, and my own in the other. On my eleventh wedding anniversary, I file for divorce.

Part of me is glad my parents are gone. My divorce would have destroyed them. I build myself back in San Diego, one day at a time.

*

Many Punjabis have shared their stories with me. No one has been as candid as Sheila has been about her love for Vidur.

"He's had an engineering company in LA. His sons still run it."

I hear the pride in her voice, for a man who never was her husband, who remained married to another woman. What matters to her is this love. Thirty-eight years together, and yet not.

"Why didn't you marry him, once you both realized . . . ?" I ask, curious.

Laughing, Sheila adds, "Why bother? We were committed. He stayed with me when he could. Till he got sick, he was with me."

She adds, "At this point in my life, why would I try to hide this? He was the love of my life. I was his. He used to say, 'Sheila, you and I are meant to be together. The rest of world means nothing.'"

"Then why didn't he divorce his wife?"

"Children," she said.

There is a resigned tone when she speaks again. "He didn't want to hurt his family. I didn't create a fuss."

What she got from him was all she wanted. They don't ask each other why. Or what if.

Vidur often reminds her, "You were meant to be mine."

She retorts, "I'm still not yours!" laughing.

*

Punjabi-Mexicans love to tell me their stories. Of their parents, their food, their religions. Of their marriages to Anglos and Mexicans. That they are happy. No one shares deeply personal stories like Sheila has.

Curious, I ask Sheila, "You've never publicly talked about Vidur. Why now?"

"Ah, but Madrooshi, no one asked me about me. They only wanted to know Sheila, daughter of the Punjabi-Mexican family. I told them that story. But Vidur and I? Our story was, is special. You asked. I told you."

In her bedroom on the shaded street near campus, there's a gold-framed photo of an older man, serious, with glasses; a black-and-white photo. It isn't a photo of her ex-husband. For thirty-eight years, this remains Sheila and Vidur's secret. Their love.

In 2009, Vidur dies; he is eighty. Out of respect for his wife and grown children, Sheila doesn't attend the funeral.

Almost a decade and a half later, Sheila still lives in the same house she did in the sixties. The house is filled with photos from her childhood. Sheila with Teja in his farm in Phoenix, 1951. Sheila holding onto her mother's skirt, El Paso, Texas, 1938. Teja and Marisol in formal attire in their Phoenix home, Christmas, 1952. A young Sheila, short hair, rouged cheeks, a studio photo, 1950.

Sheila's younger daughter watches her mother closely as she reminisces. As the daughter of an older mother usually does.

Sheila brings the coffee pot, filling the fine china cups with the hot brown liquid slowly. They look like the ones Ma had saved for special occasions in our Delhi home. I don't know where they are anymore; my sister and I had packed up the place in a few weeks after Ma died in 2009. Sometimes, all that remains are memories, and we make our peace with the things we leave behind.

Sheila's dining table is covered with a well-worn maroon block-printed tablecloth, likely from India. The milk is in a ceramic dispenser shaped like a cat.

Everything, much like Sheila, is whimsical.

**

Desi Rice (My Version)

Ingredients

1 cup basmati rice
2 tablespoons clarified butter or ghee
1 inch cinnamon
2 or 3 green cardamoms
2 or 3 cloves
2 or 3 black peppercorns
1 bay leaf
½ cup thinly sliced onions or 1 medium-sized onion
½ to 1 teaspoon sugar or ½ to 1 teaspoon raw sugar
1.5 to 2 cups water, or as needed
Salt as required

Recipe

1. Soak the basmati rice 1:1 rice to water for half an hour; drain the water and set the rice aside.
2. Heat ghee in a flat-bottomed pot, add cinnamon, cardamom, cloves, and black pepper plus one bay leaf. Fry till the spices are fragrant, lower flame.
3. Fry the sliced onions till they are translucent.
4. Add sugar and fry the mixture till onions are browned.
5. Add the rice, plus two cups room temperature water, with salt, and stir at medium-low flame.
6. Cover the pot with a tight-fitting lid and cook on medium-low till rice is cooked.
7. Stir the rice carefully to loosen the grain, and add more fried onions before serving hot.
8. Serve with daal or beans.

12

Sheila, the Pie-Maker

I tend to become friends with the people I interview. It isn't that I reach out to them with the express intention of doing so. I start my interviews with Sheila much like a nonfiction writer would. Questions. Answers. Polite asks. Photos.

But then, she calls me one day out of the blue.

"Madrooshi!" she exclaims on the phone. "How are you? I was thinking of you."

Her voice sounds genuine, and the ask is what my Ma would do. Even though I usually go on a tirade when people mispronounce my name, I don't even think to do so with her.

Our friendship, familyship, whatever you may call this, starts with a call and blossoms. She's more than a subject of interest to me, and I don't take that lightly. When her daughters tell me they don't want any identifying characteristics of their mother or her life exposed, that they prefer if I keep the names, cities, and people confidential, I agree. Sheila still gets to tell her story, and her daughters get to keep their privacy. The world gets a glimpse of a strong woman straddling many lives, histories, and representations.

I realize it's time to share my life, and my person, with Sheila now.

I hesitate because I haven't even shared this news with my own family. Let's call him GSG, shall we? We have been friends for years, and this friendship has developed into something I am unable to label. What do we call it now, and why? I'm fearful of such entanglements.

That Christmas I bring GSG along—my label-less partner, road trip accompanier, bringer of flowers, bread, and cheese every Friday—with me to meet Sheila.

For more than a year and a half, I don't, I won't acknowledge him as a partner. For a decade since my divorce, I have been a free woman, living alone, thinking alone, surviving alone, thriving alone. I don't need anyone, and I mean it. Then he transforms from being a friend to someone dear, when I don't expect anyone, least of all him.

At the beginning of the relationship, I resist like no other.

"I don't need love," I tell him.

He says he will love me even more.

"I won't tell my family about you," I say.

"Okay, Madhushree."

"I won't introduce you to my friends, the ones who matter," I say.

"Okay," he says.

What am I to do with someone like this? He has entered my life and doesn't care if I acknowledge him at all. Is he good? Yes. Is he without flaws? Oh, goodness no. Are we two middle-aged people trying to figure out life? Yes. Yes, we are. For now, this will have to do.

*

On my way back from Stockton, we stop in Los Angeles, at Sheila's. She welcomes us in, with a smile and a hug, as always.

GSG shares the photos from the gurdwara with her.

"We used to go there every year," Sheila tells him. "That was the only gurdwara here."

I didn't, hadn't expected this easy of a conversation between a Black man and an eighty-eight-year-old Californian of Punjabi-Mexican heritage. What are these relationships and roots we resist to acknowledge?

"I have dessert," Sheila breaks my reverie.

She brings out her pizza apple pie. We drink dark coffee with a splash of cream. We take photos of ourselves looking at photos of people long gone.

"More coffee?" she asks my label-less partner.

"I'd love that," he says, extending his cup.

When we look high and low for family, for connection, perhaps we need to take a pause. Sometimes paths intersect and we create relationships, not realizing how deep they can be. Maybe we should give this a chance?

We eat the food our ancestors made in places far away, and as the food morphs, so do we. Is my journey intersecting with this Punjabi-Mexican and this man telling me of journeys we've all taken to arrive at this place?

We sit down for a meal, connect over coffee, and for a while, live.

**

Sheila's Apple Tart (My Version)

Ingredients

2.5 cups white flour
¼ teaspoon salt
¼ teaspoon baking powder
1 tablespoon sugar
10 tablespoons butter
1 egg
8–10 tablespoons ice-cold water
3–4 medium green (Gala) apples, peeled
¼ teaspoon ground cinnamon

$^1/_8$ teaspoon ground cloves

1 tablespoon marmalade (or brown sugar)

Recipe

1. Mix the flour, salt, baking powder, sugar, and butter, and add the egg and butter.
2. Add ice-cold water, one tablespoon at a time, to make the dough pliable.
3. Roll out dough onto a 14-inch pizza pan, and crimp the edges.
4. In a separate bowl, mix the sliced apples with the spices.
5. Place them in circular orientation on top of the dough.
6. Brush with extra marmalade and cinnamon.
7. Optional: Add a few blueberries before baking.
8. Bake at 350 degrees F for 15–20 minutes.
9. Cool and use a pizza cutter to cut slices.
10. Add an optional dollop of cream to serve with coffee.

13

Sheila, Now

November 2024.

The long drive is always worth it when I turn onto Sheila's street. I've created a new routine of taking Sheila to a restaurant of her choice each time we meet. This time it's a Persian restaurant.

Her sense of direction is better than mine; but, well, anyone's sense of direction is better than mine, really. We choose a relatively empty restaurant, Farsi Café—a place she hasn't tried yet. I ask if she can walk to the door.

"Of course, Madrooshi," she says. I still don't have the heart to correct her pronunciation. "Walking is what got me to ninety!"

We order eggplant badamjaan, bread, and kababs with fluffy Persian rice. Her appetite is as robust as mine.

She digs into the eggplant dip. "I know my daughters protect my privacy, especially about their father. But I've already talked about my life openly. What I haven't talked about is Vidur. You're the first one who has asked me about him."

It's been nearly a year since Sheila told me about the love of her life. Vidur is not even his name. He isn't tall, or conventionally good-looking. I write about him based on how her eyes light up when we talk about him.

I'm sure the details are all wrong. Was she sixteen when she first met him? Did she fall in love with him then? Or was it when they met at the coffee place? When she was eighteen and in college? Was it when he said marry me, but you can't work—did she think he's not the one? Maybe at that dinner party when she met him years later. I may have got the details wrong. After all, in her nine decades, does Sheila recall everything accurately?

She plays with the fork, adding, "You can write about Vidur, I'm too old to care."

"Yes, Sheila," I hesitate, "but your daughters don't want to have this out there."

"Nothing for me to be ashamed of," Sheila stops me. "I think of Vidur daily. That should tell you something."

Sheila's eyes, usually milky, focus on me. Her gaze is strong.

A love story, a complicated story, a story that could be hidden and lost. A story that needs to be told.

*

It is February 2025. Sheila's house is filled with people. Her tiny kitchen is bustling with her son-in-law cleaning two big slabs of pink salmon, ready for baking. Sheila's daughter rushes from the sink to the table, assembling the salad. In the far end, Sheila's younger daughter, her eyes glinting with impish joy, selects a piece of fruit from the salad that she isn't supposed to touch.

"Shh," she hushes me, as she steals fruit slices, mischief on her lips. I'm not supposed tell on her to her sister. I am put on salad duty.

"How many people are coming?" I ask.

"Twenty-five? Thirty?"

"Oh, we won't be ready on time, oh no!" the elder daughter announces, panicking.

Her husband calms her down. "Don't worry, it's all good."

Sheila enters, her hair coiffed into a nice fluff, a saffron scarf around her neck. They put you to work, eh?" She checks the vegetables in the oven. The doorbell rings. "Ah, people are on their way."

It's Sheila's ninetieth birthday celebration. A few weeks late southern California in early 2025 had been through horrible fires that leads to frightening evacuations.[1] Postponing it a few weeks later, it's on a beautiful sunny day. Sheila's friends are here to celebrate her.

Dr. Leonard arrives with her granddaughter, son, and wife. Jayasri, the Bengali filmmaker who has worked with Sheila for decades, arrives wearing a blue sari.[2] She looks like my cousin Didibhai, and for a second, I wonder if she is. Jayasri waves at me, even though we've never met. This community embraces all who know the First Wave. This quest for belonging connects us all.

People arrive with bouquets, baked dishes—chili rellenos, salads, gifts for Sheila. The place fills with people of all ages.

Sheila's younger daughter's rescue puppy longingly stares through the mesh door. "Wait," I tell him, and head to the backyard. "I'll sit with you."

Jayasri joins me with her plate. We talk about how us two Bengalis got interested in the story of Punjabi-Mexicans.

"Ah, I've known Sheila for decades now, you're the new addition," she says in Bengali.

Yes, I'm the new addition. Perhaps this yearning to belong to people who've experienced this otherness is an apt one. Perhaps this is where we all belong.

The daughters have baked a beautiful two-tier cake with vanilla frosting. The salmon on the sideboard is almost finished, Sheila's roasted vegetables are a huge hit, the salad I helped assemble, also gone . . . it's a party when food is appreciated, dishes are empty, bellies are full.

Sheila stands in between her two daughters. She's shrunk dramatically over the years. But her eyes haven't lost the twinkle as she hugs her girls.

The nine on the cake slides slowly into the chocolate base. The elder daughter, ever the perfectionist, fusses over it, making it sit right to represent a nine and a zero. Sheila wears a happy birthday tiara.

"Should I blow?" Sheila asks, holding the cake knife.

Most have their phones up, cameras on. She blows out the candles. Her daughters help her cut the cake.

The smell of coffee brewing envelops the living room. The cake is soft, springy with the right amount of chocolate and frosting.

I get up to leave for home. Rising from the couch slowly, Sheila hugs me like my Ma would have.

I take a picture of the two of us. I want this moment to last forever.

For that moment, I feel like I belong.

*

Sonia Chopra of *Eater* writes extensively about Rasul's El Ranchero.[3] She notes, "The Punjabi-Mexican 'old-timers' thought of themselves as modern—more American—than the provincial new immigrants, who in turn did not approve of the established community."

But on a February day, weeks after the ferocious fires race through the state, in a little house close to the university campus, a Punjabi-Mexican brings together her friends of seven decades, and a Bengali daughter of refugees to celebrate her life in a city that adopted her as much as she did.

**

A Desi Green Salad (My Version)

Ingredients

2 bags of organic mixed greens
2–3 medium green apples, sliced
2 bunches radishes, thinly sliced
3–4 Persian cucumbers, sliced
Salt and pepper to taste
1 lemon
1 cup olive oil
1 cup feta cheese, crumbled
2 tablespoons chaat masala
Optional: ½ cup carrot strands, ½ cup zucchini slices

Recipe

1. Toss the greens into a large bowl.
2. Add the rest of the vegetables, salt and pepper.
3. Squeeze the lemon juice.
4. Drizzle olive oil over the salad.
5. Toss the salad with a large spoon.
6. Add the feta cheese with optional zucchini and carrot strands.
7. Add chaat masala.
8. Refrigerate before serving.

PART THREE

THE SECOND WAVE
The Gurdwara, the Women

Street art on utility box depicting a Punjabi woman holding peaches, Yuba City, 2022. Courtesy of the author.

14

The Second Wave Women

For us to understand the children of the Second Wave immigrants, we must learn about the Second Wave families of Yuba City. And for that, we must meet the women who married the men who came to Yuba City as farmers.[1] The Second Wave wives.

A few years after India's independence, many Sikhs arrive in and around Yuba City in Northern California. In the late 1940s and early 1950s, there are hardly any Sikh families to speak of in Sutter County—a few here, a few there.[2]

In 1924, Nand Kaur is the first Sikh wife to settle in Yuba City with her husband, Puna Singh.[3] She is the first Punjabi Sikh woman who arrives in Yuba City to live at home and manage a nuclear family. However, being the first nuclear family also means Nand Kaur has no support or familial network to lean on in a foreign country. In a country where Punjabi kameezes and traditional attire are uncommon, Nand learns English and becomes one of the first women to contribute to the establishment of the Punjabi community in Yuba City.

As new families arrive after the Second World War, Nand Kaur becomes the go-to person helping the young brides settle in an unfamiliar world. Both Nand and Puna are active in politics prior to India's independence, in Ghadar party activities. Respectfully called Biji, or "mother" in the community, over the years, Nand Kaur makes sure that young brides get supplies they need to set up home upon arrival. Anyone needing advice on how to adapt? Head to get groceries? Figure out doctors' appointments? They go to Nand Kaur. Soon, she's the matriarch the community needs.

For Nand and Puna Singh, the Stockton gurdwara is the only one they have for worship and community. The Stockton gurdwara in the early days is secular, as are Indians from different religions in America. Post-independence, when Indians are divided on religious lines, the gurdwara too becomes a Sikh place of prayer. From Yuba City, it takes Nand and Puna hours to drive there, and over the years, they realize the need for a place of worship, community, and sewa, devotion in their Yuba City.[4]

"We will donate land to build a gurdwara," Nand thinks. Puna Singh and she offer the community an acre to build a Yuba City gurdwara. "This way, the children don't have to be late for Stockton gurdwara programs on a Monday driving for hours to get there."

Eventually, the gurdwara is constructed on land donated by the Purewals. More on that story shortly.

Nand remains one of the first Sikhnis championing a place of worship in Yuba City to help the children be brought up with Sikh traditions.

*

After India's independence and the Second World War, many Punjabis win lotteries to get to America, an opportunity to grow crops here, and build their families. With the 1965 Luce-Cellar Act, this process becomes significantly easier. By 1975, based on public records, the Sikh population grows at least five times its original size in Yuba City–Sutter County. This then brings a localized Punjabi community in Yuba City, very distinct from other Californian agricultural areas.

I can't help but wonder how difficult it must have been for newlywed brides to arrive in a country not knowing the language, customs, or even the ways of others.

There is no Walmart, Home Depot, or Indian grocery store to speak of. Miles and miles of farmland, a two-lane road, a ditch separating farmland from the road. Acres of dark soil, weather that reminds her of home, and a husband who takes care of her. Homesickness must have gnawed at these women constantly.

The British Indian Army is a good vocation for Sikhs. Why? Good money, travel, improve your family's life. Sikhs are known for their fearlessness, their honor, their duty, so this is natural. Many farmers who arrive in Yuba City come from a military background because as Sikhs, if they don't farm, they fight for the country. Being in the British Indian Army also gives Sikhs the opportunity to earn and find ways to improve their family's economic status.[5]

Then the partition of the country leads to a mass exodus.[6]

No one talks about what happened those few months when the country was slashed into two. And then three. The colonizers break us down and leave for their homes while shame guides us.

In 1947, Mahatma Gandhi, now the Father of the Nation, gives a speech to the soon-to-be newly free people.[7] "Tomorrow, we shall be free from the slavery of British domination. But at midnight, India will be partitioned. Tomorrow will thus be a day of rejoicing as well as of mourning."

What follows is the largest migration in the history of humankind. A migration based on religion—Hindus in India, Muslims in Pakistan.[8] Four years post-independence, over 14.5 million people migrate between regions, for safety, for religious freedom, for family. Using the 1931 and 1951 population census data, authors Prashant Bharadwaj, Asim Khwaja, and Atif Mian deduce that four years after partition, 14.5 million people migrate into India, Pakistan, and East Pakistan (later, Bangladesh). Using region-specific population projections, the total outflow is about 17.9 million people. This indicates 3.4 million people "missing" or unaccounted for during partition.

Lord Louis Mountbatten claims only 200,000 people are killed. But estimates from Sir Francis Mudie, the West Punjab governor and the British high commissioner in Karachi, put the total at 800,000 Muslim deaths.

The number of missing people based on Hindus/Sikhs and Muslims appears to be similar, a range of 2.2–2.9 million. More than 50,000 women across all religions are abducted.

Ma used to tell us stories of those months before independence in 1947. Her grandfather, Bhubaneshwar Ghosh, the headmaster of Barisal High School, a well-regarded institution in what was still Bengal, tells her and her siblings, "Make sure we can sell the books you have."

When I ask what that means, Ma explains, "Oh, Thakurda, my grandfather, meant that we needed to sell the books before we left Bengal."

"What, why?"

Ma shrugs. "Books were too heavy to carry—we were planning to take boats, carts, and trains to Kolkata. If we sell them at a higher price, we get money to use in independent India."

There is a casualness of speech she uses each time she says it. I never ask about how afraid she was—she was a young teenager then—or the threats to her life. She never tells me how they traveled from Barisal to Dhaka to Kolkata. Did the entire family of multiple siblings, uncles, aunts, and parents arrive in Kolkata together? Did they come in batches? And who decided that they would find a small shotgun house in Behala, in Southwest Kolkata, with sloping roofs and slippery floors near the tubewell area next to a tiny kitchen surrounded by tall coconut trees, a couple of banana plants, and a massive jackfruit tree in the back? It is the house Ma grows up in, from where she goes to college and gets married, and the house I remember my grandmother lived in. But no one recalls how the Ghosh family got there from Barisal, Bangladesh.

The only thing Ma tells us of that time when she arrives in Kolkata is, "Well, before we left, I went to Thakurda and handed my new books to him. I hadn't made a single mark on any page, nor were any dog-eared. We got more money from my books than any of my siblings."

There is pride in how she narrates it. Education, which was so prized in our family, was for sale during the partition. And Ma makes sure her family gets the money they need when they arrive in Kolkata, displaced, landless, houseless, traumatized.

Two decades since Ma's been gone, and I still wonder what that trauma had done to her and her siblings. They didn't talk about those months except for what they lost. But she always said, "If you're educated, you can better yourself." To have a degree was to have escaped what happened in 1947.[9, 10]

*

In Punjab, much like Bengal, village elders keep their girls in check. Likely this is how.

"Don't go anywhere without your elder sisters with you."

"Always make sure your chunni covers your head."

"If you see a Muslim, walk the other way."

The young women know their place in the family. They know not to bring dishonor to them. The girl child is brought up to realize that her safety keeps the family honor safe. She will not be the reason for her family's shame. I use this assumption because this has been our culture for centuries.[11]

In *Jutti Kasoori*, a UC Davis documentary directed by Dr. Nicole Ranganath, an emotional exploration of the Pioneer Yuba City women's stories and histories, Charan Kang narrates her partition story.[12] An older grandmother with a ready and infectious laugh, she sighs, explaining, "We had very sharp spears that we were ready to use. We were not going to die without resistance." She adds: "My heart begins shaking when I recall these memories. . . . "

The violence experienced by these women is hidden in sighs, signs of prayer, or whispers. Silence is what usually captures what women like Charan may have experienced. In the fifties and early sixties, young Punjabi brides arrive in Yuba City, not knowing the language or California norms, thousands of miles away from what used to be home. They are young, married, escaping a divided nation, and completely dependent on their farming husbands.

"We didn't know anyone. We had to survive here, no choice," say the women, grandmothers in Yuba City on film. Sunil Bhatti, Harbhajan Thaker, Bakshish Mann, and Preetam Purewal—in traditional Punjabi salwar kameez and dupattas—speak almost in unison. "Our brothers could go anywhere. The girls, we didn't get to study, we never went outside."

*

Canadian psychiatrist Vivian M. Rakoff, MD, and colleagues in 1966 documented high rates of psychological distress (or intergenerational trauma) among children of Holocaust survivors.[13]

However, very little has been studied or understood in terms of trauma within the South Asian communities after the 1947 partition.

Chicago-based psychologist of Pakistani descent Dr. Ammara Khalid says, "The Partition of 1947 was the largest mass migration in history, and yet very little has been written about the mental health toll it took on the survivors and their families."[14]

In fact, what a South Asian may feel like today has its roots in what their ancestors felt yesterday. Intergenerational trauma has deep history within history and now, also, genetics.

Partition has been, and continues to remain, the Great Tragedy of South Asia—for India, Pakistan, and Bangladesh. We have borne this tragedy through repression, dissociation, and denial as a society.

In my own Bengali family, my parents reminisce of home. Big cabbages, cauliflowers, fresh fish, fragrant spices. No one talks of the fear that ran through Bengali families fleeing Dhaka for Kolkata, of Muslim rioters chasing Hindus out of the new country. Or the journey from Dhaka to Dinajpur for Baba to Kolkata's Jadavpur neighborhood. And for Ma, moving from Barisal in now-Bangladesh to Kolkata's Behala neighborhood. How many buses, rickshaws, trains, and trams did it take to get to Howrah station? Did they tell their neighbors back home, "Here, take our keys. Please water the banana trees, the jackfruit in the backyard. We'll return soon."

Did they? I don't know. My parents have been gone for two decades now, carrying those stories with them.

What my family has avoided talking about appears to be the same for other South Asian families. Most tend to shy away from discussing pain and suffering. We pay for it later through mental and physical ailments for which we have no name.

*

In Subh-e-Azaadi, poet Faiz Ahmed Faiz mourns the dawn we all ached for, the daybreak battered by night; this is not the one.[15] The partition creates grief at a national level that travels generations.

Just like in Barisal, where Bengali Hindus head toward India, Muslim neighbors start to disappear from the part of Punjab that remains in India. Overnight, people cross the border to leave for safety. Some stay back; after all, they have had generations grow up in the same village—Muslims living in their area, Hindus in the other. Religion is about life and death.

Sikhs make a choice—India or Pakistan.

Likely, conversations in Punjabi families went like this:

When the Muslims yell, "Allahu akbar," lock the kundi, the front door lock. Pick up all the stones we have lined up in the terrace, get ready.

Watch them come up our lane. Be prepared. If they climb up the stairs with knives and kattas in their hands, don't fear. Make sure you have stones ready to throw. Or the spears.

Don't be scared. Don't get captured.

Your honor safeguards ours.

The value of women during partition focuses on chastity, devotion, and reproductive ability, which makes women the battleground for the religious violence in 1947.[16] Women are raped, mutilated, paraded down the street naked, have their breasts cut off and bodies carved with the symbols of opposing religions. Curiously, it isn't always the opposite religion's men who inflict such violence. Stigma and dishonor also ensure that men within the women's own community perform honor killings.[17]

Regional Punjabi poetry and fiction capture the 1947 violence. Shiv Kumar Batalvi, a Punjabi poet, laments those days, remembering when "together, we murdered our mother."[18] Religion becomes the guide that leads India and Pakistan into contemporary times.

When Yuba City women recollect their 1947 stories, there is a flatness in their narration. It's almost a taboo topic to talk about the homesickness, what may or may not have happened during the riots of 1947 as the country was divided. Statements like, "it was hard," or "I was too young to remember" are often made, almost pushing that trauma of displacement out of memory. Or is it that they would rather focus on the stability in Yuba City after marriage instead of what they experienced in partitioned India? That they'd rather talk about homesickness in Yuba City, assimilation in America rather than chaos, violence, fear when their lives, and their family's lives, were threatened during the division of the country?

The flatness of the stories—we were young, we were fearful, we ran to safety, we were saved—remains the same, from family to family. And each woman insists that life post-partition was smooth, safe, happy. That life in Yuba City, for the ones who came post-partition, was different and good. The children were good. Life was better. Most would rather talk about how life in Yuba City was safe. It was, is safe.

Sikhs have gender-neutral names—their teachings say to treat all the same. Kaur, or princess, a girl; Singh, or lion (fearless), a boy.

Savitri Randhawa, one of the first Sikh women who arrives in Yuba City as a single, unmarried, educated woman, deduces, "Look, women weren't highly educated. And girls didn't have the right to property. That is why people thought it was important to have a boy."

The Second Wave Sikh women in Yuba City come to a city with husbands they barely know, and a country that isn't theirs. As partition survivors, they have no words to explain the trauma they experience as young brides.

Harbhajan Thaker explains: "Where were we to go? Nothing felt good then . . . there is no love at first. I had to start by telling [myself] that I had to stay here." Even though she smiles, her eyes behind her glasses look ahead, as if asking us, and herself, to understand the young bride who was too young to comprehend what she was experiencing.

Dr. Amrita Uttamchandani in 2011 proposes three models to describe the intergenerational trauma of the partition of India and Pakistan. The most prominent one is that of "the cycle of selective silence." Dr. Uttamchandani proposes that when the next generation(s) ask partition survivors of their experience during that time, survivors shut them down. The shutting down is a dismissal of what happened, a stoic acceptance, or complete disregard of the violence and trauma experienced.[19]

The next generations then either assume certain facts or lose interest. This establishes selective silence. Selective because most partition survivors can talk about the factual accuracy but not the psychological and emotional aspects.[20, 21]

Yuba City in 1949 is a two-lane highway, leading to the Stockton gurdwara, ninety miles away. In 2025, it remains a two-lane highway flanked by peach and walnut farms. In the 1950s and then the 1960s, most Yuba City Sikh brides still pray at the Stockton gurdwara. The other women in the community help a bride adjust to the new land even when she represents her pind, her village, her country.[22]

Archival photos in the Punjabi and Sikh Diaspora Archive of the women of Yuba City show a deep friendship built out of the common bond of otherness in a foreign land. They teach each other how to wear Western clothes when meeting non-Punjabis, how to grocery shop, how to drive each other when they need help.

Regretfully, Charan Kang wonders, "If only I had studied, who knows what I would be doing now?" There is a helplessness in her eyes. Now older, a grandmother, she has lived her life in sewa, in service of family, marriage, home, and the gurdwara.

Who knows what would have happened if she had been educated?

Gurmit Thakar's video reveals more than she does: "I never used to write to my parents anything negative."

There is an unsaid code that the Second Wave wives practice. Their parents have been through so much; what good would it do to tell them that their daughter is lonely and alone in Yuba City? The thread of shame and silence carries through these women's stories.[23]

Prior to independence, Hindus, Muslims, and Sikhs gather at the Stockton gurdwara for community. Five hundred miles south, the El Centro one is for Sikhs in Imperial Valley. In 1946, a Pakistani mosque is built for Muslims in Sacramento.[24]

The Stockton gurdwara transforms into one for Sikhs, with provincial Punjabi rules.

The First Wave immigrants established a westernized approach to their practice of religion—chairs to sit, eating with spoons and forks, and their Mexican wives helping cook the food in the langar.

The Second Wave arrive in Central Valley with Punjabi wives. Soon, the culture at Stockton returns to traditional roots of langar made by Sikh women, sitting on the floor, with men and women praying separately. Families like Mehar's bring traditional values to the temple.

Religion and the ways of prayer divide the house of worship that previously welcomed all religions.

Recently, Sheila asks, "Did these people tell you we—the Punjabi-Mexicans—existed before they showed up? We celebrated different cultures, religions. Do they acknowledge we were there?"

"I think so," I lie.

"Well, at the El Centro temple, they kicked the Mexicans out. Said we weren't Sikh enough."

I don't argue. Not because I agree, but because what good would it do to bring this up with the Second Wave immigrants? I don't need to start an us versus them argument. I am but a witness with my words.

By the late 1940s, however, religious division, established by the British in divided India, travels to the American West, nine thousand miles away.

*

The division between the Pioneer Mexican-Punjabi farmers and the new Sikh immigrants grows exponentially post-independence.[25] Newcomers disapprove of the Punjabi-Mexican marriages that had occurred decades earlier.

In 1970, the Tierra Buena gurdwara is built with fundraising efforts from the Punjabi-Mexican descendants as well as the Second Wave immigrants. It's the first gurdwara establishing traditional Sikh customs in America. Punjabi Sikh women cook langar food, edging Punjabi-Mexican wives out of the institution.[26]

According to Dr. Bruce La Brack, after 1950, Yuba-Sutter becomes "the center of Sikh agriculture."[27] But it is also a place that now attracts Punjabi immigrants in the Second Wave and remains so for the more recent waves.

The land becomes a space that resembles where they grew up in Punjab, and the orchards allow the Second Wave immigrants opportunities to grow financially. It is perhaps one of the first times Punjabi immigrant farmers can farm and their wives are able to stay home with the children, and not as migrant workers. Soon, the families can build homes close to their farms, land that they own.

It is land, family, community, and Wahe Guru for the Second Wave.

**

Uchche Bhaaja, Karela Fry (Bengali Version)

Punjabi bitter melon is more of a curry. Most Punjabi families cook this as a daily vegetable with roti. My childhood was karela fry, with simple spices to mix with rice and daal, a perfect bitter to counter the Bengal summer heat.

Ingredients

1 tablespoon turmeric powder
1 tablespoon cumin powder
½ teaspoon chili powder
Salt to taste
3 medium-sized bitter melons, thinly sliced
2 tablespoons mustard oil

Recipe

1. Add the spices to the bitter melon slices.
2. Add half the oil.
3. Air fry at 375 degrees F, 10–12 minutes.
4. Check the progress in 6–7 minutes; add more oil.
5. Remove from fryer, serve with rice and daal.

15

The Twenty-Six
Who Built the Gurdwara?

In 1959, Sikh farmers and businessmen of Yuba City have a problem on their hands. They are tired of traveling to worship on the one free day they have from working in the fields. While the Stockton gurdwara is close enough, it is still hours from Yuba City by car.

Every Sikh in Northern California heads to Stockton on weekends. The family piles into their trucks or cars and heads to Stockton. The highway is lined with farmlands of apricot, walnut, and peach trees. Entire weekends are spent by the Sikh families in Stockton—listening to kirtan, akhand paath, women cooking langar food, serving daily free vegetarian meals, attending weddings, and religious classes.

The women meet their friends, wives of other Sikh farmers, the only ones who speak their language in a white town. The men discuss the farming issues—labor, weather, seed, harvest, price—and, of course, the Guru Granth Sahib, the holy texts they grew up on.

*

The Stockton gurdwara is built in 1912, when Punjabi students arrive from British India—for education, to farm, and to form the revolutionary Ghadar party (in 1913).[1] Mostly young men from the farming communities in Punjab, the Ghadarites are secular. The freedom struggle, not religion, is paramount. They inform the community of the freedom fight in Gurmukhi and Urdu, languages of the Sikh farmers.[2]

The Ghadar party eventually splits into the Azad Punjab Ghadar party, headquartered in the Stockton gurdwara in 1914. The second one, headquartered in Oakland, is the Hindustan Ghadar, a Hindu-majority faction.[3]

Stockton is where revolutions start, to continue in India. The Ghadarites assemble in America, the land of the free. The Ghadarites raise the Sikh Nishan sahib flag at the gurdwara—a flag representing their people. Returning to India, they participate in "ghadar," or strategic violent attacks for India's independence.[4]

Dr. Tejpaul Singh Bainiwal, a Stockton Sikh historian, says the gurdwara is more than a place of worship: "Anyone can visit if you need shelter, food."[5]

Bainiwal grew up studying the Stockton gurdwara, where Ghadar history is taught regularly. Even when the gurdwara became a Sikh house of worship, there were spaces for Muslims and Hindus. "It continues to be an inclusive community gathering place."

The gurdwara is where the next-generation children learn about Sikh history, Gurmukhi, and religious texts. Bainiwal, and Raj Singh Badhesha, the first Sikh judge in Fresno County Superior Court, agree that the gurdwara has been transformational in their Sikh journey.[6]

"I came here as a child to take Sikh history and language classes at camps," says Badhesha. "Once you see the purity of what this religion preaches, you automatically follow the path and live for community."

At the gurdwara, marriages, celebrations of life and death are arranged. The community spends its time in sewa, service of the Sikh religion.

The second gurdwara, five hundred miles away in El Centro, services the Punjabi farmers from Imperial Valley. The First Wave immigrants with Mexican wives and Mexican-Punjabi children are slowly dissuaded from joining the prayer sessions. By the late fifties, El Centro gurdwara, a former Japanese temple, becomes a traditional Sikh house of worship.[7]

By 1965, with easier immigration laws, Sikhs immigrate to Yuba City in droves. This wave are landowners, business folks, and professionals. The Second Wave traditional Sikhs now realize they need another gurdwara in Yuba City.

Around 1965, once the Luce-Cellar immigration law is in place, the arrival of large South Asian groups of immigrants changes the identities of Sikh immigrants.[8]

Punjabi men who arrived in the late nineteenth and early twentieth centuries create an identity as Americans, in turn proudly calling themselves the Punjabi Pioneers in Central and Imperial Valleys.[9] To be "American," they adapt themselves emotionally, physically, and behaviorally to American culture—in particular, Anglo culture.[10]

For the Second Wave Punjabis, Sikh traditions are paramount. Sikhs sponsor family members, nephews, brothers, and wives to come to California. Gurdwara traditions are reestablished. The new immigrants enforce the old traditions in America. With citizenship and the ability to own land in America, the Second Wave immigrants realize they can be Sikh, and they can be free.[11]

Talking about those times, Sheila Singh shrugs:

We were used to being called "Hindus" by the Anglos. That's the insult they had for us, and we didn't pay any mind to that. But the new Sikhs said, no, Mexican women aren't Sikhs. Slowly, slowly, they made sure we were kicked out.

"Is that what happened?" I ask her again, because racism and sect-focused bias are more obvious along color lines. This narrative may not be what the Second Wave Sikhs would like.

Sheila nods. "None of us Mexican-Punjabi second-generation folks go to the gurdwara anymore. We stick to other Mexican-Punjabis because we feel safe there. The new Sikhs drove us out because we were half-Sikhs and our mothers were Catholic."

Decades since the Second Wave Sikhs took over, I can still hear the longing to belong in Sheila's voice.

Bainiwal, however, refutes that. "No, that didn't happen that way at all. Sikh religion welcomes everyone."

The thing with history is that the truth likely lies somewhere in the middle. Punjabi Mexicans probably felt they weren't valued when the new Sikhs arrived. Perhaps the Second Wave Sikhs saw the half-Sikh, half-Mexican second-generation children as foreign, too Anglicized, and therefore not "true Sikhs." Such a conflict likely led the Punjabi-Mexican families to further "assimilate," marrying Anglos, or each other, eventually moving away from traditional Sikh communities.

*

The gurdwara off Tierra Buena Road faces walnut trees that have grown for decades. Three doors to its left is Hollywood actor Guy Branum's mother's house—one of the few Armenian Jewish families in Yuba City.

"It's interesting to be in a brown neighborhood as a white, gay minority," he laughs loudly, shaking his head.

"I didn't know any better," he says of his Sikh classmates, growing up. "We knew they ate differently, prayed differently, and they hung out with their own. Oh, and their sisters certainly weren't dating white folks!"

The Second Wave Sikhs arrive as family units. Many arrive from the same Indian village to Yuba City and raise families in their traditions.

To say the Sikh community is close and tight-knit, and continues to be so, is an understatement.

*

It's cold in Yuba City, and while the elders have tried meeting in each other's homes, homes are too small to hold so many.[12]

The Sikh farmers meet at barns on their farms. "We need a place for our people to pray."[13]

Yes, the elders nod, shivering in the cold.

Punjab winters were cold, but Central Valley temperatures are a different thing altogether.

"Our own Yuba City gurdwara! Like in our villages," they nod in agreement.

Brothers Bakhtawar and Udham Singh Purewal speak, almost in unison. "Three acres. Our almond orchard land, we will donate that to our community."

The elders applaud. Bhai waah, such devotion to the faith. Purewal family members were religious Sikhs, and now they prove it.

*

Guy's mother is worried her street will be named Gurdwara Road because now Didar Bains's son, Karm, is a city councilor and wants Sikhism recognized everywhere in Yuba City.[14]

"It's kinda strange to see Karm—a kid I grew up with—as the guy who takes care of 'his people,'" Guy says, smiling. "I don't mind being a white kid who grew up with this Sikh who's now one of the most powerful men in Yuba City."

Guy and I head to the gurdwara after he parks his car at his mother's driveway. The gurdwara is a large, one-story building made with thick marble and a white domed roof with turquoise blue tips, striking against the gray December sky.

Sikh gurdwara dome architecture combines Islamic and Hindu curved ceiling structures with Sikh symbols of peace. This gurdwara is built with the best marble, stone, and gold embellishments that money can buy. Kirtan prayer music plays on a loudspeaker. We grab a few blue headscarves from the bin labeled "clean" and cover our heads. I put my shoes in the slot labeled "for women." He puts his on the "men" side. The divisions of gender are strict and rigid.

"I haven't been inside since high school," Guy admits.

"Why?"

Guy shrugs. "I mean, as a white guy, you kinda know what's meant for you and what's not. I was lucky, I'm gay, and therefore considered safe. They trusted me."

Lines were drawn, Guy says. It wasn't that folks weren't welcome, but everyone knew where they stood in this walnut-tree-surrounded land. It was respect; it was a swim-in-your-swim-lane small town. It still is.

*

By the mid-twentieth century, there are ten thousand Sikhs in California. Building that Yuba City gurdwara is imperative. Much like in India, they canvas for donations, chandaa, knocking on door by door. Every evening, when the farmers return home, wash up, drink a cup of chai, and head out. The chandaa collectors ask for donations. But just like in India, each knock means they are welcomed inside.

"Sat sri akal, come sit," and so they do.

It would be rude not to; after all, atithi devo bhava. The guest is like god.

The women, heads covered with dupattas, eyes averted, a sign of respect, bring tea, and nashta—fried pakoras sometimes, biscuits, or even parathas.

In 1959, farmers are primarily daily wage earners earning less than $2 an hour.[15] The Sikhs are proud, but in America, they are also poor. But the elders persist. They drink tea, eat nashta, and ask for help to build their gurdwara. Money is collected, donations made, the community is activated. It takes ten years.

In Punjabi villages, they construct their gurdwaras by asking their people to donate. This is no different. Knock on a door, and another door, and another door. It is just that the land is America, and they are assimilating because that's what the government wants. They grow walnuts, almonds, peaches, and rice. Hard work is all they have, money is hard to come by, but they always have faith.

Every evening, they knock on doors once the man of the house returns from work. They drink tea, eat nashta, wait to bring up the topic of donation. It would, after all, be rude to drink chai and then say, "Okay, give us money." That isn't the Sikh way. They sit. Drink tea. Eat nashta. It takes at least an hour per house.

The elders are getting older. It isn't a good thing to keep meeting in barns and then drive for hours to Stockton for events and festivals. Money-collection is slow. They need a temple in Yuba City. They have a problem on their hands.

To be a Sikh in Central Valley is a matter of pride and honor. But it is taking forever to get enough funds to build this gurdwara that will be the third one in the country, in service of community and Wahe Guru.

Finally, the elders admit, "At this rate we will never have a gurdwara!"

Now, it's not like this is a new issue. They've been trying for years. But what to do? Whites in Central Valley weren't welcoming to Sikhs. Their large turbans, flowing beards, their women covered in dupattas and salwar-kameezes handling the children, following their men a few paces behind, were suspect. Practicing Sikhism is dangerous in America in the mid-twentieth century. Outsiders think they are a cult, an unknown religion, an insulated one. Why would anyone help them build a gurdwara?

Ganda Sing Heir, a longtime Marysville resident, now a prosperous farmer–business owner, has been saving money for the gurdwara.[16] After a few years, he has $2,000. His grandson, Sewa Singh Heir, is a young boy. What better glory than to have your name and your own grandson's name associated with the Gurus?

One meeting, when the elders complain that the gurdwara would remain a dream for them, he stands up, fed up with the lack of urgency. "Arre, why don't we get more contributions? Like hundreds, thousands of dollars?"

The elders laugh at him. "We are poor, Ganda Singh ji. Who has thousands of dollars, huh?"

His hand in the air to stop the complaining, Ganda Singh Heir declares, "Two thousand from me. Two more in the name of my dear Sewa Singh."

The elders inhale in shock. Who has that kind of money? What is this Ganda Singh up to? Why now? Why didn't he tell us?

But once everyone calms down and realizes Ganda Singh Heir has a good strategy, the elders nod in agreement.

"Founding members," they say, "we need founding members for the gurdwara. Anyone giving a big donation is a founder, yes!"

"But Singh ji, two thousand is a whole lot," they surmise.

They settle on a thousand dollars. Twenty-six members gather their savings over the next few months. The Purewal family donates three acres of land. Others give what they can afford. They have $100,000 from the community. They get a loan from the bank, because they are prosperous farmers and the Anglo-owned banks are willing to give loans. The banks know a Sikh's promise is their honor. They know the Sikhs will repay the loan. They do.

The gurdwara isn't a dream anymore.[17]

In October 1969, on the five hundredth anniversary of Guru Nanak, the first Sikh guru, the Yuba City Tierra Buena Road gurdwara groundbreaking ceremony is hosted by twenty-six Sikh founding member leaders. The next year, the Tierra Buena Gurdwara is opened to the Sikh community.[18] The landowning farmers, some businessmen, have made it in America. The gurdwara is proof.

The initial seed money is helpful, as is the land. But they need more land so they can have a park, a school, a place to unfurl the Sikh flag.

One of the Sikh founding members, a shrewd businessman, the Peach King of California, Didar Singh Bains buys the neighboring land for the gurdwara.[19]

"Didar Singh Bains isn't known as the Peach King for nothing. Look how didar, how generous he is!" the elders say, applauding his generosity.

He waves them off. "Arre, all for wahe guru, for our Sikh brothers and sisters."

*

Here is how the gurdwara happens. It isn't only the twenty-six founding members.[20] It is the Purewals' donated land. It is Didar Bains's contribution. It's the women who operate the gurdwara. Like Ganda Singh's grandson's wife, Pritam Kaur, an Amritdhari Sikhni—trained in all the Sikh tenets—who brings the Guru Granth Sahib scriptures to Yuba City in 1953.[21] Women like her hold kirtan prayers in their house during construction. She fights to keep chairs in the gurdwara so the elders may pray without having to sit on the floor.

It is Nand and Puna Singh's initial offer of an acre of land to build a gurdwara. It is the Sikh women who run the langar and make food for anyone who is hungry and in need of shelter. It is sewa, it is community, it didn't happen because of one man. But it is a marvelous building, with marble, gold, and blue designs—the khanda on top and the Sikh Nishan sahib flag fluttering in the wind—that makes it a place Yuba City Sikhs are proud of.

In 1970, the gurdwara opens to the Sikh community in Yuba City.

*

A decade after the gurdwara opens, Didar Bains proposes that there be a nagar kirtan—an annual Sikh parade through the Yuba City streets. It is greeted with fear, apprehension, and trepidation by the non-Sikhs—after all, is this a cult? What's next?

According to Karm, Didar's son and Sutter County supervisor, "My dad wanted to tell people who we Sikhs are. We are fellow Americans . . . we want the same you want for your kids."

The Central Valley Sikhs now grow roughly 50 percent of total peach production, 20 percent of raisins and grapes, and 5 percent each of almonds and pistachios in California.[22] By the nineties, Didar Singh is the richest Sikh farmer in America, owns ten thousand acres of land, growing fifty thousand tons of peaches worth at least $13 million per year. He is an agro-entrepreneur and conducts himself as a king of Yuba City. People listen to him.[23] The nagar kirtan parade becomes a Yuba City annual highlight.

Since 1980, the nagar kirtan parade is held the first weekend of November. Attracting over one hundred thousand Sikhs from all over the country, the community wearing traditional outfits marches from the gurdwara through the city. It is the largest Sikh gathering outside of India, providing free food and beverages for all.[24]

Within the community and among California politicians, Didar is very influential.[25] In 2017, at a large Sikh gathering in town, Governor Jerry Brown thanks Didar Bains for the contributions he has made to the Sikh community and California. Karm remains proud of his father's community work and his vision.[26] To have enabled the Bains family, the extended members, and fellow Yuba City Sikhs to grow into a politically powerful and extremely community-focused group is something to celebrate. For a young man with only a few dollars in his pocket to arrive in Yuba City and convert it into a Punjabi success story in California is a dream few achieve. Didar is proof.

Even after his death in 2022, Didar's influence in Yuba City remains solid. The Second Wave men have established themselves in a way that is part of the land forever.

"All of this with God's grace," Karm, his son says. "We're just here as stewards of the land to tend to [the fields] for the time being."[27]

*

In 2022, when I first drive to Yuba City, it is a long, ten-hour drive through traffic, pelting California rain, LA traffic. Central Valley smells of farmland—fertilizer, animal feed, and clean air. It isn't familiar, and certainly not a city.

In December, Yuba City winter is primarily rain. The gurdwara is on a huge plot of land, a majestic blue-white-gold structure that tells the world Sikhs live here and have built a world for many decades here.

At the entrance to the Tierra Buena Gurdwara, a solid metal plaque holds the names of the twenty-six whose seed investment in their community's gurdwara has made this a landmark place of worship in Central Valley, California. The names are:

Bakhtawar Purewal
Amar Samra
Paritam Poonian
Ganda Heir
Ujagar Cheema
Otam Bains
Karnail Takhar
Udham Purewal
Didar Bains
Mehar Singh
Fakir Chima
Swaran Takhar
Malkiat Johl
Rattan Sahot
Sohan Singh
Bhagat Thiara
Pakhar Bath
Sewa Heir
Gulzar Bains
Rajinder Dhami
Kartar Khera
Major Punian
Harbhajan Johl
Davinder Bains
Gurdawar Dhillon
Lal Rai

There are no names of women on the plaque.

In a *Comstock's* magazine article in 2017, I read an interesting line about immigrants: "For the first generation of immigrants, the goal is to survive and for the second to achieve economic success for their families. For third generations and beyond, the focus is on living a full life."[28]

Politics and religion, as familiar as they are in India, also thrive in Yuba City with all the generations of Punjabis who settle here. They learn to live with both as they did back home.

I wonder where the mauna Sikh in 1993 on the Thai Airways flight from New Delhi to LAX is. Is he still in Yuba City, still a farmer, and perhaps, I will see him at the Tierra Buena gurdwara during ardas services sometime?

**

Punjabi Aloo Saag (My Version)

A Punjabi staple curry, this is a version of a starchy-greens vegetable dish accompanied with rice or roti in every Punjabi household. The women of Yuba City made langar food as part of their community sewa, feeding anyone who was hungry at the gurdwara. Here is my version of a spinach-potato curry that you may find at any gurdwara, should you have the good fortune to go.

Ingredients

3 tablespoons vegetable oil
2 teaspoons cumin seeds
5 garlic cloves, sliced
2 green chilies, finely chopped
1 medium onion, finely chopped
1 tablespoon ground coriander
1 teaspoon ground turmeric
14 ounces chopped spinach
7 ounces mustard greens/fenugreek leaves
4–6 medium Dutch potatoes, peeled, cut into large cubes, and boiled until tender
1-centimeter or ½-inch piece fresh root ginger, cut into slivers
Salt to taste

Recipe

1. Heat the oil in a large saucepan, add cumin seeds with garlic and chilies.
2. On medium-high flame, add the onions and fry with constant stirring for 5–7 minutes.
3. Add the coriander powder with turmeric, cook for 2 minutes, and add the greens on medium heat.
4. Stir and cover on low-medium flame for 2–3 minutes so the greens cook down.
5. Add the boiled potatoes and ground ginger, and adjust oil to cook on medium for 5–7 minutes.
6. Serve with makke ki roti, wheat rotis, or rice with a dollop of butter or ghee.

16

Daughter of Second Wave Families

Name-calling and slurs are part of their education. They are used to it. Decades ago, the First Wave Punjabi-Mexican children were subject to bullying. "Hindoo," "Indian," "dirty" is what they were called; that is what Sheila Singh has told me.

In Yuba City, the bullying gets worse because now the children are Sikhs—not Punjabi-Mexicans. And as Sikhs who abide by the faith and rituals, the boys wear their long hair in a top bun, and the girls don a head scarf or dupatta that is distinctly of the Sikh faith. The Second Wave children face bullying not only for their color but also for practicing their religion.

San Jose–based Pushpinder Kaur, a California public school educator, author of The Boy with Long Hair, highlights how differences, especially in Sikh young boys' hair, should be celebrated and treated with dignity as they represent the faith.[1]

But when it comes to dealing with daily bullying, silence remains the mainstay because it's not just about how to survive, it's about how to continue to survive in Yuba City.

Dr. Elyssa Barbash highlights the two kinds of trauma one may experience, that is streamlined to explain the violence and repercussions of the same during the partition of India in 1947.[2]

There are two kinds of "t"s. Small "t" trauma is the kind of distress, albeit severe, that reduces our ability to cope with our normal psychological functioning. It is at the personal rather than universal level. But large "T" trauma is usually a result of global, universal events, affecting the personal and overall societal levels of coping. Examples of that would be when one is in a natural disaster like a flood, or a man-made one like a forced mass migration.

I meet Jes Nijjer in the country of our colonizers. In their main city, London. It is January 2025. My partner and I are at Kwant, a fancy bar of social media fame of which I know little else. In an utterly frivolous manner of decision-making, we decide to spend an unnecessary number of English pounds on a couple of fruity drinks in the darkened restaurant, the first week of the new year.

I am not an extrovert, no matter who thinks or tells you I am. I try to mind my own business, drink my drink, peer at the darkened bar. The bartender crafts drinks that look like liquid gold with spritzes of lavender mist on honey-coated sage leaves. Or so I think. I am tired and London is cold, so my mind isn't on anything intelligent right now. I am certainly not in the mood to talk to anyone or seek out a conversation.

My very extroverted partner looks across the tables and waves at someone pointing at his Fuji camera. "Camera twinsies!"

I glare at him. Now we have to be polite. By us, I mean me.

The woman, a tall dark-haired girl with a self-assured look and a beautiful smile, waves back at him, "Yeah, Fuji, man, the very best!" She holds a Fuji herself.

Her accent tells me she's American. Great, to come all the way to London and to meet yet another American really isn't what I want, but here we are.

"Jes," she says on her way out, by way of introduction. "I'm a photographer."

This certainly perks my partner up. "Oh, what do you do?"

"Food, I photograph food."

And that perks me up.

I smile at her. "I'm a writer who uses food to talk about social issues."

That starts one of the most organic and the most randomly refreshing connections that I've ever embarked on. Jes Nijjer—granddaughter of Bay Area Punjabis.

*

In 2017, Berckmoes and team interview mothers who had survived the 1994 Rwandan genocide, and their children.[3] The study finds direct as well as indirect impacts of the trauma associated with the genocide. The direct effects are ways these mothers usually communicate with their children regarding the trauma, ranging from maintaining total silence to exhibiting hope that similar events do not take place in the future.

Compromised parenting demonstrated as lack or reduction of maternal sympathy, abusive or demeaning language, punitive silence, or preferential treatment among the children.

The Rwanda two-generation trauma study highlights that children are not passive recipients of the legacies passed on by older generations.[4] Children of trauma victims—in particular, genocide and forced migration—actively interpret and exist in the world around them while taking on their parents' generation's experiences as their own.

*

As a First Wave daughter, Sheila reminisces about the role of male children in her own family:

> Oh, yes, when my elder brother got married, my father, Teja, gave him two acres in Phoenix to build a house. Then my next brother, who I was very close to, got married to that awful gold digger, Magdalena, he gave him an acre and a half. I asked my father, what about his girls, his daughters? He said, wait, wait, all in good time.

Decades later in California, Sheila continues to lament that despite all the love Teja had for his youngest daughter, it didn't translate into bequeathing any land to her.

"I was the daughter," she explains sadly.

It didn't matter that she "made it." The regional Punjabi patriarchal hierarchies Teja came from stood the trials of time, and even though the sons never were as successful as Sheila, she remained the daughter and hence undeserving of property.

With Jes Nijjer, granddaughter of Second Wave immigrants in a London café, January 2025. Courtesy of Gary S. Greer.

Decades her junior, Second Wave daughters and their daughters continue the same legacy in Sutter County and beyond.

In London, Jes, my partner, and I bump into each other in all parts of the town quite by accident. At a chai shop in Notting Hill, at my favorite Bengali restaurant, at yet another fancy unaffordable cocktail spot. If you like food, you try them all. And if you're a food photographer, of course you do the same.

From Ottolenghi's café in Marylebone, I text Jes, "Hey, I'm here, how come you're not here?" and she sends me a laughing emoji.

We realize a connection over distance and serendipity, and we don't question why. The universe must want us to hang out, so we do.

By the end of our trip, we have sat down for countless meals and coffee breaks and make plans to meet in San Diego. It is easy, natural, and effortless, this new friendship.

Jes says, "I just connected with my half-sister, and she lives there. I'd love to visit you."

Half-sister? Indian family? What? My fifty-four-year-old judgy mind overreacts. She laughs and adds, "Yeah, my parents divorced when I was very young, so I didn't really have a relationship with my dad for decades. My mom and I moved away to Indiana, so yeah, I'm reconnecting now."

It's refreshing to see a Punjabi, an Indian, have a straightforward attitude toward broken marriages and to know that she is getting to know her siblings, her father's children.

I offer her my home when she comes to San Diego. We make plans. My partner announces to anyone who will listen that he's so good in connecting like-minded people. I roll my eyes at him.

*

Caruth interprets Freud's "historical trauma," or trauma that is cultural and collective in nature. This trauma represents a community psyche as an intergenerational and transhistorical latent shared response over generations.[5] Mambrol in 2018 notes in "Trauma Studies" that "perspective trauma's transhistorical potential means that a cultural group's traumatic experience in the historical past can be part of the psychic landscape of the contemporary individual who belongs to the same cultural group."[6]

By the time Jes visits, San Diego winter is cold, but not really. We sit outside, soaking up the pale sunlight, she marveling at how not cold my town is, me excited to show her my favorite haunts. I introduce her to my friends in the San Diego food world—editors, magazine leaders, chefs, and restaurateurs.

Jes used to be a nurse and now freelances as a photographer. She's been one for nearly a decade now. Her pictures of croissants shining orange-gold with dark shadows and stripes of light make food look like celestial objects. She quietly takes pictures of me cooking in my kitchen: the chutney ladles thrown in haste; my kitchen towels, used, with turmeric and chili paste stains thrown on the floor. She captures the chaos before I feed people. I love how she represents my frenzy without intruding in my process.

The few days she stays in my spare bedroom we spend hours chatting about food, family, friends who become family. The conversation is easy.

"To think we had to travel thousands of miles to meet and now we're hanging out in your kitchen," she says, laughing.

Impulsively, I ask her if she would like to join me to visit the Imperial Valley Punjabi-Mexicans. "Your people, Jes," I entice her.

I don't have to try too hard, really. She's ready to tag along, camera in hand.

Imperial Valley is about two hours from my house, and Jes is a good navigator. As the I-8 west turns closer to the United States–Mexico border, and the winds pick up heading to Brawley—I am visiting the cemetery there where the Imperial Valley Japanese farmers lived—Jes tells me about her childhood.

"My mom was a nurse too," she says, "but my mama-ji, my mother's brother, and my grandmother are who I'm close to."

Punjabi women tend toward nursing careers, an extension of their sewa or consideration for their community. Jes still has her nursing license, even though she's been a photographer for high-end restaurants for years. So why isn't she close to her mother?

Her father's family is from Selma, near Fresno. He still has farms there, where his own father worked with other Fresno and Sacramento Sikhs to build gurdwaras in different cities in Central Valley. He grows grapes to convert to raisins; also almonds and walnuts. Typical Central Valley farmland work.

This seems like a usual family that's Punjabi, with usual California farming problems. Or nursing lives.

I try not to ask too many questions. Everything doesn't need to be heard.

In 1986, Boyajian and Grigorian study Armenian genocide survivors and report that most experienced or reported to have experienced anxiety, frustration, and anger across generations. Children of these survivors then observe anxiety and guilt over not having done more for their (survivor) parents.[7]

Most First and Second Wave children I've met speak of their parents with love, respect, and regret. Regret that they couldn't do more for them. That their parents experienced a longing for India till their last days. A longing the children understand but cannot measure since they are American.

Jes's father is the son of a Second Wave immigrant. Her grandfather builds his farming business near Fresno, part of the Sikh community, growing the usual cash crops of Central Valley—grapes, walnuts, and peaches. Jes's mother comes from Punjab with a master's degree in mathematics after marrying Jes's father. Soon it's pretty obvious the pairing isn't a happy one. Infidelity, trust issues, and then the age-old problem of in-laws controlling a son.

Jes has a sense of humor about it. "So long ago, Madhushree, and frankly, who cares? They are, were, so different. It's good it's over."

"How old were you when your parents divorced?"

She knows she was very young. Jes grows up in her maternal grandparents' house in the Bay Area, two hours away from her father. Her uncles become the father figures she needs. Her grandmother is the mother who holds her love.

But, there's always a but.

We drive closer to the El Centro gurdwara. I miss the turn. She guides me back. We enter the gurdwara langar and wait to see if we can meet a religious granthi, but no such luck.

Jes covers her short hair with a scarf and heads to the kitchen. Speaking in Punjabi, she addresses one of the sewadari women. "Could we sit here for a bit?"

Bob Chell, son of First Wave Pioneers, with Jes Nijjer, granddaughter of Second Wave Fresno–Selma farmers at the Pioneers' Museum (Imperial County Historical Society) in Imperial Valley, California, March 2025. Courtesy of the author.

The woman nods her head vigorously in agreement. "Chai?"

No one says no to chai.

We sit in the dining area with chai and a sweet boondi laddoo.

Sikhism has its five Ks that signal someone is following the faith. It also considers four sins as guidelines—not part of their main religious texts, but guides in their way of life—cutting or trimming hair, fornication or adultery, eating meat slaughtered in a slow or painful manner, like the Muslim and Jewish rules for halal or kosher meat; and using tobacco, opium, or any addictive drug products. But with the newer Sikhs born into Yuba City families, there has been an uptick in "in name only Sikh" families. Newer generations are mauna who seldom go to the gurdwara unless it's a festival.

Though much lower than national averages, there has been a definite rise in divorce rates among Yuba City Sikhs. A 2018 British report on Sikhs in England shows 5 percent of Sikhs being divorced and 1 percent separated.[8] Yuba City in 2020 has Sikhs at more than 15 percent of the city's population, and chances are that while very few, separation and divorce rates likely are picking up, very similar to the rest of the country.[9]

*

After her parents' divorce, Jes moves with her mother's family to the Bay Area. For years, she doesn't see her father. He doesn't try to connect with her, either. Only two hours away from his daughter, her father makes no attempt to know her, and when she turns eighteen, Jes and the family who raised her decide to start over in Indiana, her current home.

Recently, when we speak, I ask Jes if she misses anything in her childhood that her father may have compensated for, and she is quick to dismiss that. "My uncles raised me, and that's that. Will I ever have a relationship that's close with my dad? Maybe. Maybe not. But what I can do is build a sibling bond with his children."

"Will that be enough?"

Yes, she says. "We would have broken the trauma bond of carrying our parents' and grandparents' grief into our lives."

It is the first time I realize that the next generation, the daughters of the children of the Second Wave, aren't looking for solutions through their parents. Jes is proof that what her parents have given her—broken relationships, silence, anger, divorce—isn't a gift she will accept.

At the Brawley cemetery, we silently walk to the Japanese graves—of farmers, their wives, and sometimes, tiny graves of their children. Jes photographs them with respect, a representative of the Sikhs whose ancestors took the Japanese monastery a century ago to found the El Centro gurdwara.

Away from the Japanese section, which isn't as well-maintained as the rest, we hear children laughing, chasing each other next to Catholic graves. It is a somber space, but children, and children of those ancestors, remind us of a history that ties all of us to this land through loss, anger, trauma. A history that can be transformed into a meaningful present by building instead of untying these tenuous relations.

On our way back from the cemetery, Jes warns me, "You'd better sage us, Madhushree, we Punjabis aren't meant to be in cemeteries, you know?"

I nod, "Agreed. Bengali Hindus don't wander around cemeteries either, Jes!"

Even when I continue to explore serious research in Imperial Valley, we keep our sense of humor, marveling at the absurdity of two desi women in search of Japanese farmers long gone from Imperial Valley.

The next morning, sitting at a mediocre donut shop with bad coffee, we watch ICE agents and police cars zoom into a motel across the street. The Trump administration is already in action in early 2025, checking papers and arresting people. Jes and I sit in silence. Not much to say, is there?

"How's your relationship with your mother now?" I ask, curious.

She looks up at me. "I've had to distance myself from her."

"Why?"

"Sometimes, in order to survive, one has to turn away from those who don't want you to."

*

Researchers highlight a primitive vocabulary associated with emotions within South Asian languages may have encouraged silence around the partition. This selective silence extends beyond parent and child communication, extending to communication with other survivors and relatives.[10]

We belong to a country torn apart by our colonizers. Of course, what we absorb manifests over generations.

Jes's mother, once divorced, uses Jes as a pawn in the relationship. The control she exerts is emotional, and soon financial. When Jes decides to go to nursing school, her mother too joins her in nursing. As Jes grows up, her mother restricts her movements, her money, and freedom—the control is obsessive.

Don't go out without me.

Give me all your money, whatever you earn.

You and I will live together, no questions asked.

Absolutely no boyfriends.

The stranglehold on Jes as a teenager gets even stronger. Jes's mother monitors her calls, who she meets, when she gets home, how she talks, what she wears.

Throughout Jes's teenage years, her mother tells her, "Tie your hair into a ponytail. Don't get distracted. You won't be a good student if you focus on all that, and no makeup. No nail polish."

Growing up, Jes remembers being told she's too thin. Then, as her auto-immune illnesses take over, making her gain weight, her mother says, "Too fat. You'll be 'unmarriable.'"

Jes cuts her hair. As a Sikh woman (or man), the kesh, the hair, keeps the connection to your faith and to family.

"But it's not that I'm not Punjabi," Jes explains, "it's just that I am also me, Jes. I needed a break from the cycle of parental control that was just . . . just taking a stranglehold on my life."

Most children and grandchildren of partition survivors exhibit medium levels of intergenerational trauma. Silence is weaponized to hide, reduce, or erase what happened to families in 1947.[11]

Geographically, Jes's father's family is near Fresno; her mother is now somewhere on the East Coast, she doesn't exactly know where. Jes remains literally and figuratively in the middle, in Indiana.

Look, I'm not saying everything is connected to the partition, but for us, it is. Anjali Enjeti, author of *The Parted Earth*, says, "If there is a tragedy or a failure or some horrific accident in the community, the women are shamed and blamed for it. . . . Why didn't you stop it? We carry it with us everywhere we go. It breaks some of us into pieces."[12]

What makes us—the children and grandchildren of the partition—choose ourselves over our family and our trauma? Sometimes we do it consciously, and sometimes, we actively work to hold the trauma, examine, and dismantle it.

"Have you gone to therapy, Jes?" I nudge her.

"Girl," she says, laughing as we get back in my car heading home, "therapy is what's saving me. I try not to be led by my parents' obsessions, issues, or problems. I live a life that's unconventional. But it gives me the freedom to be me, rather than as the daughter of so-and-so."

Even though Sikhism preaches women and men are equal. Even though they are equal, the boy, the son is the Singh, the lion, and the daughter is always the Kaur, the princess.

I wonder how many Punjabi Sikhs would reach for therapy—it is a taboo word in our parts of the world.

Who am I to judge? I am but a witness.

*

When we return home, I make Jes stand on my front patio, and I light my sage bundle. Ma would have been perplexed and confused if she saw me doing this, but the essence of sage used for purification in Kumeyaay land where I live represents the incense we use in my world. Jes stands still, her arms out, her eyes closed. I wave the lit sage, covering her with smoke and the smell of ashy sage. I wait a few extra steps near her head to clear her thoughts.

"Better?" I ask her.
She opens her eyes, smiles, and nods. "Better."
I am but a witness.

17

The Quietness of Those Who Leave

Punjabis' litigious nature about civil cases in agricultural areas of the Imperial Valley before the World Wars is well documented.[1] They used the court system in the Valley very aggressively, where 3 percent of all cases from 1914 through 1919 involved Punjabis, as did about 2 percent between 1919 and 1931. More than 50 percent of those cases—land and labor disputes—pit Punjabis against each other. Dr. Leonard states that what appears from their own accounts and of those who dealt with Punjabis in the early twentieth century is that they know how to get what they want from the system. The Punjabis are farmers, and they continue to control land.[2]

I wonder if being litigious is also genetic? Growing up in New Delhi, all we hear about is how the Punjabis in Kalkaji, next to our Chittaranjan Park—Jats, Sikhs, Hindus—post-partition, they fight over their ancestral land, filing cases against siblings, dividing houses so the top floor is theirs, and the bottom floor is their brother's, and how they don't talk to each other, and haven't for decades. "All agriculture, no culture," is what Baba used to call them. Is this what he meant?

*

The two-lane CA-99 highway is slick with rain when I head north to Yuba City. Alongside the narrow highway, walnut trees line the farmland on one side. On the other, pink flowers bloom on shorter trees for miles on end.

"Cherry blossoms," I think, and later find out they are peach blossoms.

Small, soft, pink flowers along the woody branches, which slowly change into plump, reddish-orange, stone-pitted fruit in late spring through early fall. But I am not a farming person; what else am I wrongly assuming?

Yuba City in spring is wet, the farmland has rain-filled patches, and fog rolling through the land when it rains. Tall trucks carrying produce up north lumber next to me. I pass large warehouse-like hangars, dairy cows in pens, agricultural equipment storage ranches, tomato and fruit canning factories. Each building, hangar, and warehouse tells a story of an agricultural town.

Closer to Yuba City, a Walmart supercenter rises like a towering façade near an in-your-face Olive Garden. A Circle K, a now-defunct JoAnn fabrics store, alongside a Kohls baby clothes store, even a WinCo grocery supermarket dotting each block tell me this is a city of working people, taking care of family.

Little India restaurant sits in a nondescript shopping complex, next to a Rent-A-Center, a thrift store, and a tired American bar. Warm gold and maroon tones of the interior greet me when I enter the space. A fluorescent pink and blue sign stating "skinny people are easy to kidnap, stay safe, eat a lot here, have a seat" is next to the kitchen. Above it, symbols of the Sikh religion, a cross, Allah in Arabic script, and an Om in Sanskrit remind us that it's a space for all.

*

I have spoken with many Second Wave women, especially in and around Yuba City. The one thing I notice is how they flatten their stories to make their parents fit in the mold that makes them noncontroversial.

That the parents struggled when they arrived here.

That when the Second Wave women were born, they were happy.

That their siblings were kind to each other.

That the bullying, while it happened, wasn't so bad.

And now, life is decent, not bad.

That they and their brothers are considered equal.

That the Sikh religion calls for equality and that they are equal.

There isn't a single conflict and everyone is fine.

This isn't what families should be doing.

This is what families do. Life isn't fair or kind, but I notice how the women born of their mothers who lived hard lives in Sutter County also live hard lives.

*

In Jutti Kasoori, lawyer Prem Hunji Turner, who is married to a non-Sikh, says, "We weren't allowed to date, not even talk to someone from the opposite sex, even in college." But later, she marries her now-husband, and says, "Well, I couldn't imagine being married to somebody who was picked out for me . . . I wanted to make my own mistake if I made a mistake."[3] She is perhaps the only Sikh woman I research who is willing to show her family a love outside of the Sikh religion that is robust and meaningful.

Jes, single, thirty-five, unconventional. Jes works toward joy, but she is the *next* generation, the granddaughter of a Second Wave immigrant.

Most Second Wave next-generation children, now in their sixties and seventies, continue to live their parents' lives. Which means, as outsiders we aren't allowed a view of how they survive(d) and certainly not what they did to thrive.

*

When buffets at weddings become the fad in Chittaranjan Park, my South Delhi neighborhood, Baba and Ma hate it. "Who eats like an animal? Throwing everything willy nilly on your plate, standing and eating, and then eating too much? Who does that?" Baba says.

What Baba means is that when you don't eat fiber and carbs and then protein in order, the digestive system gets confused. That's how most gastric ailments start. It's part of culture, which is also science.

If you went to a Punjabi house and ate dinner with them, likely the food would be simple: roti, with daal and a vegetable curry. If you go to a Punjabi dhaba, the tandoori chicken is bright, the chicken curry is creamy, the navratan korma is filled with spices.

That's the difference I see in these families. The actual food is almost hidden behind the bright buffet meals. The actual lives of hardship led by these Sikh women are never discussed, shared, or allowed to be shown to the broader world. As outsiders, all we see are happy images of people who show a full life to the world on Instagram.

*

I eat the roti with goat curry in the small Indian restaurant in a strip mall in Yuba City that wet March evening. I think of all the women in this little town who have lived, loved, and cared for their children, bringing them up despite being silenced, unhappy, and unable to break free from tradition. And of an outlier like Jes, who leaves the area, leaves her profession of nursing, moves into the fast world of photography, struggles while she does it but does it anyway. All have survived. All deal with their own complications in their lives, but at least Jes isn't silent.

Selfishly, I wish more Second Wave women would speak up beyond tradition, beyond gender roles. But four years of research in this city tells me, they are yet to break free of traditional expectations that they place on themselves. Most of them refuse to speak on record. Some actively stop me from discussing the trauma their ancestors may have experienced.

Much like the silence that was ingrained in their mothers when the country was partitioned.

There are many reasons why family members use silence. Jes's family is no different. Personal issues, sometimes money, sometimes trust. I wish I knew whether Jes and her mother will find a way to communicate, or whether Jes will thrive when her mother is absent from her life.

Small issues. Big issues. And then the last straw. Actions. Inactions. Words that hurt. Words that cannot be taken back. Silence. Oh, the silence.

When intergenerational trauma travels through anxiety, fear, silence, and retribution, these knotted roots are hard to detangle.

Losing a family is devastating. Losing a family to silence is unbearable.

*

On my way out of Yuba City, I swing past the Latter-Day Saints temple on Butte Road.[4]

Next to the church, I spot a utility box, painted with homemade art. The image of a smiling brown girl in a salwar kameez holding a basket of peaches, on a concrete sidewalk, next to nondescript beige buildings. An image that remains in my memory of what Yuba City has become—the home of Sikhs and their families, home of the region that feeds America.

What do you do with stories that feel incomplete? Not much, given life isn't always fully realized in the timeline you expect. To understand how the Second Wave children deal with life, and the trauma it has brought them, we need to understand the next wave, the Third Wave.

The Third Wave arrives after their holy leader Bhindranwale's killing and, subsequently, Indian prime minister Indira Gandhi's assassination.

All stories start in India. But they also start in the Sikh temple that is their place of community. From the Ghadar party to immigration and citizenship laws to Khalistan.

I head to the gurdwara that started this community a century ago. The Stockton gurdwara.

**

Goat (Lamb) Curry, Punjabi Version

While many devoted Sikh members are vegetarian, many still eat meat. This recipe, like a Bengali kosha mangsho, is what I make with lamb when goat isn't readily available.

Ingredients

1 pound goat meat, medium cut (substitute with lamb if goat isn't available)
1 cup Greek yogurt
1 tablespoon red chili (Kashmiri) powder
1 tablespoon turmeric powder
1 tablespoon ground cumin
1 tablespoon ground coriander
Salt to taste
½ cup vegetable oil (I use avocado oil)
4 cloves
3 medium green cardamom pods
2 bay leaves
1 tablespoon grated ginger

2 tablespoons grated garlic
2 medium onions, chopped
3 serrano chilies (as per taste)
1 cup chopped tomatoes

Recipe

1. Marinate the goat meat in yogurt, red chili powder, turmeric/cumin/ coriander powder, and salt for at least 2 hours.
2. Heat oil in a heavy-bottomed pan and add cloves, cardamoms, bay leaves, garlic, ginger, and sauté for 2–3 minutes.
3. Add onions, green chilies, and sauté the mix in medium-low heat till they turn golden brown.
4. Add the goat meat and slow-cook till the meat is tender—35–40 minutes on medium-low heat.
5. Add tomatoes with salt and water as needed, lower the flame, and slow-cook for 15–20 minutes.
6. Add the garam masala, slow-cook with the lid off for another 5 minutes.
7. Garnish with coriander leaves (chopped) and an optional dash of lemon juice; serve with roti or white rice.

PART FOUR

IN BETWEEN IMMIGRATION WAVES

The Khalistan Story

Stockton gurdwara holy granth (book) worship area, 2022. Courtesy of Gary S. Greer.

18

Stockton Gurdwara

Of Religion, Revolution, and Community

. . . jinha desh sewa 'ch pair paya, ohna lakh museebtan jhalliyan ne.
Serving one's country is very difficult, anyone who walked on that path,
must endure millions of calamities.

—*Kartar Singh Sarabha, Ghadar Party Revolutionary, executed by the British*
at age nineteen, 1915

Much like Gurdwara Sikh Temple of El Centro, 116 miles from where I live, the Stockton gurdwara—nearly 500 miles north of San Diego—is also in a quiet neighborhood street, with mature trees, manicured neighborhood lawns, and clean sidewalks. The only giveaway is the name of the street, Sikh Temple Street, which doesn't tell you much about how big or small this temple or gurdwara is.

A blue Khalistan flag flutters in the wind—the flag has the Sikh holy symbol of the khanda—a blue symbol of a double-edged sword with two smaller ones, embodying faith, courage, and justice.[1] Deeply rooted in Sikh tradition, the khanda represents the defense of righteousness and revolting against tyranny. The flag is next to a yellow Sikh triangular one, the Nishan Sahib, representing the religion. Both stand on posts next to the high-walled compound. Khalistan represents an ideology, a controversial one, and Nishan Sahib, one of the Sikh faith.

Khalistan is the land of the pure, the Khalsa, a separatist ideology for the Sikhs of India to separate from India as a sovereign country.[2] The flag represents a bloody struggle between two ideologies, two peoples, filled with violence, faith, and a separatist call. Nishan Sahib represents the Sikh religion of tolerance, faith, and identity.

In 2025, they are both intertwined so closely, it is hard to differentiate Sikhism from Khalistan ideology in America. More on that in a bit, but let's start first with the gurdwara.

*

Stockton gurdwara, 2022. Courtesy of Gary S. Greer.

The Stockton City Council designates the gurdwara as a historic landmark, number 50. Founded in 1912 by the Pioneer First Wave Sikhs, the older temple is now their library.[3] The larger Sikh temple on the same grounds is a Byzantine revival-style building that opened in 1930. This gurdwara continues to operate as a functional temple, langar, and community center, the oldest center of Sikh worship and culture in America.

"Look, the gurdwara, langar, and seva—temple, kitchen, and service—they're intertwined. Life and religion aren't separate," says Manjit Singh Uppal, a former president of the Stockton gurdwara committee who arrived in Stockton as a teenager in 1973.[4] For him, and thousands of Sikhs who visit the Stockton gurdwara every year, this place is a near-mystical center of reverence, religion, history, and revolution.

A tall man in his sixties, with a sly sense of humor, dark Sikh turban, and white beard, Uppal follows his family to Northern California, where his maternal grandfather, Dalip Singh from Punjab's Hoshiarpur district, had arrived in 1907. Dalip is an active Ghadar party member in Stockton. Life was farmwork and Ghadar, expat-resistance against British rule. Now his grandson follows Dalip's path of service.

Uppal works as a farmhand, a canning factory worker, and a paid agricultural laborer. Like many immigrants who arrive when young, he learns English and moves into the regulated American trucking business. Sikh farming communities need farm produce transported across the country.

It's an automatic step, as a Sikh immigrant, to buy a 7-Eleven. Or invest in trucking.

"As we say, if you see an Indian working for a 7-Eleven owner, rest assured he will own that store next year!" Uppal jokes. "If you drive a truck, you'll soon own it; if you work on a farm, next, you'll own the farm."

His friend, gurdwara and Ghadar historian Kuljit Singh Nijjar, laughs with him. This is a familiar joke for us Indians: we work to become our own bosses through hard work and sheer grit.

Within a few years, Uppal's sons help him manage their farmland, while the gurdwara remains constant. Uppal remembers when college students would arrive at the temple during summer break.

"They were young men, college in Chicago or San Francisco—didn't have money to go home. So, they came here. The taxi would drop them off at the gurdwara. They worked at the canning factory, slept in the temple dorm, ate at the langar. The gurdwara was our shelter. It still is."

A gurdwara in India is a gathering place, much like religious spaces everywhere. In a country where your people are few, where you aren't easily granted residency or citizenship, it's a refuge. The Ghadar party is formed here in 1913, a year after the gurdwara opens to the public.[5]

Ghadar, meaning resistance, or mutiny, is one of the first organized resistance movements through literature, activism, and awareness campaigns against British occupation. Of the 616 Ghadarites sent to India to fight for independence, 527 members are Sikhs. Seventeen-year-old Kartar Singh publishes *The Ghadar*, a Punjabi-language newspaper on this gurdwara's premises, distributing pro-independence literature.[6] The idea behind Ghadar literature is to mobilize Indian expats to take freedom from colonizers through force. He returns to India to start a mutiny within British Indian troops.

Expat Indian Ghadarites incite a pan-Indian revolt (the Ghadar conspiracy) within the British Army during World War I.[7] Miscommunication, spies, and information leaks lead to the capture of nineteen-year-old Kartar, who is eventually hanged in 1923 as part of the failed conspiracy.[8] But Kartar's essence continues to inspire other freedom fighters, including Bhagat Singh, another anticolonial Sikh revolutionary who is himself executed in 1931 by the British for his role as a terrorist against their rule.

The pre-independence revolutionaries in the Ghadar party are a coalition of Punjabi migrant workers, Bengali and Punjabi intellectuals—people of the land and the mind. Interestingly, they aren't impressed by the Gandhian nonviolent movement, emphasizing the need to seize the people's independence by force.[9]

But why do Sikhs, many of them former British Army members, form this anticolonial resistance group? The reason is very simple—the shame they experience as colonial subjects is similar to racial discrimination in Canada and the United States. They believe an independent India will lead to racial equality everywhere.

It all starts at the Stockton gurdwara.

*

"Great empires crumbled, while the ideas survived," said anticolonial revolutionary Bhagat Singh in 1929, who was executed in 1931 at age twenty-four.[10]

Over time, the Stockton gurdwara becomes a collection of buildings. The original building now houses the Ghadar revolutionaries' work, including the press used in printing Ghadar literature. Next to the press are images of freedom fighters, Sikhs, who fight alongside Bengalis like Rash Behari Bose and Bagha Jatin.

Kartar Singh likely used the printing press that made thousands of papers and leaflets circulated among expatriate Indians. It stands on a carpeted hall, now unused.

Across the well-kept iron press are the images of 1984 Operation Blue Star, a historic Sikh massacre at the Golden Temple, sanctioned by the Indian government.[11] The aftermath of Operation Blue Star has mobilized Sikhs to call for a separate Sikh state, Khalistan.[12]

The Stockton gurdwara, while acknowledging the pan-religious ideals of the Ghadarites, is now a Sikh temple, with a Khalistan flag at its gate.

The stories we tell sometimes exclude others who don't fit the narrative. Sometimes, when we glorify our ancestors, the glory is tainted with more recent violence.

The Stockton gurdwara leaders are always men, religious, bearded, turbaned. Rarely do I see women, and if I do, they are in the langar, cutting vegetables, cooking—heads covered, in salwar kameezes, subservient. While their names suggest equality, the faith has now been patriarchally interpreted to represent the keeper of the home, and the next generation.

Even though the religion calls for equality, the genders aren't equal. I grab my steel plate and stand in line. Two older men ladle rice, rotis, daal, and vermicelli kheer, a sweet pudding with nuts, vermicelli, and rose water on it. They are polite, but their eyes watch me, an obvious misfit, certainly not a Sikh. But the Sikh langars are open to all, feed anyone who is hungry. I sit down on the marble floor, with my food and a hot chai.

Both—the patriarchal segregation, and the welcoming of all people—are true.

I drop my tray off at the last counter, wash my hands, and head to the gurdwara offices.

There is a large metal vault in the corner of the gurdwara offices. The men tell me it contains Ghadar party documents over the years. They don't offer to open it. It looks like a gun vault to me, but I take them at their word.

Kuljit Singh Nijjar moves to Stockton from Punjab in the early nineties. A quiet, serious man, he smiles at Uppal's jokes, but one can see in his eyes, a lifetime of unfairness that his people have experienced. Maybe I am projecting, but I need to know what he thinks of Khalistan.

In 2025, if you're a Sikh demanding Khalistan, you are considered a separatist or a Sikh terrorist by Indians.

The question is whether Sikhs actively look to cede from India as Khalistan, the land of the pure, or are they negotiating for a powerful Punjab within India?[13]

"You have a flag of Khalistan outside the gurdwara. Does this temple represent a separatist organization?" I ask.

Nijjer shakes his head at that description. It's obvious he has answered this many times and knows his role is to continue to advocate for expat Sikhs. "Look, you must go back to where all of this started when India wasn't divided. Under Maharaja Ranjit Singh, the Sikh empire in undivided India was huge."

"Okay, but where does Khalistan come into play?"

"We had a Sikh empire under him. The British stole that from us. Then Gandhi and his people said they'll give us our land. We aligned with them, and they tore our Punjab into two during the partition. Now they take our water, our land, and call us terrorists. Khalistan is our essence, it's where we belong."

To understand the demand for Khalistan and what it means to Sikhs, especially the expat community, you must start from Bhindranwale, Operation Blue Star, and Indira Gandhi's assassination.

A story within a tale within folklore within a story. Our people are complex. Our stories are convoluted.

We need patience to go through history, almost like a jalebi—an Indian funnel cake–like dessert—circuitous, intersecting, hot, and complex.

**

Desi Jalebi

Ingredients

1 cup all-purpose flour (120 grams)
2 tablespoons gram flour (sifted)
¼ teaspoon baking soda
1 tablespoon ghee melted at room temperature
4 tablespoons plain yogurt whisked
½ cup warm water
Oil for frying

For syrup
 1 cup sugar
 ½ cup water
 1 pinch saffron crushed
 1 teaspoon ground cardamom
 1 teaspoon lemon juice

Recipe

1. Mix all-purpose flour, gram flour, and baking soda.
2. Add ghee, yogurt, and water, and mix well until the batter is smooth and set aside.
3. Add sugar, water, cardamom, and saffron to a saucepan and boil, stirring frequently.
4. Simmer for 5 minutes till the syrup has a one-string consistency, lower the heat, and add in lemon juice.
5. Pour the flour batter in a condiment bottle with the hole at least 3 mm wide for easy dispense.
6. Heat oil in a frying pan over medium heat.
7. After testing the oil temperature, squeeze the batter making spirals in the oil, starting from inside going outside in circular motion.
8. Make 6–10 jalebis in a 10-inch pan.
9. Fry the jalebis 1–2 minutes on low heat, flip, cook for 1–2 minutes, and lift the jalebis out in a slotted flat spatula.
10. Add them to the warm syrup, turn the jalebis over so both sides are coated.
11. Remove the jalebis using tongs and leave excess syrup out.
12. Repeat the process with the remaining batter.
13. Garnish with rose petals and saffron threads (optional).
14. Serve with hot tea.

19

The Bhindranwale Story
A Terrorist? A Saint?

In 2022, Amritpal Singh, a thirty-year-old religious Sikh with piercing dark eyes and unsmiling countenance, wears the religious garb of a Sikh man of faith. Unshorn hair and beard, large dark turban neatly pleated—these are the symbols of a kirtandhari religious man.[1] The familiar, blue–white outfit is of a man unafraid to say that Khalistan needs to secede from India; that the drug-addled youth of Punjab need to follow Sikhism and give up the debauched life they've been condemned to live post–Operation Blue Star.

Amritpal wears a belt of bullets, a cell phone in his hand. The Sikh youth follow him like they did when Bhindranwale rose to prominence four decades ago. Within a year, Amritpal is arrested by the Indian government because he's deemed a threat to national security. From jail, Amritpal stands in legislative assembly elections and wins. For now, he remains in jail.[2]

At the Stockton gurdwara offices, Uppal rolls his eyes when I ask him about Amritpal. "Oh, by wearing Bhindranwale's clothes and acting like him, he doesn't become him. These young people think outfits make the man. Bhindranwale was a leader; not this guy!"

Nijjer agrees, adding, "The Indian government put him in jail. They're controlling the narrative."

Both Uppal and Nijjer are the older generation, the Second Wave, who arrive after America allows immigrants to enter with families. After Bhindranwale's death in 1984, the Indian government systematically targets young Sikh men to break their spirit. They use harassment, torture, and imprisonment.[3] A young Nijjer leaves for America, and safety.

Now, as Sikh-Americans, they watch Amritpal's rise with suspicion. Perhaps they are tired of waiting for a leader who can make Khalistan happen?

Younger Sikhs like thirty-seven-year-old Prabhjot Singh Lasher, a successful trucking entrepreneur, demurs, "No, he's the real deal. We need fearless leaders. Amritpal gave us Sikhs a voice. We are rich, prosperous, and we do so much for the community. It's our time."

While there's no way to determine a black and white solution to the current Khalistan demand or the new-generation Sikhs' break from traditional Sikh philosophy, it's clear Khalistan is on everyone's mind. How they achieve it is debatable. If they do, that is.

Khalistan, land of the pure, has been a longtime Sikh separatist demand. In Central Valley, images of Bhindranwale are plastered everywhere. He is a martyr, highly respected alongside Guru Gobind Singh, the first Sikh leader.[4] On CA 99, trucks barrel past me, with images of the bearded turbaned Sikh leader painted on their side in large brush strokes. Bhindranwale is an idea, a passion, a guru.

At the local Fresno desi grocery, Bhindranwale photos are for sale, next to those of Guru Gobind Singh. Bhindranwale's image—a blue-turbaned, bearded young man in holy Sikh garb, with a bullet belt and a gun in his hand, is painted with a halo around his head. His eyes are piercing dark, his handsome face majestic, his words imprinted in Gurmukhi. He is a god in these lands. A martyr. Killed by the Indian military as a terrorist in 1984. The reason why Indira is assassinated five months later by her Sikh bodyguards.

He is the reason why Sikhs outside of India continue to dream of Khalistan.

It depends on who you ask and whose story rings true at that moment.

*

It is a regular old Diwali, the festival of lights in the middle-class South Delhi enclave meant for Bengali "displaced" families. Chittaranjan Park is where we Bengalis live—the same fish markets, vegetables resembling those from Kolkata, dessert and sweet shops with shondesh and sweet yogurt.[5] It's Kolkata in Delhi for us. You can take a Bengali out of Bengal, but you can't . . . you know the rest.

Chittaranjan Park, so named after a freedom fighter, Chittaranjan Das—of pre-independence Bengal—is a soft enclave lined by trees, separating different-income families in blocks. When we arrive in 1976, we live in a rental house with a wraparound garden in Block I, an upper-middle-class neighborhood block for Bengalis working in the government civil services. Later, we move to Block B to a house on the first floor, where the three bathrooms are arranged in a row, directly and absurdly near the front door.

B Block has a lower-middle-class look and feel. We live there for most of my childhood. Even though we could move to a posher place, we don't because Ma doesn't like change, and Baba doesn't care where he lives. Didi and I? Well, our opinions don't matter.

That Diwali, the festival of lights, we hear firecrackers. Firecrackers well before Diwali are getting increasingly common. Loud, unexpected explosions; rat-a-tat-tats; and unusual, whistling, missile-like rocket sounds.

I am studying at the dining table. In the kitchen, Ma heats up dinner. The firecrackers go off. Bang-bang-bang-bang.

"Shotti," Ma starts to grumble, "these Punjabis, all they want is noise, explosions, and crass sounds. Who needs these crackers bursting daily like this?"

Didi and I don't react. We are used to Ma complaining.

Unlike other seminary students, Bhindranwale is a married father of two in 1977.[6] He leaves his family life to become a religious leader. Traveling the countryside, he sorts disputes, gaining popularity among the villagers, proselytizing the Sikh faith. Circumventing the bureaucratic Indian justice system, Bhindranwale's sermons are popular, as are his rural material dispute settlements.[7]

Five years later in 1982, Bhindranwale, now the fourteenth Jathedar leader of the ultraconservative Damdami Taksal Sikh group, launches the righteous war, the Dharam Yudh Morcha.[8] It's a call to return Sikh youth to their faith. He aligns with the Akali Dal, a Sikh-centric, center-right party in power in Punjab.

Recognizing Bhindranwale's popularity, especially among rural Sikhs, Prime Minister Indira Gandhi and her ruling Congress party also form an alliance with him against the Akali Dal.[9] Bhindranwale aligns with both, but says he answers only to Wahe Guru, the Sikh gurus.

In the United States, similar alliances continue to be fostered, including US–Noriega or US–Saddam Hussein pacts that our current government pretends we never forged.

Bhindranwale criticizes the Congress party's egregiousness as well as the Akali Dal's moderateness. He focuses on Sikh values as the guiding light. Indira's party funds Bhindranwale and his loyalists. Cleverly, Bhindranwale refuses to contest elections directly, but ensures his loyalists win them by aligning with both the Akali Dal and Congress parties, endearing him even more to the Sikh community.

Author Khushwant Singh begrudgingly notes, "He [Bhindranwale] . . . exhorted every Sikh to kill 32 Hindus to solve the Hindu–Sikh problem. Anyone who opposed him was put on his hit list and some eliminated." But the author also said, "The [men] not only saved money they had earlier squandered in self-indulgence but now worked longer hours. . . . They had much to be grateful for to Jarnail Singh who came to be revered by them."[10]

Bhindranwale's power over the Sikh people is undeniable. Gandhi and her Congress party are worried.

*

We hear the commotion on the street outside our house before we realize what happened.

Our landlord, who lives downstairs, calls out to Ma: "Sila-di, Sila-di, where is Ghosh da?"

In our culture, everyone, older or younger, is given the designation of a relative, if you respect them. Our landlord addresses my parents with the "di" and "da" designation, di meaning elder sister, and da, elder brother.

"Na, I don't know, in the market likely, why?" Ma says, unworried.

"There's been a shooting. In Market I."[11]

*

While Bhindranwale loyalists are rural Sikhs, he's also surrounded by ex-military men. Allegedly, the Pakistani intelligence arms him with guns; some say it was the Soviets. Meanwhile, the Indian government consults with the

British intelligence to determine how to eliminate him. Through money, guns, and handshakes, alliances forge. There is peace.

Of course, such idyllic peace is short-lived.[12]

The seventies through the nineties in India is a perfect example of when good and evil merge.

You know all this starts with land and water ownership. It always does.

Punjab—the land of five rivers—was, is, the California of India. Water, grain, and food make a state rich, and Punjab is rich. Indira's government needs water rights for other states. She uses Punjab geopolitically, given its proximity to Pakistan. In return, the central government gives Punjab minimal rights. Education takes a backseat. Sikh youth are targeted with rampant drug distribution. Having learned "divide and conquer" from the British, the Indian government divides Sikhs and Hindus in the new nation.

*

Ma, Didi, and I wait in the front room. Firecracker explosions now sound like gunshots, so who knows if they, the terrorists, are still out? We don't question if the gunmen are Sikhs. In the eighties, we know they are.

"Shotti, ki jhamela, what chaos," Ma worries. "Your Baba and his market wanderings."

Baba has a routine, much like Ma. After work, he drinks his tea and heads to the market. Sometimes he returns with fish and vegetables, even chicken, something Ma never asked for.

Before leaving for the market, he says, "Sila, bajaar theke ki chaai?" What do you need from the market?

Ma diligently gives her list. He diligently ignores it and brings home whatever he wants to eat. It's their routine. Then he heads to the market a second time, stopping to talk to neighbors and vegetable and fish sellers before finally returning when Ma has given up. He isn't going to change his routine for a few pesky terrorists, is he?

As usual, Baba returns after an hour. We are frantic and inform him that we are.

But he tells us, "Sixteen people, sixteen people were shot down. I was near the fish market area, not on the street, so I missed it."

Ma nods, realizing how lucky we all are.

A neighbor of ours is shot in the arm. He has been rushed to the hospital. A young child, her father, and uncle are shot point blank. The militants on a motorcycle ride through the narrow lane leading to Market Number 1, shouting Khalistan slogans, shooting at pedestrians. They use pistols and AK-47s.

We are bheetu Bengalis—scaredy-cat Bengalis. We pontificate on politics, we are cerebral. What do we know about fighting with arms? The middle-class neighborhood is under curfew. We are stuck in our homes as the Delhi police search for the assailants.

*

The Akali Dal, the Punjabi political leadership, proposes the Anandpur Sahib Resolution, a list of demands to the central government.[13]

The demands are simple—recognize Sikhism separate from Hinduism; enable Punjab to function independently, rather, an autonomous governance within India; move Chandigarh, Punjab state's capital city under the central government's rule, back to Punjab. The resolution also demands water rights reclamation, while conceding foreign, defense, currency, and general communications to be under Indira's government's jurisdiction.

A bold move, the resolution asks the central government to pay attention. Indira announces that this call is one of sedition from India by the Sikhs. News media announce that the Sikhs want Khalistan, a country of their own. This is terrorism.

*

Delhi is under lockdown before the festival of lights. This festival happens after we Bengalis celebrate the badass goddess Durga. Durga rids the earth of evil.

But in this Bengali middle-class neighborhood, people who do middle-class things like shopping for the best fish and vegetables are gunned down. By people in turbans, fearless in their pursuit of a free state, who kill fearful Bengalis, collateral damage, to get the Indian central government's attention.

*

The world interferes craftily in Indian politics. The Soviet KGB manufactures evidence that the CIA and Pakistani intelligence are providing arms and weapons in the Khalistani movement to the Sikh separatists.[14] Indira and her party are convinced Bhindranwale and his Damdami Taksal faction of Sikhs are, in fact, terrorists. The threat appears greater than it is.

In 1983, Bhindranwale and his AK-47–toting loyalists occupy the Golden Temple, the holiest of Sikh shrines. There is civil unrest, Sikhs and Hindus attacking each other, and soon the president's rule is imposed on Punjab. Negotiations between him and Gandhi as well as the Akali Dal fail. Everyone is against him and his loyalists. After fourteen months, Indira's party fails to negotiate a ceasefire.[15]

In June 1984, Indira orders the Indian Army to storm the temple and "flush the terrorists" out. Army Chief Vaidya reassures her, "There will be no civilian deaths. He will surrender."[16]

Once the army is poised to attack, Bhindranwale mourns, "This bird is alone. There are many hunters after it."[17]

Operation Blue Star is initiated in June 1984.

Years later, in 1992, opposition leader Subramaniam Swamy states, "Operation Blue Star became necessary because of the vast disinformation against Bhindranwale by the KGB and repeated inside Parliament by the Congress Party of India."[18]

Here is a timeline of how Operation Blue Star came to be:

1. 1978: Bhindranwale's faction orchestrates Sikh sectarian violence.
2. 1982: Bhindranwale is invited by the Akali Dal to take shelter in the Golden Temple. He moves in with two hundred loyalists.
3. April 1983: Akali Dal accuses Bhindranwale's group of assassinating General Atwal, an Indian (Sikh) military leader at the temple.
4. October 1983: Bhindranwale's loyalists kill six Hindus on a bus in Punjab. President's rule is established in Punjab.
5. December 1983: Bhindranwale is asked to move out of the temple. He moves to the Akal Takht, where Sikh holy books are kept. Indira Gandhi says the temple is a "terrorists' den."
6. 1984: Operation Blue Star is initiated after Gandhi–Bhindranwale talks fail.
7. June 1984: Indira Gandhi agrees to Blue Star upon Indian military advice.

In our neighborhood, the two terrorists on the motorcycle shoot indiscriminately. Their AK-47 jams. Fleeing, they turn near Market I and crash into a ditch—if you're not familiar with our neighborhood, you too would crash. The lanes are too narrow for speeding motorcycles.

With guns, they board a DTC public bus. Passengers likely don't protest, fearing for their lives. The bus slows down for the police at a checkpoint.

The two men open fire. The passengers cower in their seats, hoping to live through this. In the ensuing gunfire, one of the Sikh men, not more than twenty years old, is killed. They arrest the other man. All we know is he's a Khalistani.

The police announce that the dead Sikh's name is Subadar Singh. The barricades set up by the Delhi police are huge concrete barriers along all main roads in Chittaranjan Park. We are blocked in.

The truth of Operation Blue Star isn't black or white. In a no-win situation, the militants in the temple fortify it. Then the Indian military attack the temple to get to Bhindranwale. Here is the Operation Blue Star timeline.

While it takes a few days to kill Bhindranwale, the long-term effect on the Sikh community is catastrophic.[19] With a media blackout right before Operation Blue Star, only state-run media were allowed to report. Civilian casualties were significant as pilgrims were still permitted to enter the gurdwara, it being a holy day for Sikhs. Witnesses note that some were used as human shields by the Khalistan militants.

Sikh soldiers, recent recruits, mutiny after Operation Blue Star in many different parts of India. According to Associated Press correspondent Brahma Chellaney, who managed to stay back despite a foreign media embargo, 780 militants plus civilians, and 400 troops perished in Operation Blue Star.[20]

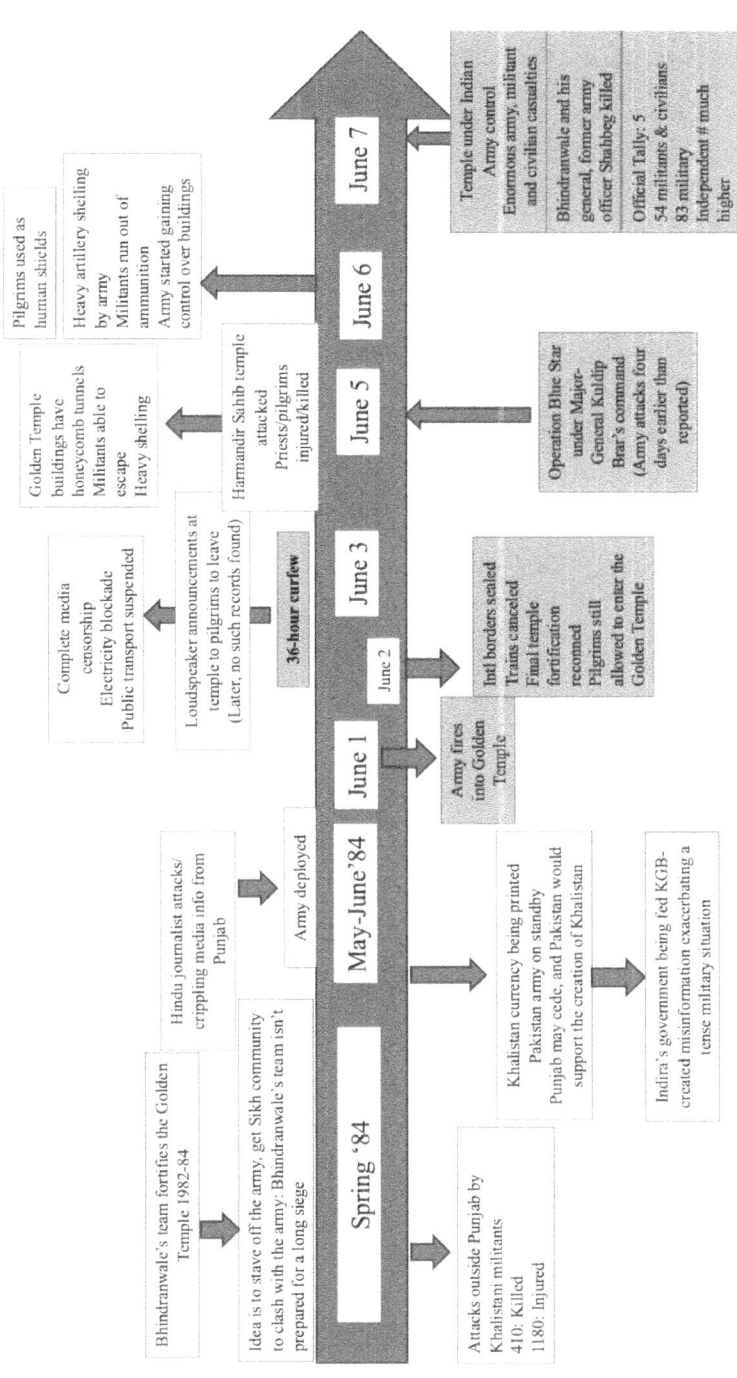

Timeline of Operation Blue Star (spring-summer, 1984). Created by the author.

Countless human rights violations by the military are noted. Chellaney is charged with sedition by the Indian government, a charge later overthrown.

The army also uses civilians as human shields during inspection of the temple premises.[21] Dead bodies are discovered in canals and water tanks in the temple complex, their arms tied. Survivors are forced to drink water from the same canals.[22] The Indian Army responds by stating their only loyalty is to the nation and their troops.[23]

In 2023, the call for a separate Sikh state rises again. It gains steam first from Sikhs outside of India, and then the rural Sikhs. Lieutenant General Kuldip Singh Brar, the Sikh military man who stormed the Golden Temple in 1984, speaks about Operation Blue Star: "No one wants an op [operation] but what do you do? Indira Gandhi allowed him [Bhindranwale] to become Frankenstein. You could see what was happening. But when he reached pinnacle, finish him—too late. . . ."

Brar, an eighty-nine-year-old Sikh from the same region as Bhindranwale, is now old, with white hair. His unapologetic eyes are still piercing, as his age-worn fingers scroll his cell phone while talking. "I am an army man," he says dismissively. Meaning, he follows orders.

In 1984, he is asked to cancel his vacation and conduct reconnaissance at the Golden Temple. Noticing men with bullet belts, AK-47, he knows the temple has been militarized.

Shabeg Singh, Brar's former boss and now the Khalistani commander, spots Brar and warns Bhindranwale, "Brar is up to no good; why is he in civilian clothes?"

Does it start with religion, move to ego, then humiliation? And if the warring people are military men, is it easier to annihilate each other because they're trained to?

When Brar returns to the cantonment, he says, "Militants have taken over the temple. We must remove them by hook or by crook."

Bhindranwale preaches, "Amritdharis [baptized Sikhs] can be shastradharis [weapon-carrying Sikhs]."[24]

What's curious is the politics of what's right, wrong, or what's hidden. KGB disinformation to Indian central government, Pakistan's involvement (or lack thereof) influences Operation Blue Star and how botched it finally was. To be fair, foreign groups enable weapons entering the temple, but it's unsubstantiated.[25] Around the time of Operation Blue Star, Bhindranwale says in 1984, "I have no fear from my enemies. It is my friends and family who make me fear them."

In 2022, while driving through Central Valley, I see this quote in Gurmukhi script painted on many long-haul trucks taking produce from California to other parts of America. Bhindranwale, then cornered in 1984, roams free as a Sikh martyr, lionized in Central Valley.

In 1984, however, the Akali Dal steps back from being his ally. Bhindranwale is trapped.

All in all, this war is justified.

Of the Operation Blue Star outcome, Brar remains unrepentant of how it was conducted. It was necessary to flush out a few of the misguided youth who turned to terrorism.

Not all Sikhs are bad. After all, he is one.

The assault on the Golden Temple is carried out for three days in June 1984, starting on Guru Arjan Singh's martyrdom day. Arjan Singh, a Sikh guru, fought against the Mughals for the Sikh faith in 1606. The date for Operation Blue Star is planned to break the Sikh spirit. Official figures estimate 575 people died. Other reports suggest at least 3,000 people, including devotees caught in the crossfire.[26]

Shabeg trains his Sikh men to fight guerrilla.[27] The generals later grudgingly agree that the militants, with limited firepower, had inflicted unprecedented damage on the troops.

"They had kattas—homemade pistols—and automatic weapons the government themselves had given them," says Brar. "It was impressive how they defended the temple with practically nothing."

But the loyalists are no match to the army firepower. Once Shabeg and Bhindranwale's bodies are found, bullet-ridden, fighting till the end, the siege is over. The army controls the Golden Temple.

"It was fanaticism," said General Brar.

The terrorists are dead; long live India.

*

After the embargo is lifted, Operation Blue Star has the opposite effect of reducing terrorism in Punjab. Thousands of young men (and women) in Punjab and outside India are radicalized as pro-Khalistan sympathizers. Khalistan is an idea, a passion, a need to keep the Sikh faith alive in a free state that is fully Khalsa, fully Sikh.

In 2025, Uppal tells me, "Once we have Khalistan, our people in the Sikh country will never have to work. Because we, the expat Sikhs, we finance and keep that state wealthy, like Israel."

"What do you mean, Israel?"

He shrugs, "Every Jewish person who lives outside of Israel, feeds Israel with funds. We are surrounded by Pakistan, India, and China. We are persecuted like the Jews. But now, we are like the Palestinians, attacked for our religion."

"How would you fight?"

"Look, negotiations have been going on for decades. We—the Sikhs—must be ready when Khalistan comes. We need a constitution, a governance body. We need to tell the Hindus, Christians, everyone, that Khalistan is the land of the pure, but you're welcome to stay. We don't discriminate. Our faith doesn't allow that."

Between 1984 and 1992, more than twenty thousand Sikhs have been killed in encounters with law enforcement. Punjab—the land of plenty—has become hunting ground to shoot-at-sight any shifty-looking Sikh men or perceived shiftiness.[28] Their turbans, their beards give them away.

Chittaranjan Park in 2025 still has concrete barriers limiting access to neighborhood streets. There are three checkpoints to Pocket 99, where my parents built their house that Didi and I still own. There, you are greeted by security and a barricade. The men are paid by the Bengali neighborhood to guard us against terrorist threats. They take our names, numbers, and the information on whose house we are visiting.

Last time I visit, they ask sternly, "Which house?" peering into my rental car.

I want to scream at them, "This is my neighborhood, my house."

But they're doing their job, I guess.

The street dogs follow the car in suspicion. The night sky remains bright because of the light pollution for which Delhi is famous.

The gurdwara towers across from Market I off the neighborhood main road. The Punjabis have been living next to us, two separate refugee neighborhoods—them, since 1967, and us as East Pakistan Displaced Persons Colony since 1964.[29]

Two sensibilities. Two cultures. Together apart.

*

In General Brar's book, *Operation Blue Star: The True Story*, he emphasizes how Operation Blue Star couldn't have predicted the strength of Sikh militancy. Since then, there have been several assassination attempts on him and his family.

By 1990, India purchases the most military equipment from the UK. In 2014, it is revealed that the UK secret service was advising the Indian government on the "Sikh crisis." Against their advice, the Indian military attack the Golden Temple in 1984, sledgehammer style.[30]

Operation Blue Star—botched, bloody, violent—has radicalized many Sikhs, especially those outside of India.

But why want a separate state now?

Nijjer insists, "We've always been considered foreign in India. We Sikhs didn't belong. We've been patient. No more. No more."

Uppal emphasizes, "Look, it isn't just about Bhindranwale. Or even a separate state. When you destroy a holy temple, *completely* destroy it with bullets and tanks, walk in with boots on, then specifically target Sikh men to kill, how are citizens to feel? Aren't we Sikhs part of India? Well, they've shown we don't belong. Ever. So yeah, we fly the Khalistan flag high on our gurdwara."

*

In 2023, Amritpal becomes a leader of Waris Punjab de, a Sikh political faction.[31] Waris Punjab de literally translates to "heirs of Punjab." Amritpal says Bhindranwale is his hero. He dresses like him, talks like him, walks under heavy security with men in Sikh religious garb and guns.

The Sikh youth are mesmerized, in India and in Fresno.

*

The Golden Temple massacre leads to many Sikhs answering the call to violent action by Khalistani separatists. The assassination of Indira Gandhi is first. Then in retaliation and a coordinated Congress party–sanctioned sectarian pogrom, nearly three thousand Sikh civilians are killed in 1984.[32]

Next to my Bengali neighborhood, in the summer of 1987, gunmen open fire at a birthday party killing four, injuring many.[33] That year, Khalistani separatists and Indian security clashes lead to more than four hundred deaths in Punjab, including more than three hundred civilians.

This starts some of the bloodiest years for India and the government's fight against Sikh separatists.

**

Vermicelli Kheer (Served at Stockton Gurdwara, My Version)

Every happy occasion needs a muh meetha, or "sweeten your mouth," with dessert kind of ending. Vermicelli kheer is a dessert that arrived in India through Arab countries, with Islamic influence. Here is my version.

Ingredients

1 quart milk or coconut milk
5 tablespoons sugar
8 cardamom seeds, ground
1 (8 ounce) package vermicelli pasta
2–3 saffron threads
8–10 raisins
5–10 cashews, raw
1–2 tablespoons ghee
1 tablespoon rose petals, optional
1 teaspoon cardamom powder, for garnish, optional

Recipe

1. In a medium saucepan, bring milk, sugar, and cardamom seeds to a boil.
2. Reduce the heat to medium-low, and add in broken vermicelli.
3. Add saffron threads and turn off flame.
4. In a separate pan, sauté the raisins and cashews on low heat in ghee.
5. Add the raisins and cashews to the pudding, and stir to mix well.
6. Add rose petals and sprinkle cardamom powder.
7. Serve cold or at room temperature after a meal, or with chai.

20

Indira and the Sikh Genocide

In 1984, I turn fourteen, and Indira Gandhi, the first woman prime minister of India, the world's largest democracy, is assassinated by her Sikh bodyguards in New Delhi on a bright, crisp October morning.[1]

In class, I heave a sigh of relief when the teacher says, "School is dismissed. There has been a shooting." It is a civics test that I am certain I'll not do well in. This is good, I think in a fourteen-year-old, selfish way.

My classmates and I celebrate. Celebrate that we don't have to worry about school. The shooting? Well, that's been part of our lives since we were children. Khalistan is an idea, a demand, a separatist movement that we are familiar with even if we don't understand the motivation. While we don't pay attention to it, we avoid crowds, watch for riffraff, make sure we return home before dusk, don't touch anything shiny like transistor radios that could be bombs, and stay in our Bengali neighborhood.[2]

We have no idea how our lives are going to change.

*

For Americans, it's the JFK assassination, the Watergate scandal, 9/11, and now January 6 that define our generations. For us, it's the partition, the wars with Pakistan or China, Operation Blue Star, and the Gandhi (both Indira and her son) assassinations (1984 and 1991, respectively).

Indira's assassination points to complex history and yet informs us of the motivation of Sikh expats in America. Bear with me as we go through this history lesson. History continues to be repeated, and no matter how many books we read, we just aren't programmed to learn. Especially when history is written by the victorious.

On October 31, 1984, sixty-six-year-old prime minister of India Indira Gandhi, with her trademark streak of white hair across her stylish black bob, her sari a muted orange handloom, walks across from her Safdarjung Road bungalow to her offices. R. K. Dhawan, her assistant, tries to catch up, managing multiple files in his arms. Gandhi's walk is legendary—quick paced, decisive. Her voice is quiet, thin, but authoritative.[3]

India, nearly four decades post-independence, has settled for a hierarchy like a monarchy—Indira's father, Jawahar Lal Nehru, a Kashmiri pundit high-caste Hindu, governs the country in 1947. He's followed by Lal Bahadur Shastri, who dies within two years as prime minister. The country brings in Nehru's daughter, because if the father could be such a visionary, his daughter would be the same, right? Initially, the ruling Congress leadership thinks a quiet, submissive woman can be controlled. As Indians, we have an almost genetic tendency to lean toward leaders who become monarchs, and that monarch, post-independence, is Indira.

Indira's dark eyes, short hair, handloom saris, and Kashmiri sharp-angled pundit features, much like those of Nehru, her father, endear her to Indians, especially die-hard Congress party supporters.[4] Indira rises to political power with her antipoverty, prosocialist stance. Her decisive role in defeating Pakistan in the 1971 Indo–Pakistan war seals her leadership.

In 1975, Indira seizes power by declaring emergency for twenty-one months, arrests her opposition leaders, conspires to mute or "disappears" hundreds, and ensures forced sterilization of the poor as a population control measure.[5] Yet she is "Mother Indira," who advocates for the (low-caste) Dalits, women, and education, and implements very successful industrial and agricultural initiatives for a rising India.

Indira remains contradictory and problematic, but that's the country's leadership I grow up with. In 1980, she returns to power with a twenty-point program for development. Garibi hatao, Desh bachao (eliminate poverty, save the country) is launched to invigorate the economy, reduce government spending, reduce population.[6] All noble, socialist-leaning thoughts for a poor country with minimal foreign aid or support.

She is beloved. She is a leader. She is reviled. She is revered.

We haven't even talked about the "Punjab problem."[7]

*

Documentary filmmaker Peter Ustinov waits to interview Indira in October 1984. He is filming India's fierce female prime minister in action.[8] Indira's security detail, five jawans, commando soldiers stand about seven feet away. Of them there are two Sikh bodyguards: twenty-five-year-old Beant Singh and twenty-two-year-old Satwant Singh, who exchanges his guard duty to be with Beant this morning.[9]

"Namaste" is what people say she greets Beant Singh with.[10]

Beant Singh steps forward, a.38 pointed at her: bole so nihal, sat sri akal.

Whoever says these words is eternally happy, eternal is the Great Lord.
As he pumps three bullets into her abdomen, Satwant Singh pulls out his semi-automatic weapon, lodging thirty of the thirty-three bullets in the sixty-six-year-old woman. Dark blood stains on her sari, Indira collapses, her jhola bag falls next to her.

Turning to the bodyguards, Beant says, "You do what you have to, for I've done what I had to."

The assassins are interrogated. Beant lunges for a guard's gun. Meanwhile, Satwant pulls out his kripan knife from his turban—the knife that every Sikh carries to protect their religion. The guards shoot, killing Beant. Satwant is critically injured.[11]

Outside the prime minister's house on Safdarjung Road, the world remains clueless. Hearing the gunshots, Ustinov is unaware of the death of the subject of his documentary. Later, his film shares Indira walking past, the screams, and pandemonium.

*

Indira is a reviled target when she orders the Indian military to enter the Golden Temple in June 1984 to eliminate Bhindranwale. Wearing combat gear, shoes, guns in hand, bullets in reserve, the trained military men enter.[12]

Kuljit Nijjar is a young man when the Golden Temple is desecrated. He is one of the countless Sikhs who are harassed and tortured by the police, treated as a threat and terrorist, enough for him to seek refuge outside of India.

Four decades later in Stockton, Nijjar, his eyes filled with rage, comments, "There was a news blackout. We didn't know what the Indian government was going to do. Which government shoots bullets into their own people? Are we Sikhs not part of India?"

"Yes, but the terrorists were in there, no? Regular devotees were used as shields, no?"

Nijjar isn't convinced. "Sure, but did you know Bhindrawale, the Sikh granthi, the religious leader that the Congress party aligned with, they turned on him when he didn't do their bidding? All politics."

They were friends? Bhindranwale and the ruling party?

"They were allies and when he wasn't compliant, they killed him."

Sitting next to him at the Stockton gurdwara, Uppal adds, "What happened to the gurdwara, a sacred place, radicalized us. Especially us expats. We thought our Golden Temple was safe. That our faith was safe. What they did killed our souls, and in a way, made us all—Sikhs in America—want our own safe space, Khalistan."[13]

*

After Operation Blue Star, her cabinet urges her to remove Sikh security guards from her team.

Indira rejects that. "We can't claim to be secular if I don't have Sikhs in my detail. I don't believe I have anything to fear."

The same bodyguards kill her to avenge Operation Blue Star. In October, the prime minister's car drives the dying leader to the All India Institute of Medical Sciences hospital in South Delhi, sirens blaring. Countless pints of blood are pumped into a lifeless body. Ninety minutes after the bullets were shot into her, the prime minister is pronounced dead by her doctors.

The war has only started.

*

It's geography class in St. Anthony's Senior Secondary Girls High School, South Delhi. News isn't instantaneous in 1984. It is almost noon.

Mrs. Veena Singh, an army wife who prefers soft georgette fabrics with pastel flowers, and with hair in a fashionable coif resembling Lady Di's, teaches us about monsoons. Low- or high-pressure waves in the Pacific Ocean didn't interest me then and don't now, four decades later.

Mother Pia, our principal, a middle-aged nun in white habit and outfit, with a stern face, beckons Mrs. Singh, who steps outside.

Then Mother Pia, her eyes sad, comes inside with Mrs. Singh, asking us to pray. "Pray for Mrs. Gandhi. India's daughter was shot today by her own bodyguards. Very sad day, ask Jesus for her well-being."

We know our role in asking Jesus for favors, all of us Hindu, Muslim, and Christian girls. We ask Jesus for help on grades, on clothes, on trips. Now we ask Jesus for Indira's health, because we have been asked to by a nun.

Mrs. Singh wipes her eyes, trying to compose herself. Mother Pia leaves. Mrs. Singh stares out of the window facing the Osho meditation center. Because we're impertinent teenagers, we giggle among ourselves. Mrs. Singh doesn't stop us.

The bell rings. Shaking herself out of her reverie, Mrs. Singh says, "Class, please form a line. The school will update when you can return."

Hesitating, I stay near her. She smiles, but her brown eyes are tragic, broken.

She tells me about the Sikhni—I don't know why, maybe because she needed to talk, and I was there? The Sikhni, a student a few years junior to me, two braids tightly tied with blue ribbons, serious, an elder sister who always held her kid sister's hand when they walked into school. A good student. A good girl. "They can't reach their father. He's a Sikh. Two Sikh soldiers shot at our prime minister. We aren't safe."

I don't know who she means by "we."

I climb into the school bus to Chittaranjan Park. From the window, I watch Mrs. Singh. She looks ahead without seeing. Her mascara doesn't drip.

The Sikhni's father was an army man returning on the Rajdhani express train from Kolkata heading back to Delhi. The mob attacks him when he tries to save his people—strangers. No one knows what they may have done to him.

The Sikhni and her younger sister leave the school and the city. I think they head to Canada. For that day, uncertainty is the only certainty we all know.

*

I tell this story of the Sikhni a few years junior to me in school and her father in many versions. I tell the story of Mrs. Singh over and over. I write about them because I cannot forget. That's the least I can do. After all, people of the religion I was born into, a patriarchal, nationalist religion I don't practice, have systematically killed people of the other religion because their queen, monarch, leader, was killed. It becomes a tit for tat for tit for tat, over and over. We are numb to this, as newspapers and media share photos of people crying, dying, dead.

I tell you these stories because we lived them, but also, if we talk about them, perhaps we can learn to unlearn?

*

Ma's smile when she opens the door to me is unexpectedly large. She doesn't hug us—we are Ghoshs, after all. Professing affection is frowned upon.

The television blares rapid-fire Hindi announcing that Indira was shot by her own. Rajiv, her son and reluctant political heir, is the presumed prime minister.

Congress party members scream outside the hospital where the doctors work on Indira, "Khoon ka badla khoon!"

Revenge for blood is blood.

Around the dining table, my parents speculate, "This will be like the partition."

Every time things get difficult, violent, or unsafe, they bring up the partition. There was distrust of Muslims by Hindus and vice versa, and it continues. Now it includes Sikhs. Refugees then, my parents continue to live the life of refugees even when they are Indians and have been for decades.

Religious alignment is paramount once revenge is in the air.[14]

*

West and North Delhi erupt in violence. The low-income neighborhoods targeted by non-Sikhs are Sultanpuri, Mangolpuri, Trilokpuri.[15]

After the curfew is lifted for a few hours, Baba heads to the market. He returns with a few stalks of greens, okra, and eggplant.

Ma heaves a sigh of relief when she sees him. Then she says, "Oh, no meat, no fish, huh?"

He shakes his head. "This is the only thing there. I think looting will start soon."

But violence, as always, starts in the lower-income neighborhoods.

*

The first Sikh is killed the night Indira dies.[16] The government denies that the violence is state-sponsored or permitted. Later, Congress party leaders Jagdish Tytler and Sajjan Kumar are implicated in cases where people saw them or their team distributing kerosene and hundred-rupee notes to light Sikh homes on fire.[17] Sikhs are easily identifiable—their long hair, beards, kara bangles; the women in their distinct salwar kameez outfits.

Lower-income neighborhoods are targeted, where rioters are swayed by the promise of money. While we expect the first death, it's shocking when it's announced on the government-run TV channel.

Didi and I head to our terrace. Delhi is burning. We smell tires burning, rubber, wood; we see smoke. Downstairs, on our black and white TV, pictures flash. Indira's body rests in a state mansion, ceremonious, head covered in a sari, eyes closed, and dignitaries paying their respects.

Sikh men are dragged out of their homes, tires thrust around their necks, kerosene poured, and lit on fire. Women are chased down streets, raped, murdered, or let loose, walking terrorized. Children, orphaned, wait near the destroyed lanes for their parents. Mobs, mostly illiterate, are given voter lists to review and check last names that tell you which house is a Sikh's. For illiterate people high on liquor and bribes, an "S" is drawn on doors of Sikh homes, for ease. Ease of attack.[18]

Police vans drive past our house, men announcing on the loudspeaker: "There's a curfew. Indira is dead. Stay inside."

*

Across the park from our house is the Punjabi neighborhood, Kalkaji. Hindu-Punjabis and Sikh-Punjabis. A Hindu temple is across the Sikh gurdwara.

The next morning, we wake up to the sounds of bole so nihal. Sat sri akal.

At our Hindu temple, cymbals clash, priests sing om jaya jagdish hare, swami jaya jagdish hare, our gods' names.

Baba says, "The Sikhs are ready with weapons. This is a battle cry."

Ma protests, "No, maybe all they're doing is praying."

"That's what everyone thought that Bhindranwale was doing in the Golden Temple. See what he did, that terrorist?"

Ma doesn't argue but she whispers to me as she makes more tea, "Yes, but after they killed him, his people killed Indira, so it was all for nothing, na?"

I'm not sure that I have to take sides, in politics or at home.

We eat because there's nothing else to do. Rice with potatoes in a poppy seed–spice mix. Poppy seeds. Which makes us sleepy, and it's easier to sleep than to think of people dying.

*

Rajiv Gandhi, the sole surviving son of Indira, wipes his dead mother's brow. His two children, fair like their Italian mother, sit obediently on the floor next to their grandmother. World leaders place gardenia wreaths in respect. They look around, uncertain, unused to Hindu customs. Outside, the police announce on loudspeakers: "Violence is expected. We have shoot-at-sight orders."

On November 4, 1984, Indira's body is consigned to flames by her son, per Hindu tradition.[19] Two days prior, the army is deployed to stop the violence, and the riots subside somewhat.

A total of 2,773 people are officially confirmed as murdered during this time; the unofficial number is 30,000.[20] Four decades later, the Widows Colony, a government-established area in the low-income neighborhood of Trilokpuri in West Delhi, has 1,300 widows from the Sikh riots and over 4,000 orphans who wait for justice.[21]

In November 1984, Rajiv Gandhi as prime minister says at a filmed public gathering, "There were a few riots, skirmishes after my mother was killed. . . . After all, when a big tree falls, the earth shakes." This statement is considered a justification for the genocidal killings after his mother's assassination.[22]

*

Ten fact-finding committees are established in the four decades since the Sikh massacre. The Nanavati commission notes, "local Congress leaders and workers had either incited or helped the mobs in attacking the Sikhs."[23] The report emphasizes that the Delhi police remained passive and did not protect its people during the riots. But the report also excludes high-level Congress party leaders including Rajiv Gandhi in instigating the mob to kill Sikhs.

In 2002, Vrinda Grover presents her analysis of the 126 trial court cases to the Nanavati Commission, of which only eight convictions result, with 118 acquittals, and two overturns by the Delhi High Court, indicating a less than 5 percent conviction rate.[24]

The years after Indira's assassination, the Sikh genocide, and multiple commissions to bring justice have been long, and frankly, without resolution. No wonder Nijjer and Uppal feel they haven't got their due.

Khalistan, previously a call for a free state, is now the flag flying in Stockton.

An idea that the next generations of Sikhs—millennials, Gen Z, and beyond—have decided they will make it happen. Khalistan.

21

Khalistan, the Idea

Now What?

On March 23, 2025, a nonbinding Sikh referendum is held in Los Angeles.[1] Thirty-five thousand Sikh-Americans vote to create Khalistan in the state of Punjab. Thousands of Sikh truckers, a huge majority in the California trucking industry, roar through the streets, Khalistan flags on full mast. A week later, nearly twice as many Sikhs do the same in Sacramento, the state capital. The next one is in August in Washington, DC.

The referendums won't do anything but establish a right to self-determination. Sikhs outside India hope to show Sikhs in Punjab that they deserve a say in their state's governance, that the 1984 Sikh massacre was genocide. Will anything come of this? Maybe, maybe not. But it raises global awareness, so the Indian government can understand the power of Sikhs even as a minority in India.

Given the Modi government's no-tolerance policy to extremists (like Khalistani activists) and its close alliance with the current Trump administration, the referendums have been more measured.[2] This may be due to Donald Trump's strict stance on national security. The tone of these referendums in 2025 is showing dissent through democratic means, rather than a rabid political show of dissent as the activists have previously demonstrated.

Most Khalistan supporters are from outside India. Which begs the question—who really wants a Sikh state, and why? Activist groups like Sikhs for Khalistan raise warning signs of how the current Hindu nationalist Modi government is targeting minorities.

In 2024, the FBI charges Vikash Yadav, a former Indian intelligence officer in a foiled murder-for-hire plot to assassinate Gurpatwant Singh Pannun, a US-Canadian citizen, and a fierce Khalistani advocate. The Indian government later claims that the agent is no longer employed with them and "acted on his own."[3]

Yadav's indictment is the first time the Indian government is directly implicated in the attempted murder of a dissident outside of India.[4] In 2022, Khalistan separatist leader Hardeep Singh Nijjar of British Columbia is gunned down by masked men near a gurdwara in a Vancouver suburb. A year later, Canadian prime minister Justin Trudeau accuses India of killing Nijjar, a Canadian citizen, propelling a diplomatic rift between the countries.

Khalistan doesn't exist on any map. But Khalistan as a Sikh homeland has gained significant global traction.

*

During my own safar journey in the United States and the UK highlighting the Sikh migration, most Sikhs are curious about my curiosity. The non-Sikhs don't understand it.

"These are Sikhs, so different from Bengalis. Their history isn't yours, you're Bengali."

Or, "How can you reconcile with the fact that they killed Hindus, and say they're not Indian?"

Or, "Are you pro-Khalistan now? Do you want India to give up Punjab to these terrorists?"

Meanwhile, Sikhs remain mystified by my interest. They are also, justifiably, suspicious of my motivations to talk about the Sikh history and the subsequent Khalistan story. I am of Indian origin, and hence, suspect. Not because I have shown that with my actions, but because Sikhs, treated as second-class citizens in my home country, have earned the right to mistrust non-Sikhs.

Do I support the Khalistan cause, now that I have heard from so many Sikhs? Especially the younger expatriate Sikhs in Central Valley? Do I oppose the Khalistan cause, because of what Sikhs did to my city, the neighborhood I grew up in? For that answer, it all goes back to the partition.

My parents—refugees, Hindus by birth—flee their homeland with practically nothing. In Kolkata, as children, they both grow up middle-class. They carry the trauma of losing everything in their childhood throughout their lives. They move with a slow-burn hatred of Muslims, for the lands and homes that were taken by them. They tell me awful things Muslims have done to them, their families, their lands, their homes.

In the mid-eighties, a cousin, Baba's favorite, marries a Muslim—this cousin, he falls in love with her in graduate school in America. It's that simple. They return to India to get our family's blessings.

Baba spends days finding the best sari for this new bride—the bride of his favorite nephew. Her being Muslim matters, but Baba's love for his nephew is far greater. Religion, while given respect, doesn't matter when you celebrate the wedding of a beloved nephew.

Which is a roundabout way of my telling you, it's not that simple to say I am anti-Khalistan or pro-Khalistan. Ultimately, as I move downhill on this roller-coaster of life, I acknowledge the people who make impressions on me. The fact that they are Sikh, of another religion—women like Sheila Singh, Jassi Saini, or Jes Nijjer—matters. The fact that their people may have voted on the Khalistan referendum matters.

The fact that Jassi calls me didi, elder sister, matters more. That Jassi and her family make sure I get my favorite Punjabi kadhi when I visit their San Diego restaurant makes me say, yes, Khalistan the idea matters. Violence, and how it impacts families, matters. Genocide, the acknowledgment of it, matters. My love for a community stripped of dignity, and justice, remains strong. Even as I acknowledge the violence that some Sikhs have bestowed on my people.

Both can be true. Both are true.

From Stockton, I head back to America's Finest City. Here is Jassi and her story.

**

Potatoes with Poppy Seeds (Posto Aloo)

When Indira Gandhi died, curfew for nearly two weeks meant scarce access to food and fresh produce. Potatoes, in general, last long and that's what Baba brought. Posto aloo is a simple Bengali potato dish that is quick, easy, and fills our stomachs. Posto aloo reminds me of the 1984 curfew days.

Ingredients

1–2 tablespoons poppy seeds (posto)
2–3 green chilies, sliced
½ cup mustard oil
½ cup chopped onions
2 medium dry red chilies
¼ teaspoons kaalo jeere (nigella seeds)
6–7 medium potatoes, cubed
Salt to taste

Recipe

1. Soak poppy seeds in water for two hours, strain and grind in a blender with green chilies and enough water to make a coarse paste.
2. Heat mustard oil on medium-low, add the onions and cook till brown and soft; set aside.
3. To the remaining oil, add red chilies, nigella seeds, and potatoes; fry for 5–7 minutes on medium-high, stirring frequently.
4. Add the poppy seed paste, and salt to taste.
5. Cook on low heat till the raw poppy seed smell dissipates, stirring frequently.

6. Cook the curry on low heat for another 5–7 minutes, till the potatoes are medium-soft.
7. Add the green chilies, with more mustard oil.
8. Keep the curry on the stove for 3–4 minutes for a slow cook.
9. Serve hot with rice.

PART FIVE

THE THIRD WAVE, JASSI, THE AMRITDHARI, AJIT'S MOTHER

Jassi Saini with a photo of her son, Ajit, 2025, San Diego. Courtesy of the author.

22

Diwali and the Face
of Punjabi Tandoor

Jassi

On a bright midday in March, the lunch line snaking outside the building, which used to house a bank but now is the Sorrento Valley home of Punjabi Tandoor, is long. Twenty-eight-year-old Jaspreet Saini—Jassi—opens the door, head covered with a gray-green dupatta, hair in a black cloth, no makeup, wearing a salwar kameez—loose pants, looser shirt, the uniform of many Sikh women.

"Come in, didi," she says, her eyes lighting up. Didi, or elder sister, is a sign of respect to elders from the part of the world we come from.

Punjabi Tandoor has been a San Diego fixture for decades.[1] A no-frills dhaba, or diner, with locations in Sorrento Valley, Mira Mesa, Carlsbad, and Orange County. Its menu has been the same since it started. The prices may have changed over the years, but a two-dish vegetarian or nonvegetarian plate is always around $12–$14. A combo vegetarian meal may be hefty scoops of daal makhani—three types of lentils simmered in spices, ginger, cream, and chilies, saag paneer—delectable, blended spinach with homemade ricotta cheese, in soft spices of cumin, ginger, or a bright navratan korma, which translates into a slow-boiled multivegetable curry rich in spices, butter, and cream. A nonvegetarian one likely is a spicy chicken curry, like my mother used to make, or tandoori chicken curry, made with chicken barbecued with spices in a hot tandoor lending its familiar red color, or even a lamb curry, soft yellow, with lamb cubes slow-cooked in ginger and garlic onion paste, with tomatoes, garam masala, and the four Cs—cumin, coriander, cloves, and cardamom—giving it the familiar dhaba flavor.

The Saini family patriarch, Jagjit Saini, his beard white, in a check shirt tucked into well-worn khakis, his customary turban tied neatly around his head, hurries past me with a quick nod—it's lunchtime rush hour, and he's busy.

In a city where new food fads, expensive cocktails, and new takes on old food are the norm, Punjabi Tandoor continues to steadfastly reflect middle-class South Asian sensibilities, with a California vibe.

My first Punjabi Tandoor visit two decades ago is by accident, when I find its smallest location on Activity Road on Mira Mar Road—home to mostly working-class Asians—and fall in love with the people, and their food. Through job changes, divorce, moves to different neighborhoods, I continue to visit, pour my heart out, and they listen. And celebrate. And commiserate.

During one such visit to their smaller Carlsbad location, twenty-five miles north of San Diego, Lucky, one of the younger-generation Saini men, tall, long beard, thick turban, happy eyes, whisper-mimes, "Chai?" as he serves a line of hungry customers.

Of course, I say yes.

Since then, no matter which location I go to, the family always brings me a cup of hot milky tea to drink while I wait for my order.

In an adopted land that feels like home and sometimes not, this family and their food tell me that they, and I, belong.

*

For an agnostic immigrant and the daughter of Bengali refugees, there is one Diwali tradition I gladly hold onto: mishti mukh in Bengali, muh meetha in Hindi, which translates to "sweetening the mouth." It's a Diwali tradition where we eat homemade dessert to celebrate new beginnings.[2]

Growing up in the '1970s and '1980s, Ma's only guidance is, "Study hard, and focus on doing well."

Everything my Bengali family does is around food. But my role as a student and as a Ghosh daughter is to study. My textbooks are spread on the dining table—my makeshift, almost permanent study table. In the kitchen, Ma prepares two dishes simultaneously—the pressure cooker whistling the steam out as she seasons the daal. Baba returns from the fish market with fresh rohu or pabda. I inhale the fragrance of haldi mixed with cumin made into the paste that Ma adds to mustard oil, making the sauce for the fish that Baba cleans.

In between dishes, Ma asks, "Did you finish your math questions?"

I rush to the next arithmetic exercise. I think memories build as life happens. A summer day with luchi-aloo, or keema goat mince with slices of potatoes and peas. A winter evening with carrot soup spiced with ginger and freshly ground black pepper. Festivals. Weddings. What we wear. What we eat.

But Diwali, the festival of lights, is when we focus on desserts. The other festival is the Bengali one called Durga Puja, the festival celebrating the goddess who protects us mere mortals from evil. Both are celebrated in the Ghosh house, but we lean on Durga—with her devil-may-care fearless attitude. I identify with her even more as I grow older.

Diwali—a universal Indian festival—again, a celebration of good over evil, is when we eat tons of sweets, desserts, and all things made of milk, cheese, sugar, molasses, and jaggery. Guilt related to food isn't tolerated. While both festivals are a win of good over evil, for me, the festivals are about food. That's what my childhood memories offer. Food bests religion any time. Food bests rituals every day. Food creates comfort, a deep-in-the-pits-of-stomachs feeling that we crave as adults.

It's easy to accept that good is what we do, not evil. White. Black. Left. Right. Good. Evil. Why wouldn't we? That's the story of myth, folklore, religion, and tradition. But as we live through 2025, we know it isn't quite true, is it?

What is good, what is evil? Well, that's quite problematic now. How can we discern when they both look the same? It feels like evil wins over and over. Or what we thought was evil looks so much like good that we aren't sure.

For me, Diwali is this—light candles, and diyas, oil-wicks in earthen plates, plus all the dessert. In my Bengali family, Diwali is special, because while it is a Hindu festival, we rely on joy from food that connects us back home.

Diwali reminds me that my short-lived childhood was happy. I hold onto Diwali as I grow up.

*

Jassi is a tall woman, by Indian standards. "Five-eight," she says, smiling, with the knowing look of yes, who would marry such a Nawanshahr girl?

Nawanshahr, a town of over half a million people, in the state of Punjab—the land of five rivers, in India. Every family has someone living in America, Europe, or Australia, sending money back.[3] This district has a female literacy of 71 percent, above the national average of 59 percent, and while I don't find direct census data related to it, I know that Nawanshahr produces many women who get medical and nursing degrees. Jassi is one of them.

According to a 2024 article in *Nursing Times*, Sikhs are strongly represented in nursing. The faith emphasizes selfless service or seva, and compassion that aligns very well with nursing tenets. Many Sikhs see caring for others as a direct way to serve God and humanity, making nursing a fulfilling career path.

Jassi knows nursing will also serve her faith. But as a young woman, to be married and have a family is what she wants. Most Sikhnis are nurses—perhaps a combination of sewa, service of others, and a profession in line with respectability, honor, and religion.

When Jassi turns nineteen, her mother tells her, "Chalo, it's time."

It doesn't matter if you're trying to finish your studies. If the call, or a rishta, comes in—a marriage proposal—then you don't defy your parents. You get married.

"Ma-ji, but I'll be at school, can't come home," she tells her mother.

Jassi knows getting married, that too to a restaurant-owning Sikh family, means it's a far cry from her nursing training. And yet, not.

Nursing school in Nawashahr is highly competitive. Jassi's lucky to study there, but she's good. And she hopes to be a great nurse.

"They are a good family, the Sainis," her mother tells her, "we—your father and I—will speak with them first. Then we will see how they can meet you."

Jassi's mother, Kulwinder, is a tall, quiet Sikhni, a woman educated in life. Life has made her bear sorrows with patience. Kulwinder's mother-in-law hasn't treated her well. That woman, dark eyes, darker heart, has lived to ensure Kulwinder serves her 24/7 and it's never enough. Over the years, Jassi's mother's eyes lose joy; her voice, always soft, is now defeated.

But of this, Kulwinder is sure. That her beautiful and educated daughter, Jassi, finds a home where not only the husband but his family is kind. Kindness over wealth. A family that will be kind to Jassi and be good Sikhs.

Twenty-three-year-old Harpreet is Jagjit Saini's younger son. Harpreet's mother, Satwinder, has worked alongside Jagjit, raising her children, helping extended family members settle in California while managing Punjabi Tandoor for years.

Harpreet knows his role. To be a good son, a good Sikh. His married elder brother has two children and lives separately in a house close to theirs. Now, it's only him, and Harpreet needs to take care of his parents.

The first girl they see is Jassi. Harpreet is tall, fair, with a neat Sikh paghdi turban. He knows he is good-looking. But he is a true Sikh; looks don't matter. Kindness and service. Two things for the Sikh family to grow in America. Jassi will be the only girl Harpreet meets. Because when he sees her, he says yes. It is done.

As is riwaaz, the tradition, his parents head to Punjab to meet her parents with him.

"Sat sri akal, ji, thank you for coming," they say.

Harpreet touches their feet in respect.

"She's studying to be a nurse," Kulwinder says quietly of Jassi.

"I will be happy by what the elders decide," Harpreet replies.

The younger generation may have mobile phones and fast cars, but the devotion to the patriarchal family—the choice, if that, is clear. It's best for the family.

Arranged marriages start with the premise that elders know best. That religion, wealth, and values should take care of everything.

Later Jassi tells me, "Look, on paper, if someone looks good, his parents are good, his education and your education match, then good, na?"

"But . . . but, what if—?" I have so many questions.

She nods. "Sure, you have no guarantee it'll work. But then, you also don't have guarantee that it won't, right?"

Yes, I nod. "Look at mine," I joke, "I fought with my parents to marry the man of my nightmares."

We laugh because my jokes are wicked, but Jassi gets my humor.

Across the dining table, Kamaljeet, her mother-in-law, adds, "Yes, for some it ends in divorce, and for some, in death. We carry on, because who knows what wahe guru has in store for us?"

I can't argue with that.

*

In 2017, Harpreet says yes to Jassi and she to him. A few days later, Harpreet visits her with his parents at her hostel where she's finishing her final year of nursing school. Guru Nanak School of Nursing is a renowned nursing institute near Dhahan-Kaleran. A rural college southeast of Amritsar, its nursing graduates work in Canadian and US hospitals.

Jassi must get permission from the schoolteachers to step out of the hostel, even if it's only for five minutes. When they tell her the Sainis are waiting at the hostel gates, she rushes out. Covering her hair with her school uniform purple dupatta, she runs to the front gate, her long legs covering the distance in seconds. The Sainis watch their daughter-in-law-to-be heading toward them. Kamaljeet nudges her husband, Jagjit. "Kudi changi hai, nahi?"

Yes, Jagjit nods, yes, she's good. A man of few words, Jagjit's nod is enough for his wife to say, yes, time for muh-meetha. We have a wedding to prepare for.

Jassi touches Harpreet's parents' feet. She moves to her mother's side, her eyes firmly on the ground. It won't do to look up and check out her husband-to-be.

Jagjit turns to her father. "My son says yes. Your daughter is our daughter. No dowry, no money exchange. May both our children be blessed by wahe guru."

When she looks up, she sees Harpreet looking at her, then quickly averting his gaze before anyone sees him. She smiles. All she knows is Harpreet, three years older, is taller than her. This is who she will marry. Nothing else to talk about, is there?

"Our children will be strong and tall," she thinks, and blushes.

*

Diwali, the festival of lights, marks the time when the citizens of Ayodhya welcome their rightful king, Lord Rama, the ideal son/husband/king, back to his throne by lighting the path with diyas, lamps. These lamps ensure he returns safely to Ayodhya after vanquishing the king of Lanka, Ravana, who dared kidnap Lord Rama's wife, Sita. Rama returns victorious, wife and brother Lakshman in tow, and good wins over evil.

We Ghoshs don't celebrate Diwali for its religious significance. Ma asks us to question blind faith. Diwali—the story of the ideal god, Ram, the ideal son, king, and husband, and how he rescues Sita, his beloved wife, from Ravana, the ten-headed demon god of Sri Lanka. But, but, but . . . did Sita need rescuing? Isn't Ravana intelligent, and an equal match to Rama? Is Ram really the good guy, given once he returns to Ayodhya with Sita post-rescue and resulting war between his and Ravana's armies? Influenced by his advisors, Ram questions Sita's "purity." Or whether she was faithful while imprisoned by Ravana. Why did she let herself get kidnapped, to begin with? Was Ravana the evil one? Didn't he pretty much leave her alone post-kidnapping? Wasn't he doing this—using women as collateral—to show Ram the rage one may feel if one's women are hurt? In Ravana's case, his sister Shurpanakha is mutilated because she made eyes and unwanted advances at Ram. As a result, Ram decides to cut Shurpanakha's ears and nose, to show her who's boss.[4] A story of violence against women, of victim blaming, of man's or god's egos, and of women who continue to be massacred for a man to emerge victorious.

Instead, could we celebrate Diwali as a festival of joy, of family eating together, of parents blessing us? Yes, of course we can. In our family, we focus on joy. And food.

*

Jassi and Harpreet marry in the spring of 2017. Jassi pampers herself with a professional wedding makeup session. Wearing traditional red, her salwar kameez adorned with gold thread, her eyes large, her smile dazzling, Jassi looks like a movie star. And her new husband is a dashing Sikh prince. He matches her wedding red outfit with a red paghdi, and a red bow tie. Photos of them in the village, her mother serious, her father worried, and her in-laws beaming with joy. Of her school friends giggling. Of Lucky, Harpreet's cousin, a new groom himself, with his bride, Kamaljit, a young girl from the same village, dark eyes, round face, wavy hair, and a deathly fear of dogs. The photos are highly stylized, posed, and arranged by professional Punjabi wedding photographers.

Both brides, Jassi and Kamaljit, wear the traditional chooda bangles—white and red—signifying the Punjabi symbol of marriage, fidelity, fertility, and prosperity. They have dark henna paisley designs on their hands. Celebrating unions, the beginnings of a new life.

Both couples look young. Both couples look happy.

We focus on joy.

*

Nearly a decade later, Jassi and I flip through her massive wedding album with frayed in-built handles in her home on Black Mountain ranch in San Diego.

"We look at these photos often," Jassi says flipping through the glossy pages. About her makeup, she smiles, "I know, I was a different person then."

Her mother-in-law adds, "My son brought me a daughter back home. What a wonderful daughter our Jassi has been to us. . . . "

We focus on joy.

*

Every Diwali, Ma makes sabudana payesh, or tapioca pudding—slow-cooked milk with jaggery, saffron strands, with ghee-roasted raisins and cashews.[5] We sit on the floor, the plate of payesh, and a small diya in front of us. Ma and Baba bless us with a stalk of green grass, unhusked rice, signifying new life. Didi and I touch their feet in respect. They bless us with a good life. These simple actions convey how we continue that tradition. Then we light our diyas and wish for peace for all. Then dig into the payesh. Simple. Solid. Family.

Ma also makes narkel naru, or coconut balls with a hint of cardamom, held together with gur/jaggery and molasses. I pop one in my mouth every time I pass by the plate on the table. The idea is to eat and eat well.

*

After the wedding, Jassi returns to school, and Harpreet to San Diego. Jassi will head to America after her nursing degree exams.

The Sainis are now her parents. Jassi belongs to the Saini family, and leaves India much like the Pioneer First Wave immigrants did, much like the Second Wave immigrants did. This is the Third Wave—a South Asian bride, arriving in a new country, following her husband, holding her faith, celebrating her duty of sewa for her people.

I asked her if she was scared.

"Why would I be? I married into a good family. My husband took care of me."

The Punjabi culture, even the contemporary one, is significantly different from my Bengali upbringing. Perhaps I'm not that trusting of a higher power handling my future.

But all the Sikh women I've met over years in this safar possess an unwavering belief that their Wahe Guru will keep them safe, even when they travel over continents to an unknown country.

A century after the First Wave Pioneer Punjabis, Jassi flies to America's Finest City, a place she will call home.

I don't meet Jassi till the middle of the pandemic, because her plan was never the restaurant. She meant to be home. She makes sure her in-laws have hot rotis and daal when they return, and to pray at the gurdwara, every Wednesday and Sunday.

Harpreet is kind to her, and as young couples are wont to do, they plan a future together.

"Maybe we can open the nursing home for older Sikh parents?" he offers one day. He knows she misses nursing.

"Ah, but I'm here taking care of your parents, na?" she counters, even though her heart skips a beat, excited.

His smile has a heartwarming effect on her, and he knows she knows. "Achcha, achcha, of course take care of them. If I can quit this restaurant business, and run a nursing home business, won't that be nice?"

Yes, she agrees. "We can both commit to sewa."

Sewa. Caring for others who cannot take care of themselves. Jassi beams with joy the whole week after that. They decide that they will have children, but not now. They have time. Not before thirty, they promise each other. They have time.

*

For years, a month before Diwali I call either Jassi, or her brother-in-law, Lucky, and they usually answer with, "Accha, Diwali dinner? The usual?"

Yes. The usual. Chicken curry. Saag. A spicy daal. Cauliflower curry. Okra dry fry. Naan. Gulab jamun. Flaky jeera basmati rice. Standard dhaba fare. Made with love for my people.

Diwali remains a festival of family, of joy, and of hope. Even when my family is no longer held together on this earth, friends become family—the transformed Bengali desserts hold the same sweetness that Ma's naru and payesh used to.

*

A year into her marriage, Jassi skips a period. She doesn't feel good, she knows. She knows.

When she tells Harpreet, his excitement is more than hers. "Chal, it's the will of wahe guru."

Their nursing home plans are on hold. Their son is born nine months later.

"Ajit," Harpreet names him, "Our son will be the victorious one. The unconquered."

Sweets are distributed at the Poway gurdwara. "A son has graced us," Jagjit tells his fellow worshippers.

"Badhaaiyan," the Sikh families congratulate the grandfather.

A time of joy.

*

As Sikhs, Diwali isn't as important a festival to them as it is to Hindus. But the beauty of immigrants connecting in an adopted country is that we celebrate each other. Every Diwali, Lucky brings in aluminum trays filled with just-fried samosas with tamarind and coriander chutneys, flaky naan, curries, and rice pudding a couple of hours before my friends-who-are-family come over.

Lucky puts his hand out, his eyes twinkling. "Coconut naroo?"

He has a sweet tooth, as do most Indians. I pack a few naroos—a quintessentially Bengali dessert—for his family, his newborn son.

Later, Jassi texts, "Heard that your people liked our food. Chalo, that's good."

It's good indeed.

*

I'd love to tell you stories of fancy chefs, amazing state-of-the-art kitchens, spectacular knife skills, and plating. But I'd rather tell you stories of kindness, perseverance, joy, and yes, love in America's Finest City.

Jassi Saini. Go say hi to her at Punjabi Tandoor. The one on Moorehouse Drive in the Sorrento Valley neighborhood. Tell her I sent you.

**

Gulab Jamun (My Version)

One of the desserts you can get in any Punjabi buffet in the United States is a simple gulab jamun, which is a sticky-sweet fried cheese/dough dessert. I offer that at every Diwali party and the Punjabi Tandoor cooks make a great version.[6] Here's the recipe.

Ingredients

For the syrup
4 green cardamom pods
½ cup sugar
4–5 strands saffron
1 tablespoon chopped pistachios

For the gulab jamun
½ cup full-cream milk powder
¼ cup plain flour
½ teaspoon baking powder
1 tablespoon sugar
6 green cardamom pods
4 tablespoons ghee
4–5 tablespoons whole milk
1 teaspoon lemon juice
Oil for frying (avocado or sunflower)

Recipe

To make the syrup
1. In a medium saucepan, heat the ground cardamom, sugar in 3 cups water till the sugar has dissolved.
2. Simmer for 10 minutes, and cool the syrup.
3. Add saffron and set aside.

To make the gulab jamun

1. Sieve the milk powder, flour, and baking powder into a mixing bowl.
2. Stir in sugar and cardamom mixture (ground).
3. Add in ghee and mix till it resembles coarse mixture.
4. Add milk and lemon juice in small batches to form a soft dough.
5. Oil your hands with vegetable oil and shape dough into small, walnut-sized balls.
6. Heat ghee or oil in round-bottomed karahi or wok to fry the gulab jamun balls in batches.
7. Fry over medium heat; remove using a slotted spoon to drain on kitchen paper.
8. Add to the warm sugar syrup, soaking for at least 3 hours.
9. Serve warm with a sprinkle of ground pistachios and extra sugar syrup over the gulab jamun, with chai.

23

Jassi, Now

Ajit isn't fussy, but then, neither are his parents. It isn't a surprise. After all, both his parents are happy people, right? Jassi's world is Ajit's food, first steps, showing him how to pray even when he doesn't understand it. Lucky's wife also has a baby boy. The Sainis are busy with life and new additions. But they meet every week at the gurdwara. The Sikh temple, for over a hundred years, a gathering place, remains the center of this community in the new century.

The gurdwara in Poway is a commercial building, distinct in its A-frame roof and church-style architecture.[1] The large wooden entrance resembles those of many churches in the San Diego middle-class neighborhood. A suburban architecture to attract Christians to church in America, it becomes a Sikh symbol in San Diego when the Sikhs make it their own. Very similar to when the Japanese monastery in Imperial Valley became a Sikh gurdwara decades ago.

Mr. Saini, a well-respected member of the community, is swamped at the gurdwara temple entrance. Community members asking for his advice, or blessings for their children's marriage, or births. He doesn't take this respect for granted. Life is good, but service to Wahe Guru is more so. Now with Ajit in the family, he's sure life can only get better.

"Bachche, kneel down," he urges Ajit.

The young boy, his uncut hair tied in a knot on his head, covered with a white cloth, holds his hand and kneels down like his grandfather in front of the Granth Sahib, the holy books.

Mr. Saini says, "Mattha tek, mattha tek," to his grandson.

Ajit bends to touch his forehead to the ground.

Behind him, in the section reserved for women, Jassi smiles with pride. Her son is going to be a good Sikh.

Then, the Great Pause arrives.

*

Punjabi Tandoor's business crashes, as do other businesses during the Great Pause.[2]

According to author Mayukh Sen, "The pandemic has laid bare the restaurant industry's creaky foundations. Media coverage focuses on celebrity chefs with lofty net worths. . . . This means the pandemic could wipe out eateries that showcase immigrant fare."

The Sainis hustle, as always. Lucky texts me, "We've seen bad, we've seen worse. This too shall pass."

He has the brash confidence of a young man who can handle any unfortunate circumstance because he works hard.

I personally sequester in my house with my Dalmatian. It is the best of times for the canine and me. Late evenings, we walk in the neighborhood when everyone is home at dinner. Cotton masks and latex gloves become my uniform because we still don't know that we need N95 filters or that gloves are unnecessary. Working in diagnostics gives me an advantage. I get the information on vaccines, on testing, on shortages, and on the disease in real-time. I know not to panic because panic doesn't help any, though I do succumb to buying excess toilet paper.

I have spent most of my years traveling for work. I am a work road warrior who thinks that's a badge of honor. But during the Great Pause, I learn to Zoom much like everyone else. I don't hug a human for almost sixty-four weeks till I get my vaccine.

In 2025, no one wants to talk about those years when the world stopped. If anything, we'd rather talk about the high school and college-going generation's mental health. Their ability to adult. But GenX-ers like us? The ones who have lived through wars, famines, migration, immigration, and epidemics? The ones who remember how life used to be, how we adjusted to the silence half a decade ago? And yet, again, we and our crises—mental, physical, spiritual— are forgotten. Our trauma is minuscule because the newer generations need attention. It will be decades before we face the horrors that we have internalized.

I turn fifty with my dog for company. My dear friends stop by for two hours, separated by masks, six feet in a backyard get-together. We pretend to be happy, planning when the Great Pause is over.

Only the Dalmatian is excited to have so many people around. Lucky drops off the food near the front steps. We wave from across the glass door. This is our new normal.

*

Two months into the Great Pause, Jassi gets a call.

"Your husband was involved in an accident," is what she remembers.[3] But maybe it was Mr. Saini who got the call? Or did her mother-in-law's wails tell her what happened? She doesn't remember. In May 2020, twenty-nine-year-old Harpreet dies in a solo car accident, leaving Jassi behind, with her fifteen-month-old son, Ajit.

Years later, Jassi's eyes are calm, belying the devastation in her heart. "What can you do, didi?" she says, leaning forward across the table covered in faux wood patina in the restaurant. "We wanted to start a family in three, maybe four years, but Ajit arrived a couple of years into our marriage. Sometimes, the universe decides for us."

Ajit's crooked smile is similar to his uncle Lucky's and his aunt Perminder's. At the restaurant, he greets me with bole so nihal before turning back to his iPad. All he knows is his mother and his grandparents. And that their love fills his world.

For two years, Jassi focuses on her child, the gift from her beloved. Her in-laws hold grief with love. Her social media handle has her and Ajit's names. She posts Ajit's progress—her son at the gurdwara; in school; in a police uniform for Halloween; a Father's Day photo of Ajit as a baby, on his father's shoulders.

When her mother calls her from India crying, "Jassi, come home, I can't bear this sorrow you're in," Jassi consoles her, saying, "My home is here, with Harpreet's parents. My son is here. He is American and a Sikh. I will raise him like his father wanted him to be."

Jassi's strength that everyone else sees is because of her faith, she says.

"But, Jassi," I protest, "your life hasn't even begun—"

She stops me with a smile, "No, didi, I am a Sikh mother."

Jassi's quiet confidence tells me that age isn't a criterion of one's maturity. For this agnostic, I admire Jassi's trust in her Wahe Guru. I don't have that kind of faith in the unknown. To me, the concept that good things happen to good people is alien. But Jassi believes it, even when bad things happen to good people like her.

*

Baba is a man of traditions, not religion.

Every Ashtami, the eighth day of celebrations for the goddess Durga, Baba wearing his best dhuti kurta, heads to the temple to eat bhog, the vegetarian food offered after prayers. Much to Ma's chagrin, he makes me his co-conspirator. "Let's eat at home, then head to the temple and eat again. Gods won't want us to be hungry, na?"

Ma's eyebrows knit together in disapproval. We repeat this routine till 1993, when I leave for America. Baba and I are joined at the hip in our irreverent, irreligious shenanigans.

The late journalist and essayist Christopher Hitchens in his *Slate* essay "Religion Poisons Everything," which he expanded in his book *God Is Not Great*, says, "Human decency is not derived from religion, it precedes it."[4]

What, then, do we do when religion, Sikhism in particular, guides its followers to live by service and decency to all?

I don't have to believe in religion to believe in Jassi and her right to believe in it.

*

A year after Harpreet dies, Jassi tells her family, "I would like to take the vrat."

The amritdhari vrat.[5] Amritdhari, or the one who takes/drinks amrit, the immortal nectar prepared by the panj piyare, the five Khalsa holy men at the gurdwara, is an initiation ceremony by which a Sikh joins the Khalsa. One can be a Sikh by being born into the family. To be part of the Khalsa is to be part of the pure. To be Khalsa, one must realize the responsibilities of adhering to the faith.

Jassi is ready.

That trip to the gurdwara is a day of celebration. The panj piyara Sikhs—holy Sikhs who guide the ceremony—kneel around the iron bowl of kada prasad, the holy offering of ghee, sugar, and flour made in the langar under strict guidance from the Khalsa, blessed by reciting the holy verses. Using their own kripans, they bless and affirm the salutation. They affirm each salutation of how Jassi will now follow the path of service within Sikhism.

"From now on, you will serve through prayer, service, and time."

Jassi kneels in front of them, her hands folded. Her mother-in-law holds Ajit's hand. The family supports her choice. It is an honor. It is a sign of respect.

"From today, your individual existence is no more. You live as a Khalsa, supporting the Sikh life. Guru Gobind Singh remains your father, and your spiritual journey makes all Sikhs your brothers and sisters."

Very similar to a Christian profession of vows for nuns, as an amritdhari Sikh, Jassi now commits to her faith.

When I meet Jassi, she has been living this life for a few years. Her eyes are determined yet joyful. Her hair is covered under a black headscarf, over which she loosely throws on her dupatta. As an amritdhari, she doesn't cut her hair, eat meat, or show immodesty, not that she ever has shown immodesty.

I remark again, "You were a different person in 2017."

"Yes," Jassi says, beaming with pride. Across us, her son tries to get our attention, showing his "I love you, Dad!" photo of him in school holding the banner against a crayon-drawn rainbow background.

She smiles at Ajit.

**

Kada Prasad

Holy whole-wheat sweet offering at Sikh gurdwaras, cooked in langar kitchens. An offering blessed by the Khalsa Sikhs, served to all gurdwara visitors.

Ingredients

1 cup sugar
1 cup ghee
1 cup whole wheat flour
3 cups water

Recipe

1. Heat water in a large pan on medium-low heat.
2. In a separate heavy-bottomed pan, add ghee and, once melted on medium-low heat, add the flour.
3. Stir and mix.
4. Fry the flour, stirring nonstop on medium-low (5–10 minutes) till the flour turns a shade of dark gold.
5. Add and mix sugar solution in small batches on low flame to prevent sputtering.
6. Cook till the kada prasad is thick.
7. Top with cashews and raisins (roasted, optional).
8. Serve warm with chai.

24

Jassi, the Third Wave Immigrant

The accident that takes Harpreet from the Sainis is a solo spinout. To date, the cause is unknown. A short news article in the *San Diego Union Tribune* mentions that he is alone in a white sedan driving north on the 163 freeway when he likely loses control of the car. Perhaps he was speeding? Or maybe he was distracted while texting? No one knows. All that is available are broken bumper and mirror parts strewn across the road. He is twenty-nine. Life, despite this, continues to move on.

Harpreet's death changes Punjabi Tandoor. The Saini family could have easily collapsed with grief. But Jagjit picks up where his son left the business, working throughout the pandemic. He and Kamaljeet keep their promise—Jassi is their daughter. With Harpreet gone, the house is now a shrine to him. Gurbani, the voice of the Sikh gurus, plays on repeat. The gurus wouldn't have taken Harpreet from them if they didn't have a bigger purpose for the Saini family, would they?

*

A few months later, with her in-laws' blessings, Jassi becomes the face of their Morehouse Drive location. Their faith teaches them to be resilient, to be kind, to serve guests. In the Sikh faith, women and men are equal. She is their daughter now. She is their son.

"Didn't you want to go back home? To your parents?"

She shakes her head. "I visit my parents yearly in India. But my home is here. San Diego."

The Diwali celebrations you may be familiar with are the extravagant, joyous events choreographed in larger-than-life Bollywood musicals. Navratri, the nine nights of dancing till midnight, with the lead actors making eyes at each other, loud dholak drumbeats matching their steps, ah, Diwali. However, my childhood Diwali memories are of lighting diyas with my sister—pouring mustard oil in clay lamps and then dipping cotton wicks to light them around the balcony. Oh, and lighting phool jhadi sparklers, holding them far away so we didn't burn ourselves.[1]

*

A customer comes to the counter. Jassi rushes back to help. With her left hand, she deftly scoops rice on the Styrofoam plate, adding in liberal ladles of chicken curry, eggplant bharta, and daal.

It is lunch hour, and most homesick South Asians from Qualcomm and biotech companies dotting the Sorrento Valley neighborhood head to Punjabi Tandoor for its comfort food. The biggest decision they make there is whether they want a three-dish or a two-dish combo. Jassi guides them through it.

"Did you want the saag or the eggplant?"

"Naan? Raita or kheer?"

People from all communities stop at this buffet line, some indecisive, some focused. Jassi and her sister-in-law, Perminder, greet them with a quick "Hi, what combo would you like?" There's a familiarity among the diners, of people who have been frequenting this lunch place for years.

*

Jassi knows the customers standing in line loved Harpreet. She decides to trust the faith that they too will now know her.

"I had to make my own space after he passed away," she explains, "I did what he would have done. Welcome our customers, give them food, wish them well."

Jassi's belief is that as they work hard, the loyal customers will return.

"When being a Sikh means that when someone is down on their luck and needs help, then you follow the lead," she says matter-of-factly. "We feed everyone with service."

Her father-in-law calls her to the kitchen, and Jassi gets up to help, her sneakers striding quickly to the back of the kitchen. The love between the family members is obvious—each looking out for the other.

*

Diners continue to file in, looking at the filled containers of chickpeas, samosas, and lamb curry. Jassi ladles the food expertly, smiling at each customer, an introverted shy smile, but a smile, nonetheless. Perminder, now a mother of two, cracks jokes in Punjabi with her, manning the cash register. Set next to it, a sign printed on a tired piece of paper tells us what this family is trying to do in America's Finest City, "Good Vibes Only."

*

In early 2025, Ajit is rushed to the hospital with respiratory issues. I am to visit their home that weekend, but Jassi says, sorry, didi, wait, we are still in the hospital.

The next day she texts, "We are back, he has RSV."

She talks about respiratory syncytial virus with the clinical precision of someone in the medical field. It reminds me that Jassi may be a mother, but she remains a nurse.

"Come over anyway, didi," Jassi insists. "He's fine, just have to monitor him."

When I reach her home she shares with the in-laws, Ajit is resting, but only as a young boy can. Slightly cranky, Ajit coughs while playing with his mother's phone. Seeing me, he smiles and shares his latest sketch: That of Bhindranwale, the warrior-guru, killed in Operation Blue Star.

"He's a big fan," says Jassi, boiling the tea in the kitchen.

Ajit's grandmother scolds him for coughing without putting his hand over his mouth.

RSV appears to be an epidemic spreading from child to child in San Diego, an epidemic that has no vaccine to help reduce a child's suffering. Ajit seems happy, just a bit under the weather.

"Tell me, Ajit," I ask as diplomatically as I can. "What's so good about Bhindranwale?"

I am curious what Ajit's perspective is of a man they idolize, a man I grew up knowing to be a terrorist.

"Well, he is a saint. He is a Sikhi. Wahe guru da Khalsa, wahe guru di fateh."

To God belongs the Khalsa (the pure), to God belongs the victory.

The chant rolls off his tongue easily. He doesn't need to know Bhindranwale is considered a terrorist by the Indian government. For him, Bhindranwale spoke up for all Sikhs and died for all Sikhs. It is the sentiment of many Third Wave immigrants.

If I am but a witness, who am I to refute that? After all, in this country, as an immigrant, I too am looked upon with suspicion.

He turns back to his video game.

Kamaljeet gives me a tour of their backyard. "Yeh dekho, look, peaches, figs, mango, guava, onions. So many fruits. This tree—" she points at a young fruit tree—"my son planted it before he died. I tend it so I can return it to his son."

Grief of losing one's son, one's husband, is something I haven't experienced, but when I see the women of Punjabi Tandoor, I see how they wear their loss like shields for their hearts.

I take the guavas from the Sainis and decide to turn them into guava jelly, much like how Ma used to make.

That night when I text Jassi a thank-you note for opening her home to me, she writes back, "Oh, but it's your home too."

In a world where we treat each other with such suspicion, where we cut off ties when we don't agree on issues, to open one's home to another immigrant stranger needs a heart filled with love for the world. Or maybe it is her faith.

*

I've lived in America longer than in India. I continue to hold my childhood traditions close and have evolved them to include the life I live now. In my house, on Diwali, I invite my friends to celebrate our kind of festival. We eat, read poetry, light diyas, and wish each other well.

Every year, I make a version of Ma's sabudana payesh that I cook with coconut milk and molasses, with a hefty helping of blueberries making it as American as it is Indian. I slow-cook coconut flakes in molasses, add cardamom powder,

The Saini family, Punjabi Tandoor, San Diego, 2022. Courtesy of the author.

and roll them into small round balls. I make the narkel naru as a reflection of who I am now by adding a berry—raspberry, blueberry, or blackberry—and sprinkle coconut flakes on top. The desserts remain Bengali, Indian, and yet also very American.

**

Guava Jelly

Every summer, I've been making guava jelly that Ma used to make when we were children. A simple slow-cooking of ripe guavas in molasses or sugar, it's a great addition to breakfast. Jassi's guavas deserved my Ma's jelly recipe.

Ingredients

5–6 pounds of ripe guavas
1–2 cups brown sugar (or 1 cup molasses)
6–8 strands saffron
1 teaspoon ground ginger
1 teaspoon chili powder
½ teaspoon salt
1 tablespoon lemon juice

Recipe

1. Add cubed guavas to 6–8 cups of water in a large pan.
2. Boil on high heat for 15–20 minutes till the pulp mixes.
3. In a large mesh strainer sieve, add the pulp in batches, squeezing the pulp through—it is a tedious process; be patient.
4. Save the guava fruit pulp for vegan cookies.
5. Take the water mixed with guava juice, naturally available fruit pectin (from the guava), and boil on high heat.
6. Add sugar as needed to the liquid mixture (or molasses).
7. Add the saffron after the mixture boils.
8. Boil the liquid till the drops stick to the spoon as it thickens (20–30 minutes).
9. Add the lemon juice to balance the sweetness.
10. Store in an airtight jar in the fridge—this should last at least 6–8 weeks at that temperature.
11. Enjoy on toast.

PART SIX

ON TRUCKERS, DHABAS, AND THOSE WHO CHANGED CENTRAL VALLEY CALIFORNIA, UMA DEVI

Daljit Singh and Uma Devi in their truck stop dhaba in Fresno, 2025. Courtesy of the author.

25

Dhabas, a Love Story

After the Indira Gandhi and Bhindranwale assassinations of the 1980s, a new wave of immigrants arrive from Punjab. The violence against Punjabi Sikhs escalates in India. Sikh youth are targeted systematically, attacking their employment, education, and life options. While exact numbers are not known, according to the Sikh Coalition, thousands of Sikhs are "disappeared," likely orchestrated by government officials and the Punjab police.[1]

The Third Wave Sikhs leave India, much like the First and Second Waves of Punjabis. A curious satellite industry of the California farming communities now becomes a Sikh emblem. That of trucking.

By 2023, more than 20 percent of the US trucking industry is Punjabi-owned, according to Meena Venkataraman. Lasher Transportation of Bakersfield, LB Transport of Los Banos, or Khalsa Transportation of Selma, all from California, are Punjabi-owned multimillion-dollar companies.[2]

Challenging the rugged, lone white trucker driving through the American West stereotype visual, this industry is rapidly becoming Sikh.

That's the story I'd like to share with you.

*

In a 2019 *LA Times* article, Jaweed Kaleem writes that of the nearly 3.5 million truckers here, California has the highest number of truckers, after Texas. However, there's a shortage of drivers, given the average trucker's age is fifty-five.[3] Fresno-based Raman Dhillon, a former driver who founded the North American Punjabi Trucking Association, says, "This is where Punjabis . . . fill the gap."

Manjit Singh Uppal, the former Stockton gurdwara president, jokes about his own trucking life. "I did everything when I landed here as an immigrant. Canned tomatoes in Yuba City factories, owned land, tractors, grew soybeans, vegetables, but you know, for me, because I know English, I had more options."

"And what's that?" I ask.

"To be a trucker. Arrey, food needs to go places, right? If you know English, and you can drive, it's easy to be a trucker."

Look, being a truck driver isn't obtaining a CDL (commercial driver's license) and driving an eighteen-wheeler. It includes a lifestyle with uncertain schedules, treacherous roads, especially in rain or snow, loneliness, cramped sleeping quarters, eating truck stop food, and long stretches of time missing home-cooked meals and family. This isn't for the faint of heart.

The Sikh drivers rise to this challenge. Much as their ancestors have—whether it is farming in an unknown land or fighting world wars on behalf of their colonizers or even building their spaces of worship in a land that considers them foreign. Approximately 150,000 Sikhs now work in the American trucking industry, of which 90 percent are drivers ferrying rice, vegetables, chocolate, and other produce from the American West.[4]

It isn't all about fearlessness, though. It's also practical. Sikhs have been enterprising risk takers because unke khoon mein hain, it's in their blood. Much like the previous waves, to operate an eighteen-wheeler, and practice your religion, and provide for your family has been attractive.

After 9/11, the first Sikh is mistaken for a Muslim and murdered in Arizona. In the 2012 Sikh temple massacre in Oak Creek, Wisconsin, seven lives are taken. Now, Sikhs, who remain peace-seeking and honoring their faith, also look for employment with religious and cultural freedom. It's just safer. Trucking certainly gives them that freedom.[5]

*

On a crisp March Saturday, I drive from Sacramento on the 99 freeway, the two-lane highway I have traveled for several safars, journeys. Large trucks—tall, majestic, loud—move alongside steadily while I urge my rental to speed to Fresno.

I've stopped peering into these massive trucks, hoping to get glimpses of the drivers through their windows. They usually look ahead, bearded men with turbans, navigating the truck through narrow roads carrying goods to states outside the Golden one.

At seventy thousand, the Fresno Sikh population is the highest in a major US city. Almost the size of a Punjabi village in India.[6] Off the freeway is a sharp turn into Golden State Boulevard. The morning fog still lingers close to the fields. The frontage road is flanked by large container boxes and cargo cars.

Past the McDonald's is a large, paved truck stop/gas station with bright red lettering, "Roady's Fifth Wheel Truck Stop," and a nondescript Arco gas station. Train tracks run parallel to Golden State Boulevard, with goods trains noisily trundling by. Along the paved concrete area stands a green wood building with English and Punjabi-Gurmukhi script titled "Punjabi Dhaba" conveniently next to a laundromat and a DoT drug testing center. A hand-drawn painting of a truck with Indian lettering is painted on the green wall with a Punjabi dholak drummer in traditional Sikh garb of a turban, kurta, and a smile.

Punjabi Dhaba is yet another unpretentious diner. It's signage in Gurmukhi script on the door highlights the food and grocery sundries. Aisles of fried snacks, dalmooth, spiced chickpeas, Parle-G biscuits (five for $1.25), and desi cookies are illuminated by bright lights. The cash register proudly displays US and Indian flags. Diljit Dosanjh's loud Punjabi music plays in the background.

Roady's truck stop and filling station, next to Punjabi Dhaba, Fresno, 2025.
Courtesy of the author.

Boiling curry smells waft from the back kitchen. In the dining space, weary truckers sop up daal with a thick naan, food they likely craved for hours heading west on their truck route.

Daljit Saini is a middle-aged man, with a graying beard, dark eyes, and a fleece cap covering his unshorn hair. His three-year-old son is cranky, as children are prone to be if woken up early. Uma Devi, Daljit's wife, in a beige salwar kameez, brown sweatshirt, and the yellow tikka mark on her forehead many married Indian women wear, hushes the child.

"Come in, come in," Uma says, pushing a small stool toward me. Accompanying me, Raj Singh Badhesha, my Fresno guide and a Superior Court judge, sits in the hallway with a smile.

Blowing on the hot chai, Raj says, "dhanyavaad, ji," thank you, friend.

After all, for us, atithi devo bhava, the guest is god.

*

Meena Venkataramanan creates a Google document in 2023 on X, formerly Twitter.[7] A crowdsourced chart of Punjabi dhabas in the United States is dynamic. Each dot represents a diner, creating dot-spatter streaks across the country, following truck routes of I-5, I-10, I-80. East to west. West to east. Crisscrossing the country as the truckers deliver food to warehouses and large box stores.

The dhabas have "India," "Punjab," or "Tandoor" in their names. Almost 20 percent of these dhabas are run by Punjabis. All have sprouted along highway routes.

Truckers need to eat.

*

Daljit and I grow up in Delhi, a few years and a few miles from each other's neighborhoods. And yet our worlds are continents apart. He looks like he could be my age, but he also looks older. Life hasn't been kind to him or his body.

He tells me he started growing his hair back recently, a born-again Sikh. You are born Sikh, but that doesn't mean you practice it. Much like a lapsed Christian, you may return to the Sikh philosophy later in life when age and circumstances transform you. Daljit, uncut hair and beard, is now steeped in service. His community is truckers and their Sikh families. Punjabi Dhaba has become an Instagram magnet for food influencers.

Daljit studies in a Hindi-medium school, and English isn't his forte. Family finances aren't good, either. He works odd jobs when his father can't send him to school anymore.

Finally, in his late teens, early twenties—he doesn't remember when, the years have blended—he heads to America. The plan is what lower-middle-class families have for their children when they leave the country for work—work and send money home.

Pointing at his wife, Daljit tells me, "Arre, but look at my good luck! I ended up with a schoolteacher. She's the boss."

Uma fixes her glasses on the bridge of her nose, smiling. "Yes, I taught middle school in Punjab before I married him."

Daljit starts with menial tasks when he arrives in America. Filling truck beds with produce, the trucker's helper, then getting his CDL. For years, with no money to spare, he doesn't return home.

"I worked next to Mexicans who taught me how to cook. Daal, roti, sabzi, empanadas, tacos, everything," he says proudly.

But he hasn't been able to stay in touch. It was a lifetime ago. "As a truck driver, that's what you lose. Connections."

*

Dhabas, or roadside diners, have been a staple along Indian highways. During the 1947 partition, dhabas along Punjab heading toward Karachi in Pakistan and toward Delhi in India are shelters where refugees find a place to rest while fleeing violent mobs.[8] Since then, dhabas exist for other reasons—serving truckers, weary travelers, or drunk college students.

*

Uma Devi is a teacher in Punjab. By the time she gets Daljit's rishta, the proposal, she's considered an older match. Daljit is in his thirties, no spring chicken himself. It's time to get married. Uma is the more educated of the two. It's a marriage of arrangement, but hey, it's a marriage.

Surprisingly and unexpectedly sweet is how Uma and Daljit learn to love each other. A modest marriage, but a promise of eternal union. In arranged Sikh marriages, the unshakeable faith that their elders choose their partner makes the lack of agency bearable.

Whether I agree with it or not is beside the point.

Lately, the Hindu majority in India has influenced contemporary Sikh union events including larger weddings, dowry, exchange of cash in return for the daughter getting married.[9] Sikh marriages are usually devoid of rituals, rites, and superstitions—focusing on the union of a couple and their families, without the need for dowry or big weddings.

Uma arrives in Fresno with her husband, with faith that they will succeed in this Northern California town.

A new bride, Uma adjusts to her American life. The loudness of Punjab is replaced by Fresno silence. No one shouts, the grocery stores are quiet, the streets are well lit. Even the 7-Eleven store gives back exact change. Her new husband is absent, traveling on his truck. When he leaves to work, Daljit feels terrible, and she feels terrible when he leaves.

Within a few months, she's had enough.

"All I do is wait for you, and you are never home," she complains quietly.

Daljit worries for her. He has had a hard life in America—first with visa issues, then finding work, then finally getting his trucking license. Working long hours for years, he feels he hasn't really lived since he left home as a young man. He doesn't want his wife to feel the homesickness he felt for years.

"You listening?" asks Uma impatiently. "I can't do this anymore."

Hearing his sobbing wife, Daljit sighs.

Taking his shoes off, he sits next to Uma. "Okay, come with me on my truck from now on."

She looks up, wiping her tears, and nods.

*

Trucking life isn't for the weak. One needs to persevere—the commercial drivers' license needs training, both written and driving tests, one needs to know the US highway routes, work under pressure of weather, deadlines, sleep deprivation, and parallel park, or back into tight spaces. But more importantly, a trucker leaves his family every time and is alone on the road for days on end. So why do Sikhs lean toward trucking jobs?

The answer is quite simple. For a community used to physical labor, and being othered because of how they look—turban, hair, comb, kirpan—Sikhs tend toward employment spaces that let them be, such as farming or trucking, where they can be Sikh in religion and life.[10]

Colorado trucker Mintu Pandher says, "You don't have to take your turban off. You don't have to lose your faith while you're working hard."

There is also another reason, that of community. Like the First and Second Wave immigrants ensuring passage for their family members, people from their villages to the United States—a situation of "there's safety in numbers"—many Sikhs follow their village or townsmen into trucking because it's highly lucrative and if it works for their fellow village members, it works for them too.

*

In April 2025, an executive order commanding all commercial drivers to be English-proficient is decreed.[11] The idea is to ensure "safety on roads." Truckers should be able to interpret traffic signs and interact with law enforcement as needed. This order comes right after another, noting English as the official US language.

Now, a commercial license requires English proficiency. In 2019, a Colorado multicar and truck accident leads to four deaths.[12] Investigation into the trucking company shows multiple brakes violations, with their drivers having weak English comprehension. The driver involved in this crash is a Cuban green card holder.

There's always a story and a story behind a story. In response to the 2025 English proficiency order, the Department of Motor Vehicles officially states: "We . . . remain concerned about potential disruptions to the supply chain due to driver shortages . . . which will have economic implications for businesses and consumers in Colorado."

*

Uma and Daljit travel on the truck, crisscrossing highways I-5 and I-10 from California to New Orleans, or the I-80 from Sacramento through Des Moines to Chicago. Uma is happy, even if they eat on the road, packing tiffin carriers with rice, vegetable curries, and rotis. They use a small stove at rest stops to heat the food.

Of those years, Uma says, "It was hard, but it was nice. I spent my time with him."

But there's always a but.

"We couldn't have children." She explains softly, her hand gentle on her young son. "Wahe guru had their own plans for us."

Having a child as an older woman shouldn't be a problem, Uma thinks. Because in her community, she's met many women who've had children later in life—it's all a blessing from the gurus. Now, both she and Daljit are at a loss—this isn't what they had planned for. They head to Amritsar to visit the Golden Temple—perhaps the gurus will bless them?

*

Returning, Uma continues managing dispatch instructions. Daljit drives through the Midwest states. Her English is better than his, but she's also a great operations leader, even if she remains in the shadows. They stay united, still hopeful of being parents.

When her husband drives east from LA, Reno, or Phoenix, Uma, on the passenger seat, watches the truck stop restaurants at filling stations. Bombay, Indian, or Palace—familiar names blink in neon red or blue. Dhabas. Diners, really. Enticing truckers to stop by, eat a roti with daal. Sometimes they go to these dhabas to wash up, clean their lunch boxes before they head back to Fresno. The Indian restaurants make them feel closer to home.

Daljit tires easily. His back hurts from all the years of travel. Likely one day the conversation may have gone as such.

Daljit sighs, "I need to stop, I really do, I can't do this anymore."

"What should we do, shall we open a dhaba? Like the ones on the trucking route?"

Daljit agrees. "Good idea. I can cook, I can make the food we like to eat. I—"

Uma stops him, "No, we can both cook. Or we can hire people."

Daljit is sure of one thing. The warm rotis must be large. Truckers from Punjab crave garam roti from the hot tawa with their chicken and sabzi. They are hungry when they enter, so the roti must be large enough for famished truckers.

*

Indian dhabas are barely shacks, with thatched roofs on tired bamboo poles, open seating, no-frills tables covered with thick plastic covers, tired fans on stools, blaring regional film music, and the smell of sputtering curries. The chef, also the owner/operator, mans the tandoori oven, sticks naan to the sides of the hot oven with his bare hands, handles a roaring gas stove with bubbling daal or a chicken curry in a big handi cauldron. A young boy, invariably named

Chhotu or little one, recites the menu like a rap song, running from table to table with a tray filled with naan, sloshing curries set next to a quick-pickled onion-chili and a steel bowl of daal. A helper/sous chef tosses the naan from the oven to the steel plates rapid-fire with the precision of an Olympic discus thrower. A dhaba is a symphony in action, if the musicians are a popular garage band.

In India, there are thousands of dhabas along the highways, hyperfocused on local cuisine. Since the 1990s, however, we see the curious phenomenon of dhabas sprouting along American highways. An estimated forty dhabas dot our highways, following Sikhs in semis.[13]

The Fresno Punjabi Dhaba's claim to fame has been their fifty-nine-cent roti. A rough, whole-wheat tandoori baked bread, large as a maintenance hole cover, it's enough to feed three regular folks or one hungry trucker.

"Arrey, do you know how much time I spent on the road from one truck stop diner to another to get one roti?" Daljit reminisces. "I told Uma, and really, she's the boss. We need good rotis, and cheap, cheap."

"How much is it now?"

"A dollar ten."

Across us, a trucker at one of the booths spreads sauces and daal from Styrofoam cups onto his plate with rice, dipping his roti in chicken curry.

"That looks delicious," I tell Uma, and she grins with joy.

Punjabi Dhaba has become a staple food spot for all truckers, Sikhs, and non-Sikhs alike. Even when I-99 becomes the freeway of choice and Golden State Boulevard is relegated to a state road (SR 204), the dhaba still stands.[14]

"We exist because of word of mouth. Truckers tell each other. Even though the highway is now a mile from us, they still come," Uma says with a quiet confidence.

Raj nudges me. "Time to go, Madhushree." I get up to leave.

Daljit protests, "Wait, you have to eat our food, you can't go!"

It's an abomination to refuse food for us South Asians. But I'm full; too much chai and it's too early.

"At least see how our kitchen is, no?" says Uma, guiding me to the kitchen. Two Sikh women expertly heat up chicken masala curry in a red spicy sauce on a roaring gas stove. Next to them, the tawa holds makke ki roti, corn rotis, slow-cooked in ghee.

"How is motherhood, Uma?" I ask as we walk through the kitchen.

"Our son is three. The gurus blessed us. My husband, who didn't practice being a Sikh, went back to the faith. I kept the dhaba business going—I am good in math, accounting. He brings business, and I manage it. Our son is everything."

I can see how adored her son is.

Even though the Sikh religion professes equality between men and women, it's not quite that. Patriarchy and being adjacent to Hindu hierarchical traditions have impacted the original Sikhism teachings. Women and men, despite being considered equal, aren't so. Uma—the brains behind Punjabi Dhaba—is content staying in the background.

Her son holds up his arms, asking to be lifted. Uma bends to pick him up.

"What do you see yourself doing in five years?" I ask, curious.

Without hesitating, she says, "We are heading home."

"Home?"

Uma smiles proudly. "After I got pregnant, we bought a house in Fresno. My husband started the dhaba, and I brought my son up. We also adopted six puppies. Six! The pups decided to be part of our family."

I think of my Dalmatian, now dead for almost two years, who decided I was her person when I filed for divorce. A decade of the Dalmatian in my life transformed me, so I understand. Uma shares live-camera images of her dogs lazing in the yard.

I nudge her again. "Home . . . ?"

"India, of course!"

The dismissiveness of that answer makes me curious.

Daljit adds, "India is home for us. We can give the dhaba to someone who can carry the tradition. We'll go home with our son and dogs."

Uma nods in agreement.

*

Homesickness is a beast, I know that. Three decades away from home, and I still miss it, but I miss the 1990s India that I left. The India now isn't what I think home is. I wonder if Uma and Daljit realize that. I also wonder if it matters when the pull of the homeland is so palpable.

As we leave, Daljit asks if I saw the truck painting on the wall.

Yes, yes, I did.

"The truck license plate number is my uncle's. He's a trucker in India. . . . "

The painting is a fixture on many online food influencer posts. Daljit makes sure the India gracing his Fresno dhaba is easily recognizable.

Driving out of the lot, a large white truck pulls in. A Sikh driver heads to the gas station. He will go to the dhaba for a $1.10 roti with curries. In my rear-view mirror, I watch Uma holding her son, waving next to the image of a truck from Punjab and a Sikh man in a turban.

A quarter of a century into the twenty-first, and we have a dearth of skilled truckers in the United States. Sikhs who arrived almost fifteen decades ago, have now made the trucking world their own.

Will the 2025 executive orders all to be proficient in a language not their own? Maybe. Or maybe Sikhs, with English as their second language, hard work in their veins, will still thrive? I don't know whether this political ping-pong of executive

Uma Devi and Daljit Singh with their son next to the mural at Punjabi Dhaba, Fresno, 2025. Courtesy of the author.

orders will swing the pendulum to the other side. What I do know is Sikhs will find a way to travel the roads that are quintessentially American, and yet Sikh.

Each dot on a Google map will continue to represent Punjabis feeding truckers transporting America's produce and goods. Each dot will continue to make roti, with saag paneer for truckers reminding them of home, wherever that may be.[15]

**

Punjabi Roti (My Version)

Ingredients

1¼ cups water (at room temperature)
½ teaspoon salt
2½ cups whole-wheat flour
1 cup whole-wheat flour (to coat rolling pin and rolling surface)
1 tablespoon ghee/butter (optional)

Recipe

1. Add salt and water to the flour, mix.
2. Knead the dough by hand till the flour is evenly mixed and the sticky dough is smooth.
3. Roll the dough into plum-size balls.
4. On a flat surface coated with 1–2 teaspoons of dry flour, place a roti ball, and roll it into a round disc with a rolling pin.
5. On a tava or a cast-iron pan place a flat roti.
6. Let the roti heat up till the edges start to rise from the surface.
7. Flip the roti (after 60–75 seconds) to cook the other side.
8. Place the roti on an open flame so it puffs into a ball, and cook the other side.
9. Add a dash of ghee (optional) to each roti before serving.
10. Enjoy with daal, or curry.

26

The Sikh Age

In the summer of 2024, Governor Gavin Newsom announces a press briefing. *"Welcome to the bench, Judge Raj Singh! We're proud to appoint the first Sikh judge to the Fresno County Superior Court, who will work to protect, defend, and serve the Golden State."*

On the face of it, the appointment is standard issue, doesn't mean much. But this is historic for the Sikh community in this country.[1] Raj is the first turbaned Sikh judge appointed to the bench in Fresno County (and the United States).

In 2010, for the first time in over two decades, the US Army allows Sikh soldiers to keep their hair intact and wear a turban.[2] Two decades prior, Sikhs could serve keeping their hair and paghdi turbans, which then was eliminated by a military ruling. An entire generation of Sikhs is prevented from serving the United States even though Sikhs have served in the armed forces since the First World War.

As with most people with proximity to war and division, my own personal journey is that I don't understand the art of war, nor do I understand militarism. Jill Lepore notes, "The study of history requires investigation, imagination, empathy, and respect. Reverence just doesn't enter it."[3]

Similarly, I question the Sikhs' yearning to serve other cultures and their heads including the British, US, and Hindu and Muslim leaders in South Asia.

The fundamentally perplexing question when reviewing the stories of Sikhs in America (and the UK) has been their ability to serve a country that actively others them. Whether that country is India, British India, or the United States, is immaterial.

Ma used to say, "Men? They fight, they drop bombs. But what happens at the end? They all sit around a table and negotiate. So why can't we start at that table already?"

I've lived Ma's philosophy: diplomacy above all else. In 2025, are we right or wrong? Who gets to be? Are we pro-Palestine and therefore antisemites or not? The days of black and white increasingly have become gray and grayer. Right- and left-leaning people are alarmingly sounding alike. Is it hard? Yes, especially now.

Yet South Asians, especially Sikhs, invariably fight for countries that don't fight for them. What is this sense of belonging our people feel in a very problematic country like the United States?

*

Judge Badhesha, a forty-one-year-old practicing Sikh, dons his unshorn hair in a blue turban, bookish glasses, and a beard that hides a boyish grin.[4] He doesn't cut his hair; wears a kadha bangle on his wrist and special undershorts; carries a kangha, a wooden comb, and a kirpan (an article of faith resembling a knife)—the symbols of faith and service to his religion. When he is welcomed to the Fresno Superior Court as a judge, he gives a speech from the podium, "I am here because of your support," to the over one hundred people celebrating him. He hopes the younger Sikh community is inspired to seek higher office as well.

His wife, Upkar, and two children stand a few steps behind him. An elder, his mother, in a white salwar suit, head covered with a white dupatta, helps him into his judge's black robes.

Calls of bole so nihal, sat sri akal reverberate through the cavernous hall. "Whoever utters [this phrase] shall be happy, shall be fulfilled. Truth is the great timeless one." A call of triumph, of Sikh religious practices, but also a slogan of the Sikh community, celebrating truth.

Raj embodies the validation this community has sought for years in Central Valley. Two decades ago, as a young law school student and then an attorney, Raj's Sikh turban and kirpan likely would have prevented him from entering the courtroom premises. It has only been fifteen years since the Department of Justice's "religious freedom in focus" permission to allow religious headcoverings in judicial premises. The caveat is that the individual may be subject to further screenings.

A small victory; nonetheless a victory.

Raj, whose family moves to Central Valley from India, hadn't been a strict follower of Sikhism when young. All that changes once he enrolls in camps to study Sikh history and scripture at Stockton.

"It's not just what happened to us, or which king ruled the regions we inhabited. It's how to lead by example, with service, joy, and compassion," he explains recently.

The Stockton gurdwara—the place where the First Wave Sikhs in the early twentieth century build community, has transformed with each wave. Then a hotbed for India's freedom movement in the United States, later generations demonstrate the pride the Sikhs feel as a community in America. Now, the next-generation Sikhs like Badhesha embrace Sikhism with renewed passion.

*

I started this journey exploring food that has transformed over generations within the Sikh community. If we study immigration through the food lens, are we skewing our observations by generalizing the community? Is it that everyone operates dhabas, or works in public service? In a way, yes. None of us like to be pigeonholed. I wonder how I am fitting this community into a neat box? Are they all farmers? Restaurant/dhaba owners? Truckers? Cooks?

Raj laughs at the characterization, shaking his head. "You know it's more than that, Madhushree! I was attracted to the legal world in part because it felt right to be heard here as a Sikh."

When religion is a way of life, and joy in service, the Sikh community rightfully claims their space in America. What he means is that Sikhs—no matter which country they reside in—remain a community that's flexible. Yes, to farming, the military, dhabas, trucking, but they continue to remain Sikhs. In turn, Sikhs habitually remain persecuted for their religion, their way of life. As a result, the community is insular because of it or become so when they find safety in their own.

*

Assimilation means different things to different immigrant generations. Recently, First Wave daughter Sheila Singh says, "My father wanted us to speak English and nothing else."

Losing one's language, then one's traditions, makes you assimilate faster. It's easier when you do so willingly. The First Wave represents "assimilation" as it was implemented in the previous century. Very few children of the 378 unions from the First Wave live as Sikhs. Most move away from the Sikh culture, leaning more into the Catholicism of their mothers.

Sheila Singh is a California woman, even though she identifies as Sikh in spirit. Her father, Teja, always appears to dress in hats, smart shirts, and trousers. He's not a bearded, turbaned Sikh. To be American, to be Western, to Teja and then his children is to dress and behave Western. To them, to be Western also means to be white.

Second Wave Sikhs intentionally lean into their religion, food, and culture. "Assimilation" to this group means to exist within American communities while embracing their South Asian traditions. It isn't the assimilation and erasure like the First Wave, but for the Second Wave, they create a mainstream Sikh world outside of Punjab. This is the group that may have left after the partition, but mostly they are those who arrive at a more welcoming United States. Then they build wealth through farming, real estate, and trucking.

Second Wave granddaughter Jes Nijjer is torn between her mother's trauma of divorce, her grandparents' histories of living in America after India's partition, and her own path she chooses to follow of being a good Sikhni, even if for now she may not be the good daughter.

Jes leans into mental health, while removing herself from a family unit that isn't serving her. She forges her life in photography while owning trauma without losing herself. "I have hope," she says. "I am building my select group of friends I can be authentic with."

The Third Wave, the contemporary Sikhs, is the fascinating one. Maybe it's because they represent my story in some way, and yet not? The Sikh story is conflicting, of Sikh pride, community, and building wealth within American enterprises. Born out of intense violence and othering during the post-Bhindranwale era in India, the Third Wave Sikhs are bold, fearless, taking mighty risks in innovative businesses. They are the rule breakers, exploring professions that make wealth, and are showing ways to prosper beyond farms and dhabas.

*

I am not of the Third Wave, but I do feel an intense closeness to the community. I am not fearless. I am not religious. I am not of their community. And yet this group shows up for me in love. Perhaps they are my community, and I just haven't acknowledged it yet?

Maybe this is the story for which I have traveled for years across states, regions, and countries? To find what makes us travel, and to find that in the food of others, in the community of others?

27

The Third Wave, Now

Manpreet Singh is an army veteran and looks it. A big man with broad shoulders, a loud laugh, dark eyes holding a joke, hair in a Sikh turban, he looks formidable. But as a teenage immigrant, he is the young assistant at his father's liquor shop near Clovis.

"I mean, you're Sikh, but you don't bring religion in. You just are," he says of his childhood, grinning.

Career-wise, the military seemed a great place to be. It was that or work at the family liquor store.

We are in Clovis, near Fresno, in a new restaurant, Gulab, that he runs with his wife. Over a nimbu paani, sweet-salty lemonade with mint leaves and chaat masala, and salmon fish tikkas drizzled with coriander chutney, Manpreet smiles when I gush over the flavor explosion with each bite. "It's all my wife's doing. She's the brains, operations, and finance. I am just me."

After multiple tours to Iraq, Manpreet returns to Clovis. He doesn't think he has PTSD. In fact, he laughs when he says he has had insomnia for years, plagued by nightmares. Then he jokes about phantom gunshots that he hears in the night. Or that the only time he is at peace is when his daughter smiles. He knows he's not the same boy who went to war. The man who returned has invisible scars he received for a country he now calls his own.

Gulab in Clovis is a hip new restaurant. Manpreet knows Sikhs love their stiff alcoholic beverages. Fish and chicken tikkas go well with a scotch on the rocks.

An estimated half a million Sikhs fight alongside British and Allied forces in the Second World War. Sikhs in British troops and as part of US troops are in the world wars, even when they aren't US citizens.[1]

In its well-known 1923 case *United States v. Bhagat Singh Thind*, the US Supreme Court decreed retroactively to deny Indians of naturalized US citizenship on grounds of failing to meet the definition of a "white person" or a person of "African descent."[2] Thind, a soldier in the war, claims Aryan roots, which is not considered valid for a "Hindu." To be higher caste means access to education, in turn privilege in India. The same higher-caste educated individual when in the United States is one who now has white-adjacent privilege.

Thind's retroactive citizenship rescinding starts the Punjabi First Wave men to consider other ways to live in the United States, gain land, and live freely.

*

Manpreet Singh at his restaurant, Gulab, in Clovis, California, 2025. Courtesy of the author.

In February 2025, the Trump administration uses US military aircraft for the first time in history to deport undocumented immigrants.[3] The first plane takes 104 people in handcuffs and shackles to Amritsar, Punjab. Of the 104, thirty are Punjabis. All were seeking employment to work in America—the reason to come without papers is economic hardship.

While the United States is India's largest trading partner, and the Hindu nationalist Modi-led government would like to increase the H-1B professional workers' visa quota for Indians, Modi hardly protests how the shackled immigrants are shipped back. Indian undocumented immigrants to the United States are nearly 725,000 according to a 2022 Pew Research report, the third-largest group after Mexicans and El Salvadorans.[4] Ultra-right-wing Modi notes, "Anybody who enters another country illegally has absolutely no right to be in that country."[5]

If this is true, then most South Asian immigrants for the past century wouldn't exist in the United States. Some enter undocumented, some surrender at the border, some arrive as refugees before the land of the free permits them to live here. Few of us show up with legal papers permitting us residency in the United States.

The year 2025 is when all of what the previous generations of our people experienced viciously returns to haunt the contemporary immigrants and children of immigrants.

*

Raj's childhood friend Prabhjot comes from the very successful Lasher Transportation family, a prominent trucking group. Prabhjot runs LB Transport, with business partnerships all over the United States, Latin America, and now expanding into Europe. He walks with the confidence of a thirty-seven-year-old successful entrepreneur. Being Sikh is his identity, as is his swagger of a self-made man. "Look, if you need help in Mexico, any kind"—waving his hand around to signify all kinds of help—"you let me know."

While I'm not in need of any assistance, I get what he means. He reminds me of men who lead joint families in India—it becomes part of their identity.

Prabhjot represents the new Sikh-Americans of the Third Wave charting new ways of prosperity in America, in the American West. Raj beams proudly at him. In our culture, our friends are family, and how we help each other has a familial tone.

"I've known him when he was a little fellow," Raj says. "He's worked hard."

But Prabhjot would rather talk about his new ventures. "I work long hours. That's my only regret—no time for my family," he explains. "My wife takes care of that."

Even when there is respect for the family, the gender hierarchy is still prevalent in the Third Wave. Most are arranged marriages within the community, including Raj's and Prabhjot's. Everyone knows their place in the family. Sikh women's labor is so invisible that their contributions don't figure in Sikh men's conversations.

This also means that it doesn't matter what I, a non-Sikh outlier, think.

As I leave the Fresno Indian grocery store where I meet Prabhjot, I notice Bhindranwale images on magnet stickers next to Guru Gobind Singh's images for sale. Guru Gobind Singh, the founder of the Sikh faith. Bhindranwale, the religious leader with an AK-47. All saints.

I don't need to ask Prabhjot for his opinion. To most Sikhs in 2025, Bhindranwale remains a holy man who fought for Sikh rights.

They are all saints, even the ones wearing bullet belts. Even the ones who are trained AK-47 users. It just depends on who you ask.

**

Salmon fish tikkas. Courtesy of the author.

Salmon Fish Tikka

Ingredients

For the tandoori masala
1 tablespoon Kashmiri chili powder
1 teaspoon salt
2 teaspoons dry fenugreek leaves
2 teaspoons roasted coriander powder
1 teaspoon garlic powder
½ teaspoon ginger powder
1 teaspoon garam masala powder

For the salmon tikka
5 tablespoons Greek yogurt
1 tablespoon tandoori masala
1½ teaspoons garlic paste
½ teaspoon ginger paste
2 tablespoons lemon juice
½ to 1 teaspoon red chili powder
¼ teaspoon turmeric powder
1½ pound salmon, cut into 2-inch cubes
Salt to taste
Oil or oil spray for cooking the tikka

Recipe

To make the tandoori masala
1. Slow-roast the tandoori masala 2–3 minutes.
2. Cool and grind the tandoori masala in a coffee grinder to a fine powder.
3. Store in a cool jar.

To make the salmon tikka
1. In a large bowl, add yogurt, tandoori masala, garlic, ginger, lime juice, chili, and turmeric powder; mix to make a paste with salt.
2. Add salmon pieces to coat them fully and let stand for 5–10 minutes.
3. Preheat air fryer to 360 F for 5 minutes.
4. Add the salmon, brush 5–10 drops of oil in the basket, and cook for 5 minutes.
5. Open the basket, flip the fish, and add more oil as needed to air fry for 5–7 more minutes.
6. Sprinkle chaat masala and serve with coriander chutney.
7. Garnish with coriander and mint leaves.

PART SEVEN

THE SAFAR, THE JOURNEY, AND NOW

28

And Now

I head to Joshua Tree for a long weekend in April 2025. A dry town dotted with old spiky cacti along the desert roads. My sense of direction, never good, now is worse because I rely on iPhone maps and sometimes, even when the instructions are to turn right, I don't. It is of my own doing. As always, I am lost.

At a stop sign, I peer at the directions. It does say the Airbnb is a mile away. But where? A car pulls up next to me and I look up. A police car. The officer, in dark shades, asks me to pull over. Heart racing, I turn right and stop.

He pulls out a megaphone and yells, "Move forward, you're in the middle of the road."

I move up some more. Where is my registration? My license? On the passenger seat, I have Costco egg cartons, sourdough bread, chutneys—I'm hosting a culinary retreat. My car is filled with food prep, utensils, an air fryer, ladles, masalas. This isn't happening, is it? It is April. The 2025 Trump administration has been in existence for a few months.

The police officer says, "You stopped at the stop sign for too long. What were you doing?"

"I'm lost, officer. I was—"

"Please get out of the vehicle."

Shocked, I step out without thinking. Sometimes, you just do what you are told because you may have lived in this country longer than in your native land, but you know when you are asked by a white man in authority to step out of your vehicle, you do.

It turns out to be a "routine" traffic stop. The officer says to pay the citation and it won't go on my record. What does that even mean?

Who gets a ticket for stopping at a stop sign? How long is too long at a stop sign?

Like a privileged person, I am angry. As a brown person, I am shaking inside. He orders me to drive on. I do.

This could have gone very differently. I could have been pulled out of the car for a reason and that reason could have changed. Between the officer and me, only one of us is armed.

Later, we joke that perhaps the police officer thought I was smuggling Costco eggs. Eggs now cost more than ten dollars.

My partner says something I hadn't considered. "Did he even ask if you were okay?"

"No."

"What if you needed medical attention?"

"I didn't think of that."

"Why don't the police help the community instead of treating us like criminals?"

We rail against the incident, somewhat jokingly, but not really. What if I stepped out of my old hybrid car, and the officer thought I was up to no good? Three decades in this country and one citizenship later, I still don't belong.

Two weeks later, I get the reminder to pay the $200 citation. I do.

*

On Memorial Day weekend's Friday, the Immigration and Customs Enforcement (ICE) officials raid a popular San Diego Italian restaurant during evening dinner service rush in the upper-middle-class South Park neighborhood.[1] In a mainly white neighborhood of people in flip-flops, loose T-shirts, and an easy attitude, ICE agents enter in tactical gear, camouflage, and heavy trucks.

Nineteen staff members are detained with zip ties. Special agents note that they are executing a criminal search warrant at the location.

Citizens, mostly white, protest the violent arrests. They block the ICE agents, their vehicles, and ensure social media attention. Agents use flashbang smoke grenades to disperse the crowd. Then the Department of Homeland Security calls the San Diego police for backup. By the time the police arrive, the federal agents have left the scene.

*

In June 2025, the second largest city in the United States, the city of angels is flooded with federal troops assigned by the Trump administration to protect ICE.[2] The group is tasked to arrest immigrants and migrants for deportation. Most of the 118 arrests are made in broad daylight. They are processed without judicial warrants and have no criminal records.

Immigrant workers in Los Angeles make up 40 percent of the workforce, where 1.6 million children have at least one immigrant parent. In a state that was ceded by Mexico to the United States in 1850, the Mexican and Latino roots are deep across man-made borders.

Councilmember Hugo Soto-Martinez notes, "If you're eating at a restaurant [in LA], chances are your food is cooked by an immigrant." In 2023, California has passed a string of laws to protect immigrant workers—regardless of legal status—from retaliation, or wage theft.[3]

In the words of the great and sorely missed Anthony Bourdain,

> Despite our ridiculously hypocritical attitudes towards immigration, we demand that Mexicans cook a large percentage of the food we eat, grow the

ingredients we need to make that food, clean our houses, mow our lawns, wash our dishes, look after our children . . . our entire service economy—the restaurant business as we know it—in most American cities, would collapse overnight without Mexican workers.[4]

This isn't rocket science; nor is it about "illegal" immigration. We are in 2025, living in a Christian (evangelical)–led, white supremacy–leaning country with leadership actively hell-bent on installing an autocratic, technocratic, fascist state. While they target Mexicans and other immigrants from Latin American countries, they also target Asians in interesting ways. We are also in 2025, when Zohran Mamdani is elected mayor of the largest city in the country, on an unabashedly positive, working-class-friendly campaign to enable socialist, healthcare-, and rent-control principles to reduce cost of living burdens for people of New York City. That he is the son of one of my favorite film directors, Mira Nair of *Mississippi Masala* fame, is another joyous add. Mira Nair forced young college students like me to think of global politics, racism, and feminism, previously alien to us. Zohran is also the son of Professor Mahmood Mamdani, whose philosophy, applied to modern political systems, questions postcolonial states and their relationship with violence, genocide, and human rights. In other words, a high-high and a low-low, for us to rejoice in the next generation leading with compassion and for us to despair under the current administration's devastating anti-working-class decrees.

We are here at the crossroads—of inherent rage and hate against nonwhite people, and of hope, promise, of socialism and youth, still pushing to find a foothold in this angry country.

Our ancestors arrived here with papers that were either revoked or permitted. Or laws were changed to enable citizenship. Or civil rights fought by our Black allies led someone like me to arrive in America. There is no such thing as illegal, when documentation is what seems to be in question. We have always been in this country, pleading our gratitude, presenting our value, our goodness, us.

The Trump administration's ICE team now targets restaurants, car washes, farms, grocery stores, and big-box construction stores like Home Depot.[5]

*

A week after the San Diego ICE raid, we find out that undocumented workers are allegedly employed at the restaurant. Four are arrested and one voluntarily leaves the country. The question isn't who isn't obeying the law. The question is how does 2025 America *implement* the law?[6]

Is it normal that ICE officers in military fatigues carrying guns walk through a San Diego neighborhood on a Friday evening? Do we need dramatic arrests and detaining people with zip ties? Who is subject to this kind of treatment?

People with missing immigration documentation used to be given time to file papers and legal help to do so. Undocumented immigration was considered a civil legal matter. Under the 2025 Trump administration, this becomes a criminal issue.

My city in California, a border town, is now not a safe place. No one is safe, especially if you are brown. The question is, were we ever?

Raj declines to comment on the Punjabi undocumented workers deported to India. While the topic is urgent, he does not officially agree or disagree with the administration. Nor can he comment on the National Guard marching through California towns. He represents his people. People historically subjugated for centuries. He's representing brown people of a different faith who have the right to exist in Central Valley. The stakes are high.

When the Latino community is targeted by ICE, there's resignation. "This is awful, but what can I do?" seems to be the sentiment.

We—us people of color—are tired. Some of us brown people are scared.

Marches are organized—the summer of 2025 is the summer of protests. Again.

*

On September 15, 2001, Balbir Singh Sodhi is planting flowers around the edge of his Arizona gas station. It's to honor those who died in the 9/11 attacks. Frank Silva Roque, ranting about immigrants, mistakes Sodhi for an Arab Muslim. He shoots Sodhi five times, killing him. Sodhi is the first racially motivated hate crime victim as a direct result of the September 11 attacks. Sodhi's obituary says he lived and died in the tradition of his religion, and like Sikh gurus, he gave his life for his faith and humankind.[7]

*

On June 11, 2025, activist, lawyer, author, Sikhni, and maternal granddaughter of Sikh farmers of California's Central Valley, Valarie Kaur stands up in Los Angeles in an interfaith vigil. Her eyes fierce, her gaze infinite, she tells the crowd,

> To the agents and the soldiers on the street—you can come at us with batons . . . you can aim [the rifles] at us . . . but you cannot make us hate you. We will block your actions with one hand, and we will have the audacity to extend the other [hand] . . . so that your children may one day take it.[8]

The crowd cheers as she champions the other people of color—brown people, Latino families, people who arrived in the United States seeking employment and a better life for their families. Valarie asks for love, revolutionary love that extends even to those who hate people who look like us.[9]

*

In October 2001, I walk to work in Rockville, Maryland. I wear a salwar kameez, as I usually do for work. A long shirt with an Indian Kalamkari block-print design with a plain dupatta, loose pants. It's practical and professional. I hear the honk as I cross the street. As the driver zooms past, he yells something I don't understand. I crossed when the light turned, so I'm not sure what I heard. But sometimes, when you sense the hatred, the words don't matter.

I narrate the yelling driver incident to my CFO. He says, "Madoo, maybe it's time to stop wearing salwar kameezes from now on to work, huh?"

It's almost humorous to him, that my outfit and skin color embolden people to say things they wouldn't have this blatantly, if not for September 11. I am too young and inexperienced to refute my boss.

I stop wearing salwar kameezes to work from that day in 2001.

*

More than a century ago, Valarie's mother's father arrives in Central Valley to farm. He teaches his granddaughter the Sikh way to resist is through love. Sodhi's murder transforms the Sikh community, especially Valarie, who in 2001 is a college student. This starts her decade-long exploration through filming stories of her Sikh community, questioning unconscious bias, othering, and who counts as "one of us" in crisis.

Using ancestral wisdom Valarie now uses love to speak out for human rights. As the founder of the Revolutionary Love Project, she introduces her Sikh ancestors' historical fight for existence. The concept of sant-sipahi, or sage warrior, put forth by Valarie gains interest. The sant sees through the eyes of love. The warrior puts that love into action.[10]

"People of color survived oppression through acts of solidarity," she says.

I can't help but marvel, how life comes full circle, even if it takes a few decades to do so. Punjabis who arrived from India made new brown families with Mexican women, and then moved away from that history and the Mexican heritage. Now, through Third Wave activists like Valarie, they embrace differences and find humanity through love.

Perhaps the point of traveling through the American West is this. That we are following resilient people who have grown roots here. Their roots are their dhaba food, faith, and their adoption of Mexican genes, Mexican religion, Mexican norms and cultures, blending to create new American West norms. Their safar is a journey of yes, suffering, of othering, yes, of being isolated. But it's a journey of my people who have evolved in life, rituals, and food while making America home.

Would South Asians have headed west if India hadn't been colonized? Would I have left New Delhi if I didn't aspire to higher education in the United States? When under British rule, our forms of education and employment are purposefully altered to serve the colonial powers, raising us to be clerks, administrators, soldiers for the Empire. To learn English is a plus. To gain employment, to be white-adjacent, middle-class Indians is the goal for many.

Perhaps it would make sense for us to understand that where we came from, and who we are, tells the world how we belong.

The travels of the Punjabi Sikh community within the South Asian migration didn't start with America. We first moved to England, the land governed by the people who colonized us. Perhaps that migration made these South Asians, the Sikhs, fearless, enterprising, and formidable adventurers in Central Valley?

I don't know the answers, but the connection I feel with these displaced people who hold their faith and culture is powerful.

I decide to head to London, where it all started.

I hope to understand the American safar, our journey, by witnessing our place in the country where the royals colonized my country for centuries.

29

London, Our People, and Our Safar

London has more than seven hundred thousand Punjabis—that include Sikhs, Hindus, and Muslim Punjabis. Well-known neighborhoods like Southall are in West London, a mini-Punjab, albeit a significantly colder one. Ealing, Hounslow, and Hillingdon are Punjabi neighborhoods, except in the London suburbs.[1]

In the winter of 2024, I head to Southall. It appears frozen in the eighties—in temperatures and in traditions—where lower- to middle-class Punjabi families (from Pakistan and India) live their Punjabi lives in England.

The gurdwara on a December weekday is jampacked with people in thick jackets and socks—the women in salwar kameezes and dupattas covering their heads, the men in turbans, dark jackets, shirts, and pants. Like in any gurdwara, men and women remain in separate sections. Chants of the Granth Sahib through loudspeakers, clean floors, fluorescent lights. In the gray afternoon of a pre-Christmas day, visitors rush to pay their respects, swiftly removing their shoes in the "shoe area" before entering the prayer room.

In Southall, streets are lined with bright tinsel. Shops sell halal meat next to bright shawls and kameezes, across from oud perfumes from Arabic street perfume sellers. Women push their babies in strollers, thick jackets over their Punjabi outfits, while children pull at their mother's kameez, whining for a treat from the sweet jalebi stall.

It is India, and yet it's not. I don't think anyone on that December afternoon is thinking of how their ancestors landed in their colonizer's land. For them, this is life. Oh, also, it's Christmas.

*

Baba tells us stories of when he marched with Gandhi, part of the millions who followed him in the nonviolent freedom struggle against the British. There is a hush of reverence when Baba describes him.

"Did you speak with Gandhi?" I ask in anticipation.

"Na, but he touched my shoulder when he walked past at a march in Kolkata. He was a mahatma, a big soul." Baba's hushed voice holds the reverence.

The freedom struggle is exactly that in 1947, a struggle. Indians, like Baba, young men, have a hero to worship. Gandhi's charisma unites Indians. Him being problematic as a human, his views on Black South Africans, his actions as a man—well, that's another story. A flawed human, he leads India's fight for freedom with nonviolence. A movement that has global reverberations.

London chefs Chet Sharma at BiBi, Mayfair, 2025, and Asma Khan at Darjeel-ing Express, Soho, 2022. Courtesy of Gary S. Greer, 2025, Madhushree Ghosh, personal collection.

It's not that violent movements failed. The Ghadar movement creates havoc before Gandhi's emergence. Once Gandhi and the Congress party get center stage, with diplomacy and alliances, they are the leaders who negotiate India's independence.

Even though the movement is nonviolent, the violence during the largest human migration of the twentieth century is horrifying. The partition of India is a controversial compromise with the British that the leaders broker. The migration is responsible for twelve to twenty million displaced people with two hundred thousand to two million deaths.[2]

I am a daughter of this partition.

*

Baba takes the ferry to cross the river heading home. A friend heading in the other direction waves at him frantically.

"Hashi, Hashi!" He yells my father's name, meaning "laughter," by which all friends and family address him. "We are free now, the British are leaving."

Independence is a happy occasion, but no one really knows what that means. The British leave with a land divided into two (and then three) countries based on religion: a land depleted of its mineral, financial, agricultural, and artistic wealth. A land divided that cannot compete with Western might, a land that was allegedly 25 percent GDP precolonization reduces to 4 percent in 1947 post-independence. The India of 1947 is a poor, underdeveloped country.[3]

Didi and I grow up on partition stories. We learn to understand the nuances of history, what the British colonizers did to our land, and who wrote those history books.

*

I don't have any desire to go to England—what good will that do? Don't get me wrong. I grow up on Enid Blyton books, I study in Catholic and missionary schools, even my English is British-accented. But I have no need to go to London.

The first time I do go is in 2010, as part of my biotech work. London isn't what I presumed—rich with culinary diversity, it acknowledges people from all countries—in fact, why should it not? Given that country has colonized so many people, the UK cannot legitimately prevent the colonized from coming to their shores, can they? Welcomed by my British colleagues, I enjoy their snarky sense of humor, wry wit, and openness to collaborate.

I know the British people themselves didn't actively participate in harming my people. History tells me more about the royal family, and their ancestors' actions.

It's not personal. But isn't it, though? How many colonized people feel similarly?

Could we ever make this right? May we ever be at peace? Or should we insert ourselves in the colonizer world by being us?

*

Let me tell you the story of chicken tikka masala. Chicken tikka masala—a Glasgow dish likely made by Indian or Bangladeshi cooks in 1971 at Shish Mahal, an Indian restaurant in Scotland, or is it a dish from Karim's, a Mughal eatery in 1913, or even a dish from Balbir Singh's 1961 cookbook? England, the land of our colonizers, now calls chicken tikka masala their unofficial national dish.[4]

Isn't culinary excellence a good way to showcase what was done to us? I think so.[5]

*

The Punjabis—Sikhs in particular—move to the UK during colonization, either for jobs in the service industry, farming, or the military. Most move there as they do to the United States later, for economic opportunities, a better life, and to send money home, to India.

If they are part of the Sikh royal family, like Duleep Singh, the former maharaja of the Sikh Empire, that's a different story.[6] In 1849, the largest Sikh kingdom includes present-day Punjab, Jammu, and Kashmir, Haryana, most of Pakistan. They lose the war to the British. The Sikh maharaja, Duleep Singh is asked to gift the queen the Sikh Kohinoor diamond. A boy with no power or agency. The British to date haven't returned the diamond.

Duleep Singh, also called the "dark prince," is anglicized, turned Christian, and lives his life in England. He returns to Sikhism, briefly tries to return to India, gets his land back, fails, and eventually dies in exile in England.

That's a story of monarchs, land, privilege alongside colonization. A story for another time.

*

Outside of India, London desi food is the very best. South Asian chefs, unabashed in their inventiveness, are creating a new wave of regional cuisine in London.

I travel through London streets on trains, buses, and taxicabs in 2024. Again, no schedule, no agenda. The December Christmas lights, the crisp winter air, and the smell of baked bread and butter wafting from the countless English establishments are a surreal yet pleasantly satisfying experience.

The London of today is a mix of global cuisines, immigrant food from the many countries they colonized. There's an easy acceptance of diversity, especially among the younger generations. This is unproblematic and surprisingly heartwarming. Does it mean there isn't any xenophobia? Now, come on—let's not get *that* carried away!

*

Walking through the tall, dark doors to BiBi, one of the celebrated and well-known Indian eateries in Mayfair in the winter of 2024, I am struck by how upscale British pub-like this is.[7] The curtains at the door are plush, as are the booths. The mid-morning sunlight streams through the tall windows, while low lights at the bar illuminate the prep table. Team members carry boxes of onions and tomatoes for dinner service into the narrow hallway, apologizing when I enter for their mess, which, I assure them, it is not.

Thirty-seven-year-old chef Chet Sharma greets me informally, his dark hair a stark contrast to his white chef's jacket.[8] He has just returned from a fancy celebrity gathering but minimizes his well-deserved fame.

"One day I hang with the best of chefs, and the next day I'm hauling potatoes; such is life," he says, adjusting his jacket.

BiBi, loosely translated in Punjabi to "older woman," or "grandmother," opens during the pandemic when the restaurant industry is reeling from closures. A tagline of "contemporary flavor, exceptional produce," it's what Chef Chet calls a British establishment. "Look, we can keep looking at the past and glorify our colonial history, but the fact is Indian food now is what we— with roots back home—make it."

Named after Chef Chet's two Punjabi grandmothers, Ranjana and Kamal, BiBi's precise set menus are fascinating. They include monkfish salan, Sharmaji's Lahori chicken—an homage to his ancestors' land they left in Pakistan, and the chicken they made there, and even Ma ki daal, which literally translates to "dal/lentils Ma/mother makes."

The drinks menu reads like a barside chat between you and Chef Chet. You are educated on the colonial G&T, developed to mix quinine, an antimalarial, into a palatable alcoholic drink. The G&T becomes a quintessential cocktail hour drink adopted in other British colonies.[9] That's precisely why Chef Chet will *not* offer it at BiBi.

Instead, a Tapatío tequila with chaat masala is a BiBi Calamansi margarita, with an orange-lime citrus note, a fair nod to the Punjabis traveling out West in America, though I'm not sure if that was intentional.

Chef Chet's Punjabi family influence on his food and restaurant is obvious, but it isn't a one-note highlight. He jokes about his parents, professionals both, and not the cooking influence everyone expects them, especially his mother, to have been. While in graduate school in Oxford, where he acquires a PhD in physics, Chef Chet gains restaurant experience with part-time culinary stints at the Michelin-starred Locanda Locatelli (now defunct) in Marylebone, and the also defunct Dabbous of the clean and simple industrial-style cooking fame. He then works at the famed two-star Michelin Mugaritz in Spain under Chef Andoni Aduriz, and the late Ledbury, learning to curate dream teams in the kitchen, and in the food business. He expects his assistants to leave to start their own.

"If they have excellent culinary skills and are creative, they've got to be free to express themselves. Which means they find their own niche, eventually," he says with quiet confidence.

After all, he too gained the experience to open BiBi through apprenticeships. BiBi, a very London culinary creation, is a nod to Chef Chet's South Asian roots, celebrating his London upbringing.

All this to say, Punjabi food isn't about playing identity politics in London. Be it the British Indian–influenced Benares, or the gastropub-focused Kricket (with its adjacent desi-inspired speakeasy Soma), or the Punjabi-British Jamavar, this is modern Indian food brought by chefs with South Asian roots, built through colonization and immigrant travel, but not owned by a single story.

Does this reflect a shift in how food is reflected in the country whose leaders colonized us for centuries? Perhaps. We learn from our ancestors' stories and offer cuisines that tell those stories—of what happened to us and how that food makes us who we are.

*

I detour to Kingly Court in Soho, to the now-impossible-to-find-a-table Michelin-guide darling Darjeeling Express. Look, we can talk about Punjabi food all day long, but no trip to London works without a pilgrimage to the Kolkata-Mughlai-inspired Darjeeling Express.[10] From what started as a supper club in her London home, Asma Khan, now one of 2024 *Time* magazine World's 100 Most Influential People, is a London culinary star.[11]

Darjeeling Express is known for its biryani, and for its all-women team of housewives who encourage you to share and feast. Similar to a homestyle Mughlai dawat or feasting event of former years, Asma's pride in her Muslim and Bengali heritage is refreshing. As is her relentless championing of women culinary leaders.

I order the famous kosha mangsho with luchi—slow-cooked goat curry with Bengali gorom moshla (our version of garam masala), with puffed flash-fried bread. Ma used to make this for Saturday lunch. Or at weddings, this is part of a multicourse meal where the children sit cross-legged in a line, with banana leaves as our plates, and salt, pickle, and chilies on the side to spice up our meal.

Chef Asma says what's been on my mind lately. "Western chefs, they are tattooed, knives in hand, barking orders. At Darjeeling, it's an all-women kitchen. We didn't get trained to yell yes chef, no chef. If one of us needs help lifting a biryani degchi cookware, we ask for help. And others help. It's empowering."

Inside her open kitchen, women from many parts of the world work in synchronicity. Dishes aren't slammed on counters. Knives move with grace.

This reminds me of my visits to our Kolkata home—Shejoma, my elder aunt, cutting eggplant into soft cubes, the maid grinding cumin seeds with red chilies on the shil nora, stone metate-like mortar and pestle, Ma stirring the fish into the curry with extra mustard oil, and my sister and I sitting on our haunches, helping by adding a drop of water to the shil nora, as instructed.

Darjeeling Express brings joyous feasting from our parts of the world to the West.

Food in London is an unabashed expression of history, tradition, contemporary interpretations, and culinary decolonization. For six weeks, I flit from one neighborhood in Southall to Soho to Mayfair to Brick Lane and Shoreditch. The effect of British colonization is that these cuisines from Asia are here in London. To stay.

Is this the irony of immigration? That our food is now elevated, celebrated in the very place where we—the Indians—were called "a beastly people with a beastly religion" by Winston Churchill?[12] The prime minister of Britain, who was singularly responsible for creating the Great Bengal Famine of 1943. A famine that effectively changed our genetic makeup, a famine Churchill said was our fault because we were "breeding like rabbits." Not bad for a beastly people's food to capture the attention of the world, is it?

The casual, racist manner of our colonization to a global celebration of our cuisine is how crazy stories are built. South Asians in England may have reconciled with their safar, their journey. They have found a place—still rife with othering—in the country that occupied us. For now.

I'm not so sure we have the same dialogue in the United States in 2025.

The story of my people in London may be for another day. This is the story of my people in the American West.

*

Decades back, I embark on this journey to trace our roots in the country I now call home. I didn't focus on Bengalis' world but leaned into Punjabi and Sikh people's journeys to find legitimacy outside a colonized India. Why? Because I did not, I *do* not see a difference between Bengalis and Punjabis in what happened to us in 1947. We are communities that were directly affected by that division. The trauma has transcended generations and continues to haunt our lives.

Even as I return home, to San Diego—a city that used to be Mexico's and is now annexed by the contemporary imperialist power, the United States—I don't think I have the answer to our journeys, our migrations, our safar.

As I live in a border town that is America's Finest City, a place where immigrants—with or without documentation—can be detained with force, that my people have been here for centuries. We have moved here because we were forced to, or we moved because a better life prospect propelled us to. Be it Teja Singh on a ship headed to San Francisco, becoming as American as he could; or his daughter, Sheila, an American, a Punjabi, with Mexican roots that are weak but Mexican, nonetheless.

We have moved here like the young bride Nand Kaur with her husband, Puna Singh, even before the Civil Rights Movement enabled family immigrations. Or like Second Wave granddaughters like Jes, holding the generational trauma her Punjabi roots have bestowed on her. We hold Stockton gurdwara as our guiding place of community like Manjit Uppal and Third Wave Sikhs like Raj and Prabhjot while dhaba owners like Uma pine for home that is India.

In the end, we have moved here and called this home like Jassi, Harpeet's widow, Ajit's mother, who grows guavas and mangos in her backyard in northeast San Diego with her mother-in-law. Jassi, who returns to Nawashahr every summer, but home is here, San Diego, where her now-dead husband's parents are.

Home is how she makes me chai every time she sees me, stirring the milk into the boiled tea, sprinkling cardamom, and boiling it with ginger. It isn't what Ma used to make, which was a refined Darjeeling loose-leaf tea, with a splash of milk. But it is also home.

*

In the spring of 2025, I head to Punjabi Tandoor on Moorehouse Drive, slightly unmoored, heart-wise and mind-wise. Every day, the current administration has new ways to tell me and people who look like me that we don't belong. Jassi sets the Styrofoam cup in front of me. I adjust my laptop in a booth on the left of the still-empty restaurant. Lunch-hour rush won't start for another thirty minutes.

"Thank you, Jassi," I say, taking the cup.

She smiles. "Arre, apno mein kya thank you?" Why be so formal? You're one of us.

What makes us belong? Sometimes, it's just a cup of chai. Sometimes, it's a meal shared with people. Sometimes, it's sitting with them as they pray, even when you don't.

Later that evening, I text my thanks to Jassi because, as always, the family refuses to take my money. Jassi dismisses my concerns. "You're always welcome, didi," she texts back. "You are home."

I place a heart on her text. Perhaps I should just let this quest be.

I am home. I am home. I am home.

**

Calamansi Margarita (My Version of BiBi's Cocktail)

Equipment

1 cocktail shaker
1 measuring jigger
1 margarita glass

Ingredients

2 ounces freshly squeezed calamansi juice
Maldon salt to coat glass rim
2 ounces tequila
½ ounce orange liqueur
1 ounce agave or simple syrup

Recipe

1. Prepare a cocktail glass by rubbing the edge with a sliced calamansi lime.
2. Dip it in Maldon salt.
3. Add fresh ice, and set aside.
4. In a cocktail shaker, add the liquid, and shake for 10–12 seconds.
5. Pour into prepared glass, and garnish with a calamansi lime slice.

NOTES

Chapter 1

1   Mandair, Arvind-Pal S. 2009. *Religion and the Specter of the West: Sikhism, India, Postcoloniality, and the Politics of Translation*. Columbia University Press.

2   The Sikh Coalition. 2025, July 9. "Sikhs and Sikhism." Sikh Coalition. https://www.sikhcoalition.org/about-sikhs/faq/#.

3   Singh, Rahul. 2019, May 12. "Defining Sikh Identity." *The Tribune*. https://www.tribuneindia.com/news/archive/columns/defining-sikh-identity-771778/.

4   Bureau, United States Census. "Yuba City Census Data: Race and Ethnicity." Explore census data, 2020. https://data.census.gov/profile/Yuba_City_city,_California?g=160XX00US0686972#race-and-ethnicity.

Chapter 2

1   Singh, Simrin. 2021, April 22. "Fighting for Identity: Stories from Sikh Americans." *Sojourners*. https://sojo.net/interactive/fighting-identity-stories-sikh-americans#:

Chapter 3

1   Dalrymple, William. 2015, June 22. "The Mutual Genocide of Indian Partition." *The New Yorker*. https://www.newyorker.com/magazine/2015/06/29/the-great-divide-books-dalrymple.

2   Hark1karan. 2023, November 6. "The Punjabi City Farmers Nurturing Their Connection to the Land." Atmos. https://atmos.earth/the-punjabi-sikh-farmers-nurturing-their-connection-to-the-land/.

3   Pritam, Amrita. 1948. "To Waris Shah by Amrita Pritam." To Waris Shah. https://udrc.lkouniv.ac.in/Content/DepartmentContent/SM_65c74f52-4e90-43cf-887d-e8ff0f567598_6.pdf.

4   Mukhopadhyay, Srijani. 2025, March 1. "'I Refuse Your Partition'—Faiz to Shankha Ghosh, How Bengali Poets Captured 1947 Violence." ThePrint. https://theprint.in/feature/i-refuse-your-partition-faiz-to-shankha-ghosh-how-bengali-poets-captured-1947-violence/2112744/.

5   Satia, Priya. 2019, March 8. "Partition of 1947 Continues to Haunt India, Pakistan."
    Stanford Report, Stanford Partition Stories. https://news.stanford.edu/stories/2019/03/
    partition-1947-continues-haunt-india-pakistan-stanford-scholar-says.

6   British Red Cross. 2023, June 16. "India Partition: Our Response to the Refugee
    Crisis." British Red Cross. https://www.redcross.org.uk/stories/our-movement/our-
    history/india-partition-the-red-cross-response-to-the-refugee-crisis.

7   Staff. 2024, February 12. "Punjabi Sikh Community—Historical Research Center:
    CSU Bakersfield." Historical Research Center, CSU Bakersfield. https://hrc.csub.edu/
    punjabi-sikh-community/.

8   Dhaliwal, Deepeaka. 2018. "Yuba-Sutter: A Case Study for Heritage Conservation in
    Punjabi-Mexican Communities, December 2018." https://bpb-us-e1.wpmucdn.com/
    sites.usc.edu/dist/9/583/files/2022/10/Deepeaka-Dhaliwal-thesis.pdf.

9   Chopra, Radhika. 2018. *Amritsar 1984: A City Remembers*. Lexington Books.

10 Singh, Simran Jeet. 2014, October 31. "It's Time India Accept Responsibility for Its
    1984 Sikh Genocide." *Time*. https://time.com/3545867/india-1984-sikh-genocide-
    anniversary/.

11 Human Rights Watch. 2014, October 24. "India: No Justice for 1984 Anti-Sikh
    Bloodshed." https://www.hrw.org/news/2014/10/29/india-no-justice-1984-anti-sikh-
    bloodshed; US Commission on International Religious Freedom and Tom Lantos
    Human Rights Commission Joint Hearing on Ending Genocide: Accountability
    for Perpetrators, July 28, 2021, Statement of Bhupinder Singh and Boota Singh
    Kharoudh Shiromani Akali Dal (Amritsar) America Inc. https://www.uscirf.gov/
    sites/default/files/Sikh-written-testimony.pdf.

Chapter 4

1   Divakaruni, Chitra Banerjee. 1997. *Leaving Yuba City*. Knopf Doubleday Publishing
    Group.

2   Facebook Group. 2010. "Yuba-Sutter History 101." Yuba-Sutter History 101 Facebook
    Group. https://www.facebook.com/groups/422705781233916.

3   Chopra, Sonia. 2019, April 23. "California's Lost (and Found) Punjabi-Mexican
    Cuisine." *Eater*. https://www.eater.com/2019/4/23/18305011/punjabi-mexican-
    migration-roti-quesadilla-el-ranchero.

4   Rasul English, Tamara. 2010. "Facebook Account, Tamara L Rasul English."
    Facebook. https://www.facebook.com/kuryspice.

5   Rasul English, Tamara L. 2021, December 29. "Ali Rasul, Photo (Yuba City)."
    Facebook. https://www.facebook.com/photo?fbid=10227550713176111&set=
    gm.203671398316641.

6   Pathak, D. Homegrown.in. "Who Were the Punjabi-Mexicans of California & Why Are They Fading Away?" https://homegrown.co.in/homegrown-voices/who-were-the-punjabi-mexicans-of-california-why-are-they-fading-away.

7   Kaur, Harmeet. 2021, September 11. "A Sikh Man's Murder at a Gas Station Revealed Another Tragedy of 9/11." CNN. https://www.cnn.com/interactive/2021/09/us/balbir-singh-sodhi-9-11-cec/.

Chapter 5

1   Bald, Vivek. 2015. *Bengali Harlem and the Lost Histories of South Asian America*. Harvard University Press, 46–51. https://www.hup.harvard.edu/books/9780674503854.

2   Hart, Jayasri Majumdar. 1998. *Roots in the Sand*. PBS Media.

3   2019 Immigration History. The University of Texas at Austin Department of History. "Immigration Act of 1917 (Barred Zone Act)." https://immigrationhistory.org/item/1917-barred-zone-act/.

4   Leonard, Karen. 1994. "Contexts: California and the Punjab." In *Making Ethnic Choices: California's Punjabi Mexican Americans*. Temple University Press, 30–32.

5   Ibid., 25–27.

6   Ibid., "Early Days in the Imperial Valley," 37–38.

7   Equal Justice Initiative. "Immigration Act of 1917 Bans Asians, Other Non-White People from Entering U.S." https://calendar.eji.org/racial-injustice/feb/5.

8   Equal Justice Initiative. "Immigration Act of 1924 Prohibits Immigration from Asia." https://calendar.eji.org/racial-injustice/may/26.

9   Kawaguchi, Lesley. 2009. *The History Teacher* 42, no. 3: 367–69. http://www.jstor.org/stable/40543544.

10 Ngai, Mae. 2023. "The Architecture of Immigration Restriction, 1924." *Labor* 20, no. 4 (2023): 4551.

11 Baxter, Andrew M., and Alex Nowrasteh. 2021. "A Brief History of U.S. Immigration Policy from the Colonial Period to the Present Day (Report)." Cato Institute.

12 Tong, Julia. 2023, January 26. "In California, A Long and Pivotal History of Interracial Marriage." American Community Media. https://americancommunitymedia.org/mixed-race/in-california-a-long-and-pivotal-history-of-interracial-marriage/.

13 Provost, Nyla. 2023. "Mixing: A History of Anti-Miscegenation Laws in the United States." *History in the Making*, 16, no. 7: 75–99. https://scholarworks.lib.csusb.edu/history-in-the-making/vol16/iss1/7.

14   Caragozian, John S. 2021, April 28. "Overturning California's Ban on Interracial Marriages." *Los Angeles Daily Journal.* https://www.cschs.org/wp-content/uploads/2021/05/History-Resources-Articles-Caragozian-Ban-on-Interracial-Marriages.pdf; U.S. Constitution. Amendment XIV, section 2.

Chapter 6

1   Leonard, Karen. 1994. "Marriages and Children." In *Making Ethnic Choices: California's Punjabi Mexican Americans.* Temple University Press, 73.

2   "Sikh Temple Stockton." 2022, January 13. Sikh Heritage Education. https://sikhheritageeducation.com/sikh-temple-stockton/.

3   "East Indians of Oregon and the Ghadar Party." *The Oregon Encyclopedia.* Accessed July 19, 2025. https://www.oregonencyclopedia.org/articles/east_indians_of_oregon_and_the_ghadar_party/.

4   "The Ghadar Party." South Asian American Digital Archive (Saada). Accessed July 19, 2025. https://www.saada.org/tides/article/the-ghadar-party; Deol, Gurdev Singh. 1969. *The Role of the Ghadar Party in the National Movement.* Foreword by I. D. Sharma. Sterling Publishers.

5   Leonard. *Making Ethnic Choices,* 74–75.

6   Dang, May. 2020, October 9. "What Is Curry Powder: Stories." Kitchen Stories. Accessed July 19, 2025. https://www.kitchenstories.com/en/stories/what-is-curry-powder.

7   Gottleib, Benjamin. 2012, August 13. "Punjabi Sikh-Mexican American Community Fading into History." *Washington Post.* Accessed July 19, 2025. https://www.washingtonpost.com/national/on-faith/punjabi-sikh-mexican-american-community-fading-into-history/2012/08/13/cc6b7b98-e26b-11e1-98e7-89d659f9c106_story.html.

8   Ferguson, Edwin E. 1947. "The California Alien Land Law and the Fourteenth Amendment." *California Law Review* 35, no. 1 (March): 61. https://doi.org/10.2307/3477375.

9   Leonard. 1994. "Childhood in California." In *Making Ethnic Choices,* 134–37.

Chapter 7

1   "The Holtville Tribune—Serving Holtville CA and Imperial County since 1905." 2025, May 31. *Holtville Tribune.* https://holtvilletribune.com/; Leonard, Karen. 2016, September 9. "The Punjabi Pioneer Experience in America: Recognition or Denial?" *International Journal of Punjab Studies.* https://escholarship.org/uc/item/23964278.

2   Fernandez, Leah. 2011. "Breaking Ground: Imperial Valley's Japanese and Punjabi Farmers, 1900–1933." *Hindsight Graduate History Journal* 5 (Spring). Accessed July 19, 2025. https://socialsciences.fresnostate.edu/historydept/documents/organizations/hindsight/BreakingGround.pdf.

3   Leonard, Karen. 1994. "Early Days." In *Making Ethnic Choices: California's Punjabi Mexican Americans.* Temple University Press, 43–45; Darnell, William Irvin. 1959. "The Imperial Valley: Its Physical and Cultural Geography." Master's thesis, San Diego State College, 90–92, 95.

4   Suzuki, Masao. 2004. "Important or Impotent? Taking Another Look at the 1920 California Alien Land Law." *Journal of Economic History* 64, no. 1: 125; "Five Views: An Ethnic Historic Site Survey for California (Japanese Americans)." National Parks Service. Accessed July 19, 2025.

5   "Welcome to Pioneers' Museum." Pioneers Museum. Accessed July 19, 2025. https://pioneersmuseum.net/.

6   "A Guide to the War in the Pacific: The First Year." National Parks Service. Accessed July 19, 2025. https://www.nps.gov/parkhistory/online_books/npswapa/extContent/wapa/guides/first/sec2.htm; "The Death of Private Kauffman, USMC Sumay Barracks, Guam Island, December 10th, 1941." Warfare.gq. Accessed July 19, 2025. https://web.archive.org/web/20220411144012/https://warfare.gq/dutcheastindies/kauffman.html.

7   "A Magnificent Fight: Marines in the Battle for Wake Island (This Is as Far as We Go)." National Parks Service. Accessed July 19, 2025. https://www.nps.gov/parkhistory/online_books/npswapa/extcontent/usmc/pcn-190-003119-00/sec5a.htm; Warren, Alan. 2002. *Singapore 1942: Britain's Greatest Defeat.* Talisman; Hardie Grant Books.

8   "Executive Order 9066: Resulting in Japanese-American Incarceration (1942)." National Archives and Records Administration. Accessed July 19, 2025. https://www.archives.gov/milestone-documents/executive-order-9066;

9   "Japanese-American Internment." Japanese-American Internment, Harry S. Truman. Accessed July 19, 2025. https://www.trumanlibrary.gov/education/presidential-inquiries/japanese-american-internment.

10   Beito, David T. 2023. *The New Deal's War on the Bill of Rights: The Untold Story of FDR's Concentration Camps, Censorship, and Mass Surveillance.* Independent Institute.

11   "The Sikhs of California: Images of an Asian Culture." 2021, December 20. Sikh Heritage Education. https://sikhheritageeducation.com/the-sikhs-of-california-images-of-an-asian-culture/.

12   "Sikhs in the Borderlands: Lesson Plan Curriculum: The Asian American Education Project." Accessed July 19, 2025; " BTSD Holds Services for Imperial Valley

Ancestors: A Longstanding Memorial Day Weekend Tradition." Discover Nikkei. Accessed July 19, 2025. https://discovernikkei.org/en/journal/2024/9/10/btsd-holds-services/.

13   Sandy Sierra Staff. 2015, January 26. "How Punjabi Pioneers Purchased the Valley's First Gurdwara." Imperial Valley Press Online.

14   "Sikhism Religion of the Sikh People." Accessed July 19, 2025. https://www.sikhs.org/khanda.htm#:

15   Lal, Vinay. 2021, November 5. "The Enigma of Udham Singh." Open. https://openthemagazine.com/essays/the-enigma-of-udham-singh/#google_vignette.

16   Wagner, Kim A. 2019. *Amritsar 1919: An Empire of Fear and the Making of a Massacre*. Yale University Press, 20; O'Dwyer, Michael Francis. 1925. *India as I Knew It: 1885–1925*. Constable.

17   Tuteja, Kundan Lal. 1997. "Jallianwala Bagh: A Critical Juncture in the Indian National Movement." *Social Scientist* 25, no. 1/2 : 25–61. https://doi.org/10.2307/3517759.

18   Admin. 2024, January 30. "Rowlatt Act & Jallianwala Bagh Massacre (1919)—UPSC Modern History Notes." BYJUS. https://byjus.com/free-ias-prep/rowlatt-act-and-jallianwala-bagh-massacre/.

19   "Jallianwala Bagh Massacre." 2025, June 24. *Encyclopædia Britannica*. https://www.britannica.com/event/Jallianwala-Bagh-Massacre.

20   Venkatesh, Archana. 2019. "History Milestone: The Amritsar Massacre." Origins. Accessed July 19, 2025. https://origins.osu.edu/milestones/april-2019-amritsar-massacre-gandhi-dyer-rowlatt-acts-punjab.

21   Arden, Vishal Parmar. 2025, April 28. "He Waited 21 Years for Justice. This Is the Story They Tried to Forget." *Medium*. https://medium.com/readers-digests/he-waited-21-years-for-justice-this-is-the-story-they-tried-to-forget-fdfd3fd43787.

22   Lal, Vinay. 2021, November 5. "The Enigma of Udham Singh." Open. https://openthemagazine.com/essays/the-enigma-of-udham-singh/; Anand, Anita. 2020. *The Patient Assassin: A True Tale of Massacre, Revenge and the Raj*. Simon & Schuster.

23   "Sikh Temple El Centro California." Sikh Temple El Centro California. Accessed July 19, 2025. https://www.ivkhalsadiwan.org/.

24   Baisakhi. Accessed July 19, 2025. https://dvnetwork.org/page/baisakhi.

25   Leow, H. M. A. "The 'Mexican-Hindus' of Rural California." *Jstor Daily*. Accessed July 19, 2025. https://daily.jstor.org/the-mexican-hindus-of-rural-california/;

26   Villegas, Jordan, and Alissa Lopez Serfozo. 2022, November 18. "The History of California's Punjabi-Mexican Communities." *Latina*.

27 Bravo, Noel. 2021, April 16. "Evergreen Cemetery: Solace for the Living and the Dead." *The Desert Review.* https://www.thedesertreview.com/business/evergreen-cemetery-solace-for-the-living-and-the-dead/article_dca73026-890c-11e8-9df6-3b9e08b58d25.html.

28 "Oco & Tanaka Farms Walk the Farm: Japanese American Farm History." Accessed July 19, 2025. https://www.walkthefarm.org/jafarmhistory#.

Chapter 8

1 "The Ghadar Party." South Asian American Digital Archive (Saada). Accessed July 20, 2025. https://www.saada.org/tides/article/the-ghadar-party; "The Ghadar Movement: Fighting Colonialism at Home and Abroad: Lesson Plan Curriculum: The Asian American Education Project." The Asian American Education Project. Accessed July 19, 2025. https://asianamericanedu.org/the-ghadar-movement.html.

2 Singh, Simrin. "This Little-Known American Community Is Fading into History." Project: MS Template 2018–2019. Accessed July 19, 2025. https://ascjcapstone.com/terms/spring-2020/simrinsi/.

3 Lohman, Sarah. 2023, March 10. "Eight Flavors: Punjabi-Mexican Cuisine and the Roti-Quesadilla." fourpoundsflour.com, last updated February 9, 2023. https://fourpoundsflour.com/eight-flavors-punjabi-mexican-cuisine-and-the-roti-quesadilla/.

4 Schlachet, Joshua. 2024, March 22. "A Roti by Any Other Name Would Taste Like Home: Food Culture in the Punjabi-Mexican Communities of the Early 20th Century United States." The Recipes Project. Retrieved July 19, 2025, from https://doi.org/10.58079/w2ox.

5 "Menu." Examining Latino and Punjabi Sikh Identity. Accessed July 19, 2025. https://journeys.dartmouth.edu/finalcurationsunny/making-of-the-punjabi-mexican-community/.

6 Leonard, Karen B. 1993. "Intermarriage and Ethnicity: Punjabi Mexican Americans, Mexican, Japanese and Filipino Americans." *Explorations in Ethnic Studies* 16, no. 2 (July): 147–63. Accessed July 20, 2025. https://escholarship.org/content/qt6r2466j2/qt6r2466j2_noSplash_03ad0bb842bd4e6d80e2830c7493fb4d.pdf; Dhir, Simrita. 2025, March 13. "California's Pioneering Punjabis: An American Story." SikhNet, https://www.sikhnet.com/news/%C2%A0california%E2%80%99s-pioneering-punjabis-american-story.

7 Kale, Reva. 2022, August 20. "The Punjabi Pioneers." *Asian American Research Journal.* https://www.academia.edu/85248005/The_Punjabi_Pioneers.

8 Leonard, Karen. 1994. "Conflict and Love in Marriages." In *Making Ethnic Choices: California's Punjabi Mexican Americans*. Temple University Press, 108–12.

9   "Domestic Violence and Pets." 2025, March 19. RedRover. https://redrover.org/
     domestic-violence-and-pets/#issue.

10   Focht, Jennifer. 2024, June 13. "'Why Doesn't She Just Leave?' Barriers to Getting
     out of Abusive Relationships." National Center for Health Research. https://www.
     center4research.org/why-doesnt-she-leave-abusive-relationship/.

Chapter 9

1   Leonard, Karen. 1994. "Early Days in the Imperial Valley." In *Making Ethnic Choices:
     California's Punjabi Mexican Americans*. Temple University Press, 42–51.

2   Inani, Rohit. 2018, March 9. "Language Is a 'War Zone': A Conversation with Ngũgĩ
     Wa Thiong'o." *The Nation*. https://www.thenation.com/article/archive/language-is-a-
     war-zone-a-conversation-with-ngugi-wa-thiongo/.

3   Han, Yoonji. 2022, October 8. "The Early 20th Century Was Rife with Anti-
     Immigrant Laws: They Spurred a Flourishing Punjabi-Mexican Community in
     California." *Business Insider*. Accessed July 19, 2025.https://www.businessinsider.
     com/punjabi-mexican-community-immigrant-history-california-indian-
     hispanic-2022-10.

Chapter 10

1   "Using Jackfruit in Place of Chicken." Creatively Delish Using Jackfruit in Place of
     Chicken Comments. Accessed July 19, 2025. https://creativelydelish.com/course/
     using-jackfruit-in-place-of-chicken/.

2   Srivastava, Tanvi. 2022, August 29. "Keema Masala (Dhaba Style)." Sinfully Spicy.
     https://sinfullyspicy.com/keema-masala-dhaba-style/.

3   Leonard, Karen. 1994. "Contexts: California and the Punjab." In *Making Ethnic
     Choices: California's Punjabi Mexican Americans*. Temple University Press, 30–33.

4   "Immigration Act of 1917 (Barred Zone Act)." 2020, February 1. *Immigration
     History*. https://immigrationhistory.org/item/1917-barred-zone-act/; "Analysis:
     The National Origins Act (Immigration Act of 1924): EBSCO." EBSCO
     Information Services, Inc. www.ebsco.com. Accessed July 19, 2025. https://www.
     ebsco.com/research-starters/history/analysis-national-origins-act-immigration-
     act-1924#.

5   Walker, Shaun. 2020, August 6. "The Last of the Zoroastrians." *The Guardian*.
     https://www.theguardian.com/world/2020/aug/06/last-of-the-zoroastrians-parsis-
     mumbai-india-ancient-religion.

Chapter 13

1   MacCarthy, James, and Jessica Richter. 2025, February 5. "4 Graphics Explain Los Angeles' Rare and Devastating January Fires." World Resources Institute. https://www.wri.org/insights/los-angeles-fires-january-2025-explained.

2   Hart, Jayasri. (Dir.). 1998. *Roots in the Sand.* Documentary.

3   Chopra, Sonia. 2019, April 23. "California's Lost (and Found) Punjabi-Mexican Cuisine." *Eater.* https://www.eater.com/2019/4/23/18305011/punjabi-mexican-migration-roti-quesadilla-el-ranchero.

Chapter 14

1   Ranganath, Nicole. 2017. "Nand Kaur." Punjabi and Sikh Diaspora Digital Archive. https://punjabidiaspora.ucdavis.edu/nand-kaur/.

2   Dhaliwal, Deepeaka. 2018, December. "Yuba-Sutter: A Case Study for Heritage Conservation in Punjabi-American Communities." Master's Thesis, Heritage Conservation, USC. https://bpb-us-w1.wpmucdn.com/sites.usc.edu/dist/9/583/files/2022/10/Deepeaka-Dhaliwal-thesis.pdf.

3   Ranganath, Dr. Nicole. 2008. "Global Institute for Sikh Studies: *Journal of Sikh & Punjab Studies:* Gurinder Singh Mann, Manager." https://giss.org/jsps_vol_27.html.

4   *Tribune* Staff. 2024, August 23. "First Punjabi Women in the US." *The Tribune.* https://www.tribuneindia.com/news/punjab/first-punjabi-women-in-the-us/.

5   Shahid, Affifa. 2024, May 23. "Sikhs in the British Indian Army: Loyal Soldiers or Imperial Pawns?" Brown History. https://brownhistory.substack.com/p/sikhs-in-the-british-indian-army.

6   Zamindar, Vazira Fazila-Yacoobali. 2013. "India–Pakistan Partition 1947 and Forced Migration." In *The Encyclopedia of Global Human Migration*, I. Ness (Ed.). https://doi.org/10.1002/9781444351071.wbeghm285.

7   Rangarajan, Mahesh. 2020. "Independence Day Celebrations 1947—Google Arts & Culture." Nehru Memorial Museum and Library. https://artsandculture.google.com/story/independence-day-celebrations-1947-nehru-memorial-museum-library/; Kimta, Dr. Abha Chauhan. 2020. "Gandhi's Views on Partition: An Evaluation." *International Journal of Current Advanced Research* 9, no. 7: 22767–69. https://doi.org/https://journalijcar.org/sites/default/files/issue-files/11386-A-2020.pdf.

8   Partition of British India. Accessed July 20, 2025. https://econweb.ucsd.edu/~prbharadwaj/index/Partition_of_British_India.html; Bharadwaj, Prashant, Asim, Ijaz Khwaja, and Atif R. Mian. 2008, June. "The Big March: Migratory Flows after the Partition of India." Harvard Kennedy School Faculty Research Working Paper

Series. https://papers.ssrn.com/sol3/papers.cfm?abstract_id=1124093; Kaur, Harjyot and Pooja Jaggi. 2023. "Intergenerational Trauma in the Context of the 1947 India–Pakistan Partition." *Psychological Studies*, 1–14. https://doi.org/10.1007/s12646-023-00730-w.

9   James, Lawrence. 2003. "The Departure: Was It Too Quick? Dividing and Departing March-September 1947." In *Raj: The Making and Unmaking of British India*. St. Martin's Griffin, 608–39.

10 Tan, Tai Yong, and Gyanesh Kudaisya. 2007. *The Aftermath of Partition in South Asia*. Routledge.

11 Puri, Kavita. 2017, July 31. "Break the Silence on Partition and British Colonial History—Before It's Too Late, Kavita Puri." *The Guardian*. https://www.theguardian.com/commentisfree/2017/jul/31/break-silence-partition-british-colonial-history-south-asian.

12 Ranganath, Dr. Nicole. 2019, November 7. "Jutti Kasoori: Walking into the Unknown." YouTube. https://www.youtube.com/watch?v=mHExRo2ULjI.; Ranganath, Nicole. 2017, December. "Later Arrival: Charan Kang." Punjabi and Sikh Diaspora Digital Archive. https://punjabidiaspora.ucdavis.edu/charan-kang/.

13 Rakoff, Vivian, John J. Sigal, and Nathan B. Epstein. 1966. "Children and Families of Concentration Camp Survivors." *Canadas Mental Health* 14, no. 4: 24–26.

14 Bhat, Jyothsna S. 2025, January 20. "The Partition of 1947 and Intergenerational Trauma." Blog. *Psychology Today*. https://www.psychologytoday.com/us/blog/the-psychology-of-the-south-asian-diaspora/202501/the-partition-of-1947-and-intergenerational.

15 Chauhan, Sameera. 2022, August 13. "Revisiting Manto, Recovering Histories: Partition Violence and the 'Little People'—the IAFOR Research Archive." The IAFOR Research Archive. https://papers.iafor.org/submission62387/.

16 Yehuda, Rachel, and Amy Lehrner. 2018, October. "Intergenerational Transmission of Trauma Effects: Putative Role of Epigenetic Mechanisms." *World Psychiatry: Official Journal of the World Psychiatric Association (WPA)*. https://pmc.ncbi.nlm.nih.gov/articles/PMC6127768/; Poole, Anna K., and Ryan Ronnenberg. "Honor, Violence, and Recovery: The Stripping of Female Agency during the Partition of India." DigitalCommons@Kennesaw State University. Accessed July 20, 2025.

17 Butalia, Urvashi. 1993. "Community, State and Gender: On Women's Agency during Partition." *Economic and Political Weekly* 28, no. 17: WS12–24. http://www.jstor.org/stable/4399641.

18 Bhalla, B. M. "Loona: An 'Unwomanly Woman' or a Tragic Heroine?" *The Sunday Tribune*—Spectrum. Accessed July 20, 2025. https://www.tribuneindia.com/2003/20030504/spectrum/book6.htm.

19   Uttamchandani, A. M. 2011. "Crossing Borders and Generations: Sharing of Partition Stories among Survivors and Families of the Partition of British India." PhD diss., The Chicago School of Professional Psychology.

20   Kaur, Harjyot, and Pooja Jaggi. 2023, June 10. "Intergenerational Trauma in the Context of the 1947 India Pakistan Partition." Psychological Studies. https://pmc.ncbi.nlm.nih.gov/articles/PMC10257180/.

21   Srivastava, R., and S. K. Sasikumar. 2003. "An Overview of Migration in India, Its Impacts and Key Issues." www.livelihoods.org.

22   Leonard, Karen. 1994. "The Second Generation Comes of Age." In *Making Ethnic Choices: California's Punjabi Mexican Americans.* Temple University Press, 144–49, 167–69.

23   Bhalla, Guneeta Singh, Steve Moyer, and David Soud. 2022. "The Story of the 1947 Partition as Told by the People Who Were There." National Endowment for the Humanities. https://www.neh.gov/article/story-1947-partition-told-people-who-were-there.

24   "Stockton Gurdwara." Punjabi and Sikh Diaspora Digital Archive. Accessed July 20, 2025. https://punjabidiaspora.ucdavis.edu/contributions/religion/stockton-temple/.

25   Leonard. "Encounters with the Other." In *Making Ethnic Choices,* 188–89.

26   Summa, Robert. 2023, November 6. "A Window into Yuba City's Past: The Sikh Temple Gurdwara." *Appeal.* https://www.appeal-democrat.com/news/a-window-into-yuba-city-s-past-the-sikh-temple-gurdwara/article_38b4df3e-cdac-11ec-a2ff-f3e05f1d1b85.html.

27   La Brack, Bruce. 1980. *"The Sikhs of Northern California: A Socio-historical Study."* PhD diss., Syracuse University, 21.

Chapter 15

1   "Home." Gurdwara. Accessed July 20, 2025. https://www.stocktongurdwara.org/.

2   Deol, Gurdev Singh. 1969. *The Role of the Ghadar Party in the National Movement. Foreword by I. D. Sharma.* Sterling Publishers.

3   "The Ghadar Party: Freedom for India." Site Search. Accessed July 20, 2025. https://pluralism.org/the-ghadar-party-freedom-for-india.

4   Kaur, Pawanjot. 2019, December 26. "In Punjab, the Legacy of the Ghadar Movement Continues to Inspire the Fight for Justice." *The Wire.* Accessed July 20, 2025. https://thewire.in/history/ghadar-movement-indian-freedom; Khosla, Aishwarya. 2024, November 15. "The Enduring Legacy of Kartar Singh Sarabha and the Ghadar Movement." *The Indian Express.* https://indianexpress.com/article/cities/chandigarh/the-enduring-legacy-of-kartar-singh-sarabha-and-the-ghadar-movement-9671791; "The Ghadar Movement: Fighting Colonialism at Home and Abroad." The

Asian American Education Project. Accessed July 20, 2025. https://asianamericanedu. org/the-ghadar-movement.html; Lokapally, Vijay. 2025, July 3. "Veterinarian Rana Preet Gill Revives Memories of the Ghadar Movement in Her New Book." *The Hindu*. https://www.thehindu.com/books/veterinarian-rana-preet-gill-revives-memories-of-the-ghadar-movement-in-her-new-book/article69734496.ece; Gill, Rana Preet. 2025. *Ghadar Movement: A Forgotten Struggle*. India Viking, 10–14.

5   Jain, Mehek. 2022. "A Forgotten Revolution: Understanding the Ghadar Movement's Impact on Indian Nationalism, Castes, and Martial Troops during World War I." Accessed July 20, 2025. https://repository.rice.edu/bitstreams/296f4042-9df5-4f70-b4ef-b73cc12e5fb4/download.

6   Singh, I. P. 2024, July 13. "Raj Singh Badhesha Becomes Fresno County's First Sikh Judge." Chandigarh News—*The Times of India*. Accessed July 20, 2025. https://timesofindia.indiatimes.com/city/chandigarh/raj-singh-badhesha-becomes-fresno-countys-first-sikh-judge/articleshow/111701831.cms.

7   Gottleib, Benjamin. 2012, August 13, "Punjabi Sikh-Mexican American Community Fading into History." *Washington Post*. Accessed July 20, 2025. https://www.washingtonpost.com/national/on-faith/punjabi-sikh-mexican-american-community-fading-into-history/2012/08/13/cc6b7b98-e26b-11e1-98e7-89d659f9c106_story.html.

8   Bayor, Ronald H. 2011. *Multicultural America: An Encyclopedia of the Newest Americans*. Greenwood.

9   "Puna Singh and Nand Kaur." Punjabi and Sikh Diaspora Digital Archive. Accessed July 20, 2025. https://punjabidiaspora.ucdavis.edu/people/pioneers/puna-singh-and-nand-kaur/#; Cooke, Miriam, 2018, October 8. *Blood into Ink: South Asian and Middle Eastern Women Write War*. Routledge; Taylor and Francis. Terhune, Lea, and I. J. Singh. 2023. *California's Pioneering Punjabis: An American Story*. The History Press.

10   "Echoes of Freedom: South Asian Pioneers in California, 1899–1965: 8. Community and Religion." Library Guides at UC Berkeley. Accessed July 20, 2025.

11   Leonard, Karen. 2010. "Political Change and Ethnic Identity." In *Making Ethnic Choices: California's Punjabi Mexican Americans*. Temple University Press, 163–65.

12   Summa, Robert. 2023, November 6. "A Window into Yuba City's Past: The Sikh Temple Gurdwara." *Appeal*. https://www.appeal-democrat.com/news/a-window-into-yuba-city-s-past-the-sikh-temple-gurdwara/.

13   La Brack, Bruce. 1988. *The Sikhs of Northern California, 1904–1975*. AMS Press.

14   Fox40 Web Desk. "Sutter County Board of Supervisors to Swear in First Elected Sikh-American Member." Last updated November 24, 2020. Accessed July 20, 2025. https://fox40.com/news/local-news/sutter-county-board-of-supervisors-to-swear-in-first-elected-sikh-american-member/.

15   "Income of Families and Persons in the United States: 1959." Accessed July 20, 2025. https://www2.census.gov/library/publications/1961/demographics/p60-35.pdf.

16   Summa, Robert. 2023, November 6. "A Window into Yuba City's Past: The Sikh Temple Gurdwara." https://www.appeal-democrat.com/news/a-window-into-yuba-city-s-past-the-sikh-temple-gurdwara/article_38b4df3e-cdac-11ec-a2ff-f3e05f1d1b85.html.

17   La Brack. *The Sikhs of Northern California, 1904–1975*; Sutter County Board of Supervisors to Swear in First Elected Sikh-American Member." Accessed July 20, 2025. https://fox40.com/news/local-news/sutter-county-board-of-supervisors-to-swear-in-first-elected-sikh-american-member/; Income of Families and Persons in the United States: 1959. Accessed July 20, 2025. https://www2.census.gov/library/publications/1961/demographics/p60-35.pdf.

18   "Religion." Punjabi and Sikh Diaspora Digital Archive. Accessed July 20, 2025. https://punjabidiaspora.ucdavis.edu/contributions/religion/.

19   "Didar Singh Bains, 'Peach King' Who Built Northern California's Sikh Community, Dies." 2022, September 29. *Los Angeles Times*. https://www.latimes.com/california/story/2022-09-29/didar-singh-bains-the-peach-king-obit.

20   Ranganath, Nicole. 2024, May 30. "Women and the Sikh Diaspora in California: Singing the Seven Seas." Routledge & CRC Press. https://www.routledge.com/Women-and-the-Sikh-Diaspora-in-California-Singing-the-Seven-Seas/Ranganath/p/book/9781032384047.

21   "Pritam Kaur Heir." Punjabi and Sikh Diaspora Digital Archive. Accessed July 20, 2025. https://punjabidiaspora.ucdavis.edu/pritam-kaur-heir-4/.

22   "Punjabi-Origin Farmers Realise the Great American Dream by Dint of Hard Work, Resilience." 2012, May 9. *India Today*. https://www.indiatoday.in/magazine/international/story/20041011-punjabi-origin-farmers-realise-the-great-american-dream-by-dint-of-hard-work-resilience-789214-2004-10-10.

23   Menon, Aditya. 2022, September 14. "Didar Singh Bains' Inspiring Journey from Farm Worker to America's 'Peach King.'" *The Quint*. https://www.thequint.com/south-asians/didar-singh-bains-passes-away-sikhs-america.

24   Sutter, Visit Yuba. "Experience Culture in Yuba-Sutter: Visit Yuba Sutter." Sutter. Accessed July 20, 2025. https://visityubasutter.com/blog/experience-culture-in-yuba-sutter; MGP Staff. 2024, October 30. "All You Need to Know about Nagar Kirtan or 'Sikh Parade.'" Territorial Dispatch. Accessed July 20, 2025. https://www.territorialdispatch.com/2024/10/30/511192/all-you-need-to-know-about-nagar-kirtan-or-sikh-parade-.

25   Christine Duhaime, BA. 2023, September 25. "Didar Singh Bains, Gurpatwant Singh Pannun, Hardeep Singh Nijjar—A Look at Some Khalistan Activists in Vancouver, the Dispute with India, Iranian Spies and Habib Chaab." https://dirtymoneycrime.substack.com/p/didar-singh-bains-gurpatwant-singh.

26   Christian, Sena. 2017, July 11. "American Dreams." *Comstock's* magazine. https://www.comstocksmag.com/longreads/american-dreams.

27   Khanna, Amarpal. 2011, April. "Governor Jerry Brown at San Jose Sikh Gurdwara."
     YouTube. https://www.youtube.com/watch?v=VjqsTCPJC6E.

28   Christian, "American Dreams."

Chapter 16

1   Sikh Foundation Staff. 2004, March. "The Boy with Long Hair, Pushpinder Kaur."
     The Sikh Foundation—Community Profiles: Pushpinder Kaur. https://www.
     sikhfoundation.org/comprof0304.html.

2   "Different Types of Trauma: Small 't' versus Large 't.'" *Psychology Today*. Accessed
     July 20, 2025. https://www.psychologytoday.com/us/blog/trauma-and-hope/201703/
     different-types-trauma-small-t-versus-large-t; Qureshi, Farah, Supriya Misra, and
     Asma Poshni. 2023. "The Partition of India through the Lens of Historical Trauma:
     Intergenerational Effects on Immigrant Health in the South Asian Diaspora." *SSM—
     Mental Health* 4, Article 100246. https://doi.org/10.1016/j.ssmmh.2023.100246.

3   Berckmoes, Lidewyde H., Veroni Eichelsheim, Theoneste Rutayisire, Annemiek
     Richters, and Barbora Hola. 2017, September 14. "How Legacies of Genocide Are
     Transmitted in the Family Environment: A Qualitative Study of Two Generations in
     Rwanda." MDPI. https://www.mdpi.com/2075-4698/7/3/24.

4   Mamdani, Mahmood. 2020. *When Victims Become Killers: Colonialism, Nativism,
     and the Genocide in Rwanda*. Princeton University Press.

5   Caruth, Cathy. 2016. *Unclaimed Experience: Trauma, Narrative, and History*. Johns
     Hopkins University Press.

6   Mambrol, Nasrullah. 2020, July 15. "Trauma Studies." *Literary Theory and Criticism*.
     https://literariness.org/2018/12/19/trauma-studies/.

7   Boyajian, Levon, and Haigaz Grigorian. 1986. "Psychosocial Sequelae of the
     Armenian Genocide." In *The Armenian Genocide in Perspective*, 1st ed. Routledge,
     177–86.

8   "Tamber." SikhiWiki. Accessed July 20, 2025. https://www.sikhiwiki.org/index.php/
     Tamber.

9   Kaur, Minreet. 2019, March 15. "'I'm Divorced, so Sikh Men Don't Want Me.'" BBC
     News. https://www.bbc.com/news/stories-47562252.

10   Danieli, Yael, et al. 2015, June 23. "The Danieli Inventory of Multigenerational
     Legacies of Trauma, Part I: Survivors' Post Trauma Adaptational Styles in Their
     Children's Eyes." *Journal of Psychiatric Research* 68 (September): 167–75. https://
     www.sciencedirect.com/science/article/abs/pii/S002239561500182X; Patel, Reeya
     A., and Donna K. Nagata. 2021, June 1. "Historical Trauma and Descendants' Well-
     Being." *AMA Journal of Ethics* 23, no. 6: 487–493. doi: 10.1001/amajethics.2021.487.

https://journalofethics.ama-assn.org/article/historical-trauma-and-descendants-well-being/2021-06.

11   Kaur, Harjyot, and Pooja Jaggi. 2023. "Intergenerational Trauma in the Context of the 1947 India–Pakistan Partition." *Psychological Studies* 68, no. 3 (June). Accessed July 20, 2025. https://www.researchgate.net/publication/371471745_Intergenerational_Trauma_in_the_Context_of_the_1947_India-Pakistan_Partition.

12   Das, Kavita. 2021, May 21. "The Trauma of Partition: A Conversation with Anjali Enjeti." *Los Angeles Review of Books.* https://lareviewofbooks.org/article/the-trauma-of-partition-a-conversation-with-anjali-enjeti/.

Chapter 17

1   Leonard, Karen. 1994. "Early Days." In *Making Ethnic Choices: California's Punjabi Mexican Americans.* Temple University Press, 188–89.

2   Ibid., 57.

3   Ranganath, Nicole. 2019, November 7. ` "Jutti Kasoori: Walking into the Unknown." YouTube. https://www.youtube.com/watch?v=mHExRo2ULjI.

4   "Unity Across Faiths: Sikhs and Saints Strengthen Bonds in California." 2024, August 9. The Church of Jesus Christ of Latter-Day Saints. https://newsroom.churchofjesuschrist.org/article/sikhs-saints-yuba-city-california-youth.

Chapter 18

1   "Khanda." The Dasvandh Network. Accessed July 20, 2025. https://dvnetwork.org/page/khanda#.

2   Duggal, Hanna, and Alia Chughtai. 2023, September 27. "What Is the Khalistan Movement? How Is It Linked to India–Canada Tensions?" *Al Jazeera.* https://www.aljazeera.com/news/2023/9/27/what-is-the-khalistan-movement-how-is-it-linked-to-india-canada-tensions#.

3   "History: Stockton Gurdwara Sahib." 2014. *San Joaquin Magazine.* Accessed July 20, 2025. https://sanjoaquinmagazine.com/2014/02/history-stockton-gurdwara-sahib/.

4   Bartell, John. 2024. "U.S. Oldest Sikh Temple Is in Stockton, California." ABC10. com. Accessed July 21, 2025. https://www.abc10.com/article/news/community/race-and-culture/temple-for-worship-and-india-independence/103-d5b8b427-f03f-4446-984e-a48873b22518; Parrish, Kevin. 2012, September 22. "Sikhs Honor Rich History in Stockton." *The Stockton Record.* https://www.recordnet.com/story/entertainment/human-interest/2012/09/22/sikhs-honor-rich-history-in/49394673007/.

5   "History of Stockton Gurdwara." 2013, January 27. 100 Years of Sikhs in the USA. https://sikhcentury.wordpress.com/stockton-gurdwara-history/.

6   "Ghadar Party Hero Kartar Singh Sarabha." National Book Trust India. Accessed July 20, 2025. https://www.nbtindia.gov.in/books_detail__9__national-biography__1203__ghadar-party-hero-kartar-singh-sarabha.nbt.

7   Editors, India Empire. 2014. "Gadar Movement and its Torch Bearers: The Unsung Hero." India Empire. https://www.indiaempire.com/v1/2012/September/gadar.asp.

8   Grewal, Dalvinder Singh. 2024, November 21. "Kartar Singh Grewal (Sarabha)." SikhNet. https://www.sikhnet.com/news/kartar-singh-grewal-sarabha.

9   "The Ghadar Movement: Fighting Colonialism at Home and Abroad." The Asian American Education Project. Accessed July 20, 2025. https://asianamericanedu.org/the-ghadar-movement.html; Khosla, Aishwarya. 2024, November 15. "The Enduring Legacy of Kartar Singh Sarabha and the Ghadar Movement." *The Indian Express*. https://indianexpress.com/article/cities/chandigarh/the-enduring-legacy-of-kartar-singh-sarabha-and-the-ghadar-movement-9671791/#.

10   Singh, Bhagat. 2022, September 22. "On Bhagat Singh's Anniversary: 'Why I Am an Atheist.'" Scroll.in. https://scroll.in/article/715660/on-bhagat-singhs-death-anniversary-why-i-am-an-atheist.

11   Sidhu, G. B. S. 2022. *Khalistan Conspiracy: A Former R&AW Officer Unravels the Path to 1984*. HarperCollins India.

12   Information on Operation Blue Star. Accessed July 21, 2025. https://www.ecoi.net/en/file/local/1419263/4792_1512533280_143136.pdf.

13   Jain, Rupam, and Shivam Patel. 2023, September 19. "What Is the Khalistan Movement and Why Is It Fuelling India–Canada Rift?" Reuters. https://www.reuters.com/world/what-is-khalistan-movement-why-is-it-fuelling-india-canada-rift-2023-09-19/.

Chapter 19

1   Brar, Kamaldeep Singh. 2022, October 8. "Preacher, 'Influencer,' Ideologue: Meet Amritpal Singh, Head of Waris Punjab De." *The Indian Express*. https://indianexpress.com/article/cities/amritsar/preacher-influencer-ideologue-meet-amritpal-singh-8196944/.

2   Gupta, Vivek. 2023, March 25. "Amritpal Justifies Demand of Sikh Nation against the Backdrop of Demand for a Hindu Nation." *The Wire*. https://thewire.in/politics/amritpal-demand-punjab-sikh-nation-khalistan.

3   Burns, John. 1996, September 6. "A Decade after Massacre, Some Sikhs Find Justice."
    New York Times.

4   Singh, Khushwant. 2017. "Rendezvous with Jarnail Singh Bhindranwale." In *Captain
    Amarinder Singh: The People's Maharaja: An Authorized Biography*. Hay House,
    150–60; Sinha, Chitranshul. 2019. *The Great Repression: The Story of Sedition in
    India*. Penguin Random House India Private Limited; Juergensmeyer, Mark. 2020.
    Why God Needs War and War Needs God. Oxford University Press, 26; Deol,
    Harnik. 2000. *Religion and Nationalism in India: The Case of the Punjab*. Routledge;
    Singh, Harbans, and Sandeep Singh. 1999, October 23. "Saint Jarnail Singh
    Bhindranwale (1947–1984)." Sant Jarnail Singh ji Bhindranwale. https://web.archive.
    org/web/20070324110547/http://www.sikh-history.com/sikhhist/personalities/
    bhindrenwale.html; Kaur, Mallika. 2020. *Faith, Gender, and Activism in the Punjab
    Conflict: The Wheat Fields Still Whisper*. Springer International Publishing, 62.

5   Roy, Sidhartha. 2011, July 6. "From Bengal, but Staunchly Delhiites." https://
    www.hindustantimes.com/delhi/from-bengal-but-staunchly-delhiites/story-
    muBVCSimh2d3GZuo8DYO6I.html.

6   Mahmood, Cynthia Keppley. 2010. *Fighting for Faith and Nation: Dialogues with Sikh
    Militants*. University of Pennsylvania Press, Incorporated, 50–80.

7   Singh, Khushwant. 1991. *A History of the Sikhs: 1839–1988*. Oxford University Press,
    329.

8   Dutt, Nirupama. 2022, June 2. "Revisiting Punjab's Turmoil before and after Op
    Bluestar." *Hindustan Times*. https://www.hindustantimes.com/cities/chandigarh-
    news/revisiting-punjab-s-turmoil-before-and-after-op-bluestar-101654200315526.
    html; Deol, Harnik. 2000. *Religion and Nationalism in India: The Case of the Punjab*.
    Routledge, 2000; Sidhū, Choor Siṅgh. 2006. *Sant Jarnail Siṅgh Bhindrānwāle: Saint
    and Martyr*. B. Chattar Siṅgh Jiwan Siṅgh.

9   Tully, Mark, and Satish Jacob. 1986. *Amritsar: Mrs Gandhi's Last Battle*. Pan Books.

10 Punjab Politics: Retrospect and Prospect. n.d. Readworthy; Singh, Khushwant.
    2015, June 6. "Operation Blue Star 'Was a Well-Calculated and Deliberate Slap in
    the Face of an Entire Community': Khushwant Singh." Scroll.in. https://scroll.in/
    article/732469/operation-blue-star-was-a-well-calculated-and-deliberate-slap-in-the-
    face-of-an-entire-community-khushwant-singh.

11 Barnetsen, Denholm. 1987, October 20. "Sikh Extremists Went on a Shooting
    Rampage in a . . .—UPI Archives." UPI. https://www.upi.com/Archives/1987/10/20/
    Sikh-extremists-went-on-a-shooting-rampage-in-a/3567561700800/.

12 Mahmood, Cynthia Keppley. 2010. "A Saint Soldier." In *Fighting for Faith and Nation:
    Dialogues with Sikh Militants*. University of Pennsylvania Press, Incorporated, 51–64;
    C. Christine Fair; Sumit Ganguly. 2008, September 29. *Treading on Hallowed Ground:
    Counterinsurgency Operations in Sacred Spaces*. Oxford University Press, 39–40;

Singh, Khushwant. 2004, November 7. "Oh, That Other Hindu Riot of Passage." *Outlook Magazine*. https://countercurrents.org/comm-khushwantsing071104.htm.

13   Singh, Khushwant. 1974. *A History of the Sikhs. Vol. 2, 1839–1974*. Oxford University Press.

14   Andrew, Christopher, and Vasili Mitrokhi. 2006. *The World Was Going Our Way: The KGB and the Battle for the Third World: Newly Revealed Secrets from the Mitrokhin Archive*. Basic Books; Andrew, Christopher. 2014. *The Mitrokhin Archive II: The KGB in the World*. Penguin Books.

15   Kalra, Mahesh A. 2016, November 5. "Operation Blue Star: India's First Tryst with Militant Extremism." DNA India. https://www.dnaindia.com/india/report-operation-blue-star-india-s-first-tryst-with-militant-extremism-2270293.

16   Rao, Amiya, Vithal Mahadeo Tarkunde, George Fernandes, Aurobindo Ghose, Sunil Bhattacharya, Tejinder Ahuja, and N. D. Pancholi. 1986. *Oppression in Punjab: A Citizens for Democracy Report to the Nation*. Sikh Religious and Educational Trust.

17   Roy, Sidhartha. *Mission and Martyrdom*. Accessed July 21, 2025. https://sikhcoalition.org/documents/pdf/SantJarnailSingh.pdf.

18   Swamy, Subramanian. 1992. *Building a New India: An Agenda for National Renaissance*. UBS Publishers' Distributors, 18.

19   Hardgrave, Robert L. 1985. "India in 1984: Confrontation, Assassination, and Succession." *Asian Survey* 25, no. 2: 131–44. https://doi.org/10.2307/2644297.

20   Associated Press. 1985, September 14. "India Is Said to Drop Prosecution of A.P. Reporter in Punjab Case." https://www.nytimes.com/1985/09/14/world/india-is-said-to-drop-prosecution-of-ap-reporter-in-punjab-case.html.

21   Rao, et al *Oppression in Punjab*, 72.

22   Ibid., 69.

23   Brar, Kuldip Singh. 2014. *Operation Blue Star: The True Story*. UBS Publishers' Distributors.

24   Mahmood, Cynthia Keppley. 2010. *Fighting for Faith and Nation: Dialogues with Sikh Militants*. University of Pennsylvania Press, Incorporated, 188.

25   Christopher Andrew. 2006. *The World Was Going Our Way: The KGB and the Battle for the Third World: Newly Revealed Secrets from the Mitrokhin Archive*. Basic Books, 615–20.

26   Guha, Ramachandra. 2015, June 7. "The Bhindranwale Cult: How Politics Allowed an Obscure Preacher to Challenge Indian Democracy." Scroll.in. https://scroll.in/article/732426/the-bhindranwale-cult-how-politics-allowed-an-obscure-preacher-to-challenge-indian-democracy; Kaur, Minreet. 2024, June 8. "Sikh Families Still Suffering 40 Years after Golden Temple Raid." BBC News. https://www.bbc.com/news/articles/cw99rgv397go; "Operation Bluestar: Punjab Disappeared: Disappeared,

Denied, but Not Forgotten." 2019, August 22. Punjab Disappeared. https://punjabdisappeared.org/operation-bluestar/.

27   Singh, Tavleen. 1984, May. "An Interview with Major General Shabeg Singh May 1984. The Telegraph. Calcutta, India." 1984 Tribute. Accessed July 20, 2025. https://1984tribute.com/an-interview-with-major-general-shabeg-singh-may-1984-the-telegraph-calcutta-india/.

28   Silva, Romesh, Jasmine Marwaha, and Jeff Klingner. 2009, January. "Violent Deaths and Enforced Disappearances during the Counterinsurgency in Punjab, India: A Preliminary Quantitative Analysis." A Joint Report by Benetech's Human Rights Data Analysis Group and Ensaaf, Inc. http://www.hrdag.org/about/india-punjab.shtml and at http://www.ensaaf.org/reports/.

29   Rajput, Abhinav, and Preen Lidhoo. 2016, August 13. "Refugee Colonies Changed South Delhi's Face." *Hindustan Times*. https://www.hindustantimes.com/delhi/refugee-colonies-changed-south-delhi-s-face/story-qYpc0OQI28vP5syqnvYYCO.html; Travelwisesr. 2020, October 27. "A Magic Bengal Outside Bengal, Chittaranjan Park New Delhi." https://travelwisesr.com/a-magical-bengal-outside-bengal-chittaranjan-park-new-delhi/#.

30   Doward, Jamie. 2017, October 28. "British Government 'Covered up' Its Role in Amritsar Massacre in India." *The Guardian*. https://www.theguardian.com/world/2017/oct/29/british-government-cover-up-amritsar-massacre-golden-temple-sas-india.

31   Goyal, Divya. 2023, April 23. "Waris Punjab de: What Is the Mission of This Outfit, Floated by Deep Sidhu and Now Led by Amritpal Singh?" *The Indian Express*. https://indianexpress.com/article/explained/waris-punjab-de-deep-sidhu-amritpal-singh-8464095/lite/.

32   Ghosh, Deepshikha. 2018, December 17. "Why Gujarat 2002 Finds Mention in 1984 Riots Court Order on Sajjan Kumar." NDTV. https://www.ndtv.com/india-news/why-gujarat-2002-finds-mention-in-1984-riots-court-order-on-sajjan-kumar-1963730.

33   Barnetson, Denholm. 1987, June 14. "Sikh Radicals Kill 12 with Submachine Guns—UPI Archives." UPI. https://www.upi.com/Archives/1987/06/14/Sikh-radicals-kill-12-with-submachine-guns/7449550641600/.

Chapter 20

1   Sengupta, Arjun. 2023, October 31. "What Happened on October 31, 1984: Recalling the Assassination of Indira Gandhi." *The Indian Express*. https://indianexpress.com/article/explained/explained-history/oct-31-1984-assassination-of-indira-gandhi-9006876/.

2   Hazarika, Sanjoy. 1985, May 12. "India Seizes 1,500 as Deaths Mount in Bomb Attacks." *New York Times*.

3   Ghosh, Madhushree. 2022. "When Indira Died." In *Khabaar: An Immigrant Journey of Food, Memory and Family*. University of Iowa Press, 65–86.

4   Smith, William E. 1984, November 12. "Indira Gandhi: Death in the Garden." *Time*. https://time.com/archive/6860808/indira-gandhi-death-in-the-garden/; "Who Are the Guilty?" 2014, October 16. *Economic and Political Weekly*. https://www.epw.in/journal/2014/41/glimpses-past-web-exclusives/who-are-guilty.html; Malhotra, Inder. 2014, February 2. "The Last Walk: Indira Gandhi's Last Morning as the PM." *India Today*. https://www.indiatoday.in/mail-today/story/the-last-walk-indira-gandhis-last-morning-as-the-pm-179393-2014-02-02.

5   Prasad, Ravi Visvesvaraya Sharada. "The Story of How RSS Leaders Deserted Jayaprakash and the Resistance during Indira's Emergency." 2020, June 25. *The Print*. https://theprint.in/opinion/rss-leaders-deserted-jayaprakash-resistance-during-indira-emergency/448294; Prakash, Gyan. 2021. *Emergency Chronicles: Indira Gandhi and Democracy's Turning Point*;Kumar, Ashwani. 2025, June 30. "The Forced Sterilisations of Emergency." *The Hindu*. https://www.thehindu.com/opinion/op-ed/the-forced-sterilisations-of-emergency/article69752171; Steinberg, Blema S. 2008. *Women in Power: The Personalities and Leadership Styles of Indira Gandhi, Golda Meir, and Margaret Thatcher*. McGill-Queen's University Press, 75.

6   Memorial Trust, Indira Gandhi. "Garibi Hatao Programme by Indira Gandhi." I Am Courage—Indira Gandhi, The Iron Lady of India. Accessed July 21, 2025. https://indiragandhi.in/en/timeline/index/garibi-hatao-timeline.

7   Singh, Tavleen. 1998, June 20. "Prophet of Hate." Jarnail Singh Bhindranwale. https://web.archive.org/web/20080620164214/http:/www.india-today.com/itoday/millennium/100people/jarnail.html.

8   Ustinov, Peter. 1985. *The Gandhis of India*. https://www.imdb.com/title/tt0393316/?ref_=ext_shr_lnk.

9   "Indira Assassin 'Great Martyr': Vedanti." 2008, January 6. *The Indian Express*. https://indianexpress.com/article/news-archive/indira-assassin-great-martyr-vedanti/.

10   Mahmood, Cynthia Keppley. 2010. *Fighting for Faith and Nation: Dialogues with Sikh Militants*. University of Pennsylvania Press, 2010.

11   "Indira Gandhi Killers to Be Hanged Friday." 1988, December 1. *New York Times*. https://www.nytimes.com/1988/12/01/world/indira-gandhi-killers-to-be-hanged-friday.html.

12   "You Are Acting against Misguided People." 2004, June 9. Rediff. https://in.rediff.com/news/2004/jun/07inter1.htm.

13   "Khalistan: Why Are Some Sikhs Calling for a Separate Homeland in India?" 2023, December 1. BBC News. https://www.bbc.com/news/world-asia-india-66852291.

14   Jain, Kalpana. 2020. "With Her Head Held High." Harvard Divinity Bulletin. https://bulletin.hds.harvard.edu/with-her-head-held-high/.

15   Singh, Jasjit. 2020. "Narratives in Action: Modelling the Types and Drivers of Sikh
      Activism in Diaspora." *Religions* 11, no. 10: 539. https://doi.org/10.3390/rel11100539;
      Bedi, Rahul. 2009, November 1. "South Asia, Delhi 1984: Memories of a Massacre."
      BBC News. http://news.bbc.co.uk/2/hi/south_asia/8306420.stm; Peer, Basharat. 2001,
      May 9. "Anti-Sikh Riots a Pogrom: Khushwant." Rediff.com. https://www.rediff.com/
      news/2001/may/09sikh.htm.

16   Singh, Pav. 2017. *1984: India's Guilty Secret*. Kashi House.

17   Prakash, Satya. 2025, February 12. "1984 Anti-Sikh Riots Case: Sajjan Kumar
      Convicted for Killing Father, Son in Delhi." *The Tribune*. https://www.tribuneindia.
      com/news/delhi/1984-anti-sikh-riots-case-sajjan-kumar-convicted-for-killing-
      father-son-in-delhi/; "Jagdish Tytler: My Own Daughter Asks If I Killed Sikhs." 2014,
      February 19. BBC News. https://www.bbc.com/news/world-asia-india-26237133;
      Kaur, Jaskaran. 2006. *Twenty Years of Impunity: The November 1984 Pogroms of Sikhs
      in India*. Ensaaf.

18   News Release. "India: No Justice for 1984 Anti-Sikh Bloodshed." 2020, October 28.
      Human Rights Watch. https://www.hrw.org/news/2014/10/29/india-no-justice-1984-
      anti-sikh-bloodshed; "Chapter 6: Was It a Communal Riot?" 1985, January. Citizen's
      Committee. https://www.carnage84.com/human/truth/truth.htm; Ramakrishnan,
      Shriya. 2016, October 7. "Renewed Calls for Justice in India's 1984 Riots." *Al Jazeera*.
      https://www.aljazeera.com/features/2016/10/7/1984-anti-sikh-riots-calls-for-justice-
      in-india; Anderson, Paul. "The Body of Slain Prime Minister Indira Gandhi, Set . . .
      ". 1984, November 3. UPI. https://www.upi.com/Archives/1984/11/03/The-body-of-
      slain-Prime-Minister-Indira-Gandhi-set/6143468306000/.

19   Stevens, William K. 1984. "Gandhi Cremated as Troops Deploy to Quell Violence."
      New York Times. Accessed July 21, 2025. https://www.nytimes.com/1984/11/04/
      world/gandhi-cremated-as-troops-deploy-to-quell-violence.html.

20   Umberg, Sen. Thomas. 2023, June 14. "Sikh Genocide." https://sjud.senate.ca.gov/
      sites/sjud.senate.ca.gov/files/ajr_2_sjud_analysis.pdf.

21   Gagandeep. 2010, February 17. "India's Sikh Widows of 1984 Say Justice Mia."
      Women's eNews. https://womensenews.org/2010/02/indias-sikh-widows-1984-say-
      justice-mia/; Shafi, Showkat. 2014, February 4. "In Pictures: Delhi's 'Widow Colony.'"
      Al Jazeera. https://www.aljazeera.com/gallery/2014/2/4/in-pictures-delhis-widow-
      colony.

22   Team, DNA Web. 2018, December 17. "When a Big Tree Falls, the Earth Shakes: How
      Rajiv Gandhi Justified 1984 Anti-Sikh Riots." *DNA India*. https://www.dnaindia.com/
      india/report-when-a-big-tree-falls-the-earth-shakes-how-rajiv-gandhi-justified-
      1984-anti-sikh-riots-2697259#google_vignette.

23   Justice Nanavati. 2019, October 22. "Report of the Justice Nanavati Commission of
      Inquiry (1984 Anti-Sikh Riots): Volumes I and II." Justice Nanavati Commission
      of Inquiry (1984 Anti-Sikh Riots). https://ruralindiaonline.org/bn/library/resource/
      report-of-the-justice-nanavati-commission-of-inquiry-1984-anti-sikh-riots-

volumes-i-and-ii/; Khullar, Mridu. 2009, October 28. "India's 1984 Anti-Sikh Riots: Waiting for Justice." *Time*; Srivastava, Sanjeev, and BBC News Team. 2005, August 8. "South Asia, Leaders 'Incited' Anti-Sikh Riots." BBC News. http://news.bbc.co.uk/2/hi/south_asia/4130962.stm.

24 Deposition by Vrinda Grover: Nanavati Commission. 2002. https://www.carnage84.com/judge/analysis.htm.

Chapter 21

1 Dunya News Team. "Sikhs' Successful Referendum to Make Khalistan Concludes in Los Angeles." *Dunya News*. Accessed July 21, 2025. https://dunyanews.tv/en/World/875095-sikhs-successful-referendum-to-make-khalistan-concludes-in-los-angele.

2 Sodhi, Parminder Singh. 2025, March 18. "Khalistan Referendum: A Tactical Shift under Trump's Watch." Khalsa Vox. https://khalsavox.com/opinion/khalistan-referendum-a-tactical-shift-under-trumps-watch/.

3 Lucas, Ryan. 2024, October 27. "Sikh Separatist, Targeted Once for Assassination, Says India Still Trying to Kill Him." NPR. https://www.npr.org/2024/10/27/g-s1-29561/sikh-separatist-assassination-india; Al Jazeera Staff. 2024, October 18. "US Charges Indian Government Employee in Foiled Sikh Separatist Murder Plot." *Al Jazeera*. https://www.aljazeera.com/news/2024/10/18/us-charges-indian-government-employee-in-foiled-sikh-separatist-murder-plot; Srinivasan, Chandrasekhar. 2024, October 18. "NDTV Explains: US Charge over Plot to Kill Terrorist, India's Reaction." NDTV. https://www.ndtv.com/world-news/ndtv-explains-gurpatwant-singh-pannun-murder-for-hire-case-ex-spy-vikash-yadav-drug-smuggler-nikhil-gupta-plot-to-kill-khalistani-terrorist-6816220.

4 US Office of Public Affairs. 2025, February 6. "Justice Department Announces Charges against Indian Government Employee in Connection with Foiled Plot to Assassinate U.S. Citizen in New York City." Office of Public Affairs, United States Department of Justice. https://www.justice.gov/archives/opa/pr/justice-department-announces-charges-against-indian-government-employee-connection-foiled; Yousif, Nadine, and Neal Razzell. 2023, October 2. "Who Was Canadian Sikh Leader Hardeep Singh Nijjar?" BBC News. https://www.bbc.com/news/world-us-canada-66860510; Cecco, Leyland, and Patrick Wintour. 2024, October 16. "Trudeau: India Made 'Horrific Mistake' in Violating Canadian Sovereignty." *The Guardian*. https://www.theguardian.com/world/2024/oct/16/justin-trudeau-testimony-india.

Chapter 22

1   Ghosh, Madhushree. 2022, September 1. "On the Road, a Taste of Home." *High Country News*. https://www.hcn.org/issues/54-9/on-the-road-a-taste-of-home/.

2   Rao, Tejal, Naz Deravian, Priya Krishna, Hetal Vasavada, and Maneet Chauhan. 2023, October. "Diwali Recipes." *New York Times*. https://cooking.nytimes.com/68861692-nyt-cooking/36172702-diwali-recipes.

3   "Shaheed Bhagat Singh Nagar." Home, Land of Shaheed-e-Azam Sardar Bhagat Singh, India. Accessed July 21, 2025. https://nawanshahr.nic.in/; Devereux, Ella. 2024, March 31. "The Nursing Faith Groups Tackling Health Inequalities." *Nursing Times*. https://www.nursingtimes.net/public-health/the-nursing-faith-groups-tackling-health-inequalities-31-03-2024/#.; Landa, Amarjodh Singh, Bhajneek Kaur Grewal, and Rajinder Singh. 2022, June 12. "Sikh Religion and Palliative Care." *BMJ Supportive & Palliative Care*. https://pubmed.ncbi.nlm.nih.gov/33139306/.

4   Chakraborti, Shruti. 2022. "Subverting Patriarchal Interpretation of the Ramayan through a Feminist Lens: A Critical Study of Sita's Ramayana." Digital Commons @ Cortland. https://digitalcommons.cortland.edu/wagadu/vol24/iss1/11.

5   Swasthi. 2024, August 26. "Sabudana Kheer (Sago Kheer)." Swasthi's Recipes. https://www.indianhealthyrecipes.com/sabudana-kheer/.

6   Swasthi. 2022, October 16. "Gulab Jamun Recipe." Swasthi's Recipes. https://www.indianhealthyrecipes.com/gulab-jamun-recipe-using-milk-powder/.

Chapter 23

1   "The Sikh Foundation, San Diego ਦੀ ਸੰਖਿ ਫਾਊਡੇਸ਼ਨ, ਸੈਨ ਡਾਇਗੋ." The Sikh Foundation, Gurdwara San Diego (SFSD). Accessed July 21, 2025. https://www.sdsikhs.org/index1.php.

2   Sen, Mayukh. 2020, April 16. "The Legacy of the Pandemic: 11 Ways It Will Change the Way We Live." Vox. https://www.vox.com/the-highlight/2020/4/16/21213635/coronavirus-covid-19-pandemic-legacy-quarantine-state-of-mind-frugality.

3   Riggins, Alex. 2020, May 21. "Driver, 29, Killed in Solo Rollover Crash on SR-163 in Hillcrest." *San Diego Union Tribune*. https://www.sandiegouniontribune.com/2020/05/20/driver-29-killed-in-solo-rollover-crash-on-sr-163-in-hillcrest/.

4   Hitchens, Christopher. 2007, April 25. "Religion Poisons Everything." *Slate*. https://slate.com/news-and-politics/2007/04/religion-poisons-everything.html.

5   ""Amrit Sanchar: The Initiation into the Khalsa Brotherhood." Dasvandh Network. Accessed July 21, 2025. https://dvnetwork.org/page/amrit-sanchar-the-initiation#.

Chapter 24

1   Burnett, Christopher. 2025, March 10. "Diwali 2025: What Is Diwali?" Almanac.com.
     https://www.almanac.com/content/diwali#.

Chapter 25

1   West, Graham. 2024, October 31. "Remembering 1984 on the 40th Anniversary of the
     Sikh Genocide." Sikh Coalition. https://www.sikhcoalition.org/blog/2024/remembering-
     1984-on-the-40th-anniversary-of-the-sikh-genocide/; "Home: Punjab Disappeared:
     Disappeared, Denied, but Not Forgotten." 2019, September 14. https://punjabdisappeared.
     org/#; "How Punjab's Missing Thousands Are Being Forgotten." 2014, June 3. BBC News.
     https://www.bbc.com/news/world-asia-india-27585500; Segall, Hayley Dawn. 2020."1984
     and Film: Trauma and the Evolution of the Punjabi Sikh Identity." Digital Commons at
     Oberlin. https://digitalcommons.oberlin.edu/honors/708/.

2   Venkataramanan, Meena. 2023, May 20. "Along the Highways, Indian Restaurants
     Serve America's Truckers." *Washington Post*. https://www.washingtonpost.com/
     nation/2023/05/20/along-highways-indian-restaurants-serve-americas-truckers/.

3   Kaleem, Jaweed. 2020, January 21. "Sikh Drivers Are Transforming U.S. Trucking.
     Take a Ride along the Punjabi American Highway." *Los Angeles Times*. https://www.
     latimes.com/nation/la-na-col1-sikh-truckers-20190627-htmlstory.html.

4   The Economist Team. 2018, May 3. "An All-American Industry Changes the All-
     American Way." *The Economist*.

5   Sodhi, Rana, and Harjit Sodhi. 2020, September 15. "Remembering Balbir
     Singh Sodhi, Sikh Man Killed in Post-9/11 Hate Crime." Edited by Linya Anwar.
     StoryCorps. https://storycorps.org/stories/remembering-balbir-singh-sodhi-sikh-
     man-killed-in-post-911-hate-crime/#; Mentzer, Rob. 2022, July 28. "Wisconsin's
     Sikh Community a Decade after Fatal Temple Shooting." NPR. https://www.npr.
     org/2022/07/28/1114335390/wisconsins-sikh-community-a-decade-after-fatal-
     temple-shooting; Axelrod, Jim. 2018, November 23. "More than 30,000 Indian-
     American Sikhs Have Entered the Trucking Industry in 2 Years." CBS News. https://
     www.cbsnews.com/news/sikh-indian-americans-becoming-truckers-mintu-
     pandher-laramie-wyoming/.

6   "Sikh Population in India." Population Census 2011. Accessed July 21, 2025. https://
     www.census2011.co.in/data/religion/4-sikhism.html#google_vignette.

7   Venkataramanan, Meena. 2023, May 20. "Unofficial Map of US Highway Punjabi
     Dhabas." X.com. https://x.com/mvenk82/status/1659960128743849986?lang=en.

8   Lal, Neeta. 2022, December 3. "Indian Dhaba's Journey from Roadside Truck Stop
     to Fine-Dining Destination." *South China Morning Post*. https://www.scmp.com/

magazines/post-magazine/food-drink/article/3201769/indias-dhaba-restaurants-scattered-roadside-truck-stops-nationwide-staple-and-high-end-versions.

9   Singh, Gurmukh. 2009, January 10. "Religions—Sikhism: Weddings." BBC. https://www.bbc.co.uk/religion/religions/sikhism/ritesrituals/weddings.shtml#.

10 Mullen, Maggie. 2019, January 23. "Sikhs Turn to Trucking by the Thousands to Keep the Faith." Colorado Public Radio. https://www.cpr.org/2019/01/23/sikhs-turn-to-trucking-by-the-thousands-to-keep-the-faith/.

11 "U.S. Transportation Secretary Sean P. Duffy Signs Order Announcing New Guidance to Enforce English Proficiency Requirement for Truckers." 2025, May 20. FMCSA. https://www.fmcsa.dot.gov/newsroom/us-transportation-secretary-sean-p-duffy-signs-order-announcing-new-guidance-enforce#.

12 Miller, Blair. 2019, April 29. "Company That I-70 Crash Driver Works for Has Past Federal Violations for Brakes, English Proficiency." Denver 7 Colorado News (KMGH). https://www.denver7.com/news/crime/company-that-i-70-crash-driver-works-for-has-past-federal-violations-for-brakes-english-proficiency#google_vignette.

13 Rituparna. 2024, November 8. "Trucker's Delight: A Culinary Journey of Dhabas from India to the US." Medium. https://medium.com/new-east/truckers-delight-a-culinary-journey-of-dhabas-from-india-to-the-us-8c74dbaf17f7.

14 "State Route 204." California Highways. Accessed July 21, 2025. https://www.cahighways.org/ROUTE204.html.

15 Rao, Tejal. 2019, August 26. "A Taste of Home for California's Punjabi Truck Drivers." *New York Times*. https://www.nytimes.com/2019/08/26/dining/punjabi-dhaba-truckers.html.

Chapter 26

1   Parsons, Rob. 2024, May 7. "Badhesha Appointed as Next Fresno County Superior Court Judge." Fresnoland. https://fresnoland.org/2024/05/07/badhesha/.

2   Elliott, Steve. 2011, July 22. "Sikh Soldiers Allowed to Serve, Retain Their Articles of Faith." US Army. https://www.army.mil/article/36339/sikh_soldiers_allowed_to_serve_retain_their_articles_of_faith.

3   Inskeep, Steve. 2025, May 12. "Historian Jill Lepore Gives Her Perspective on the World the U.S. Made after 1945." NPR. https://www.npr.org/2025/05/12/nx-s1-5385328/historian-jill-lepore-gives-her-perspective-on-the-world-the-u-s-made-after-1945.

4   "Raj Singh Badhesha Becomes First Sikh Appointed to the Fresno County Superior Court Bench." 2024, July 11. YouTube CBS47 KCEE24. https://www.youtube.com/watch?v=Mjg2jQ5qWcg.

Chapter 27

1   "Sikhs in World War II." 2015, July 28. SikhiWiki.

2   US Supreme Court. 1923. *United States v. Bhagat Singh Thind*, 261 U.S. 204 (1923).
     Justia Law, 2015. https://supreme.justia.com/cases/federal/us/261/204/#214; United
     States Reports: Cases Adjudged in the Supreme Court at . . . and Rules Announced
     at . . . United States: Banks & Bros., Law Publishers. 1924; Ancheta, Angelo N. 2006.
     Race, Rights, and the Asian American Experience. Rutgers University Press.

3   Ahmed, Aftab, and Adnan Abidi. 2025, February 5. "US Military Plane Flies
     104 Illegal Immigrants Back to India." Reuters. https://www.reuters.com/world/
     us-military-plane-deporting-indian-immigrants-lands-india-reuters-witness-
     says-2025-02-05/.

4   Limaye, Yogita. 2025, March 9. "Migrant Deported in Chains: 'No-One Will Go to
     US Illegally Now.'" BBC News. https://www.bbc.com/news/articles/cx2gjjrzm54o;
     Biswas, Soutik. 2025, February 17. "Nine Surprising Facts about Indians in the US."
     BBC News. https://www.bbc.com/news/articles/c8r56vr40jvo.

5   *Hindustan Times*. 2025, February 14. "PM Modi's Big Message on Illegal Immigration
     Amid Trump's Crackdown, Arrests, Deportations India, US." YouTube. https://www.
     youtube.com/watch?v=uxcJgPistE0.

Chapter 28

1   LaVigne, Dominique. 2025, June 2. "Federal Documents on Buona Forchetta Ice Raid
     Released." Fox 5 KUSI. https://fox5sandiego.com/news/local-news/san-diego/federal-
     documents-on-buona-forchetta-ice-raid-released.

2   Clayton, Victoria. 2025, June 12. "Why Did Angelenos Swiftly Resist ICE Raids?
     Look to LA's Deep Immigrant Roots." *The Guardian*. https://www.theguardian.com/
     us-news/2025/jun/12/los-angeles-ice-protests-immigration.

3   Cal/OSHA, and State of California. 2025, June 11. "California Labor Commissioner
     Reminds All Workers of Legal Rights under California Labor Laws." https://www.dir.
     ca.gov/DIRNews/2025/2025-53.html#.

4   Bourdain, Anthony. 2014, May 3. "Under the Volcano." Tumblr: Under the
     Volcano. https://anthonybourdain.tumblr.com/post/84641290831/under-the-
     volcano.

5   Fry, Wendy, and Sergio Olmos. 2025, July 18. "'There Is No Sanctuary Anywhere':
     Border Patrol Raids Come to California's Capital." CalMatters. https://calmatters.
     org/justice/2025/07/sacramento-border-patrol-raids/; Meyersohn, Nathaniel. 2025,
     July 18. "How Home Depot Became a Magnet for Day Laborers and a Target for

ICE." CNN; Singh, Maanvi. 2025, June 16. "At Home Depot, ICE Raids Terrorize the Workers Who Helped Build LA: 'They Just Come and Grab You.'" *The Guardian.* https://www.theguardian.com/us-news/2025/jun/16/home-depot-ice-raids-los-angeles.

6   Sheets, Molly, and Jose Duran. 2025, June 3. "ICE Defends Tactics in Buona Forchetta Raid amid San Diego Councilmember Backlash." CBS8. https://www.cbs8.com/article/news/local/federal-search-warrants-reveal-new-details-ice-raid-san-diego-restaurant/509-c3826674-6940-43bb-bd56-9d4aa15af3da.

7   *Arizona Republic* Staff. 2001, September 22. "Balbir Singh Sodhi Obituary." *Arizona Republic.* https://www.newspapers.com/article/the-arizona-republic-balbir-singh-sodhi/122070157/.

8   Kaur, Valarie. 2025, June 11. "Valarie Kaur on Instagram: 'Our Dream Is More Powerful than Their Nightmare. In Downtown LA Tonight, at Our Interfaith Vigil for Immigrant Families. Ty @picocalifornia @la__voice @revloveproject #revolutionarylove #SageWarrior #seenostranger #solidarityis.'" Instagram. https://www.instagram.com/reel/DKwEZ97OeLU/?utm_source=ig_web_copy_link&igsh=MWdya29nZHYydmdxcQ.

9   Kaur, Valarie. 2025, February 26. The Revolutionary Love Project. https://revolutionarylove.org/.

10 Kaur, Valarie. 2024, September 10. "Sage Warrior by Valarie Kaur." https://valariekaur.com/books/sage-warrior/.

Chapter 29

1   Amess, David, John McDonnell, Bob Spink, Mark Todd, Dominic Grieve, and Patrick Hall. 2006, December 5. "House of Commons Hansard Debates for December 5, 2006 . . . " Punjabi Community in Britain. https://publications.parliament.uk/pa/cm200607/cmhansrd/cm061205/halltext/61205h0001.htm; Thandi SS. 2015. "Punjabi Migration, Settlement and Experience in the UK." In Rajan, S. I., V. J. Varghese, and A. Kumar Nanda, eds. *Migration, Mobility and Multiple Affiliations: Punjabis in a Transnational World.* Cambridge University Press, 105–30. Jaspal, Rusi. 2013. "British Sikh Identity, Distinctiveness and Continuity." British Sikh Identity. Nottingham Trent University. http://irep.ntu.ac.uk/id/eprint/39654/1/1315815_Jaspal.pdf.

2   Elahi, K. Maudood. 1985. *Population Redistribution and Development in South Asia.* Edited by Leszek A. Kosiński. Springer Netherlands.

3   Aiyar, Swaminathan S. Anklesaria. 2023, June 21. "Indian Nationalism and the Historical Fantasy of a Golden Hindu Period." Cato.org. https://www.cato.org/policy-analysis/indian-nationalism-historical-fantasy-golden-hindu-period#bjp-becomes-fan-angus-maddison; Tharoor, Shashi. 2015, July 22. "Viewpoint: Britain

Must Pay Reparations to India." BBC News. https://www.bbc.com/news/world-asia-india-33618621; Sullivan, Dylan, and Jason Hickel. 2022, December 2. "How British Colonialism Killed 100 Million Indians in 40 Years." *Al Jazeera*. https://www.aljazeera.com/opinions/2022/12/2/how-british-colonial-policy-killed-100-million-indians.

4 Dand, Khyati. 2024, September 21. "The Debated Scottish Origins of Chicken Tikka Masala." Food Republic. https://www.foodrepublic.com/1666379/chicken-tikka-masala-origin-scotland/; Olson, Emily. 2022, December 23. "Who Created Chicken Tikka Masala? The Death of a Curry King Is Reviving a Debate." NPR. https://www.npr.org/2022/12/23/1145119758/chicken-tikka-masala-ali-ahmed-aslam-shish-mahal; TOI Lifestyle Desk. 2024, September 5. "Debate over the Origin of Chicken Tikka Masala." *The Times of India*. https://timesofindia.indiatimes.com/life-style/food-news/debate-over-the-origin-of-chicken-tikka-masala/articleshow/113094423.cms.

5 Hay, Mark. 2018, July 26. "Who Owns Chicken Tikka Masala?" Roads & Kingdoms. https://roadsandkingdoms.com/2014/who-owns-chicken-tikka-masala/.

6 Bance, Peter. 2018. "The Lahore Durbar: Duleep Singh Family." The Wallace Collection. https://www.wallacecollection.org/explore/explore-in-depth/the-sikh-empire/the-lahore-durbar-the-court-of-lahore/legacies-duleep-singh-family/.

7 BiBi Restaurants. 2025, June 2, 2025. "Home—Bibi Restaurant, Mayfair, London." https://www.bibirestaurants.com/.

8 Prept. 2022. "Chet Sharma." https://prept.foundation/team/chet-sharma/.

9 Olivia. 2024, May 16. "The Gin and Tonic: A Short History: Sipsmith Gin." Sipsmith.https://sipsmith.com/gin-and-tonic-a-short-history-of/#.

10 Darjeeling Express. 2025. "Indian Food Restaurant in London, United Kingdom." https://www.darjeeling-express.com/.

11 Lakshmi, Padma. 2024, April 17. "Asma Khan Is on the 2024 Time 100 List." *Time*. https://time.com/6964956/asma-khan/.

12 Selby, Jenn. 2015, January 30. "The Darker Side of Britain's Most Iconic Wartime Hero." *The Independent*. https://www.independent.co.uk/news/people/winston-churchill-from-accusations-of-antisemitism-to-the-blunt-refusal-that-led-to-the-deaths-of-millions-9999181.html; Safi, Michael. 2019, March 29. "Churchill's Policies Contributed to 1943 Bengal Famine—Study." *The Guardian*. https://www.theguardian.com/world/2019/mar/29/winston-churchill-policies-contributed-to-1943-bengal-famine-study; Heyden, Tom. 2015, January 26. "The 10 Greatest Controversies of Winston Churchill's Career." BBC News. https://www.bbc.com/news/magazine-29701767.

INDEX

ABOUT THE AUTHOR

Madhushree Ghosh is the daughter of refugees and an immigrant to America. Author of the award-winning debut food narrative memoir *KHABAAR: An Immigrant Journey of Food, Memory, and Family* (2022), Madhushree uses food to discuss civil rights, social justice, culinary, community, and cultural history. Her 2023 TEDx San Diego Seeds of Change talk *What We Talk About When We Talk About Food* featured the East African refugee farming women in San Diego. Her work has appeared in *Best American Essays in Food Writing*, been Pushcart nominated, and published in *The New York Times*, the *Los Angeles Times*, *The Washington Post*, *Vogue India*, *Longreads*, *Catapult*, *BOMB*, *Writer's Digest*, the *Los Angeles Review of Books*, *Guernica*, and others. Madhushree runs the curated global literary salon and supper club *KhabaarCo*, enabling conversations on food cultures, writing, responsible travel, and mindful activism through conversations with changemaking activists, historians, authors, and chefs.

Trained in oncology diagnostics, Madhushree considers both San Diego and New Delhi home and can be reached at @writemadhushree.